"[THIS] BOOK IS TAKING THE COUNTRY BY STORM.... ENLIGHTENING."
—*Black Business Listings*

"THINK AND GROW RICH: A BLACK CHOICE is the perfect updating of a classic, a must read for Black America. Kimbro and Hill have created a sensible and powerful guide to getting ahead that will long stand as the guide to not only *reaching*. but also *explaining*, success."

—AHMAD RASHAD

"A four-star winner! Kimbro's book is alive with the *scientific principles* that will lead you to success— using the gifts and powers you *already have*. It's riveting, realistic, and supercharged with exciting stories of black achievers who discovered the real secret of wealth and success: Whatever you fix your mind on, you will become."

—*Success* Magazine

"Kimbro is a terrific speaker, and the writings are dead-on. Napoleon would have been proud."
—*USA Today*

Please turn the page
for more reviews....

By Dennis Kimbro
Published by Ballantine Books:

THINK AND GROW RICH: A Black Choice
     (with Napoleon Hill)
DAILY MOTIVATIONS FOR AFRICAN-AMERICAN
     SUCCESS

THINK
AND
GROW RICH

A Black Choice

Dennis Kimbro
and Napolean Hill

BALLANTINE BOOKS • NEW YORK

A Fawcett Book
Published by The Random House Publishing Group
Copyright © 1991 by The Napoleon Hill Foundation

Published in the United States by Fawcett Books, an imprint of The Random House Publishing Group, a division of Random House, Inc., New York, and simultaneously in Canada by Random House of Canada Limited, Toronto.

BALLANTINE and colophon are registered trademarks of Random House, Inc.

Grateful acknowledgment is made to the following for permission to reprint previously published material: Marcia Ann Gillespie: Excerpt from "Winfrey Faces All" by Marcia Ann Gillespie. © Marcia Ann Gillespie/*Ms.* Magazine, November 1988.

Alfred A. Knopf, Inc.: Excerpt from "Mother to Son" from *Selected Poems* by Langston Hughes. Copyright 1926 by Alfred A. Knopf, Inc. Copyright renewed 1954 by Langston Hughes. Reprinted by permission of the publisher.

Random House, Inc.: Excerpt from *How to Sell More Cookies, Condos, Etc.* by Markita Andrew and Cheryl Merser. Copyright © 1986 by Markita Andrews. Reprinted by permission of Simon & Schuster, Inc.

Simon & Schuster, Inc.: Excerpt from a poem by Guillaume Apollinaire quoted in *Creating Wealth* by Robert Allen. Copyright © 1983, 1986 by Robert Allen. Reprinted by permission of Simon & Schuster, Inc.

ISBN 978-0-449-21998-0

This edition published by arrangement with Simon & Schuster, Inc.

Printed in the United States of America

www.ballantinebooks.com

First Hardcover Edition: September 1991
First Mass Market Edition: November 1992

OPM 40

DEDICATION

*To Pat, my wife, my adviser, and my best friend;
to my daughters, Kelli, Kim, and MacKenzie;
to my late father, Donald Kimbro. He was right.
He missed his ship, but I'll catch mine.
And to an entire race anxiously
awaiting the keys to success.*

Contents

Foreword by Wally "Famous" Amos ... xiii
Introduction ... 1
1 Inner Space: The Final Frontier ... 17
2 Imagination: Ideas In Action ... 51
3 Desire: The Starting Point of All Achievement ... 80
4 Faith: The Prerequisite to Power ... 117
5 "By All Means—Persist" ... 145
6 What Are You Worth? ... 170
7 Self-Reliance ... 185
8 A Pleasing Personality ... 211
9 Enthusiasm! ... 235
10 A Message on Money, or Money Talks and You Would Do Well to Listen ... 255
11 Three Magic Words ... 287
12 Outer Space: Your Great Discovery ... 318
Index ... 353

Acknowledgments

Where do I begin? So much work goes into a book like this. There are so many to thank. During the years I spent developing the ideas for *Think and Grow Rich: A Black Choice*, I benefitted from the support of family, special friends, and associates. Major credit can be given to the following:

To W. Clement Stone, Bob Anderson, and Michael Ritt for believing in an unknown, unpublished writer. Because they took the first step, I was able to complete a journey of a thousand miles. A great boost also came from the Napoleon Hill Foundation, in particular Eileen Considine, who would drop everything to handle my most trivial needs.

To Wally Amos for teaching me how to raise my level of vision.

To Harvey Mackay and his fine staff at Mackay Envelope. Harvey walks what he talks and has taught me the real meaning of winning. To him I am deeply indebted.

My agent, Jonathon Lazear, and his assistant, Jennifer Flannery, could see from a distance what I couldn't see up close. Their book publishing expertise was felt throughout the entire process. A special note of thanks must go to Susan Randol at Ballantine, whose editorial touch is evident on every page of this book.

Special recognition goes to Warren Brookes, a kind soul, who taught me to "cast my nets on the right side." He really provided the insight to the three magic words. Walter Williams, whose piercing wit and keen intellect has provided much-needed alternatives for Black America, has been helpful. Maybe one day he and Tom Sowell will be given their due.

Drew Piasecki and Roy Lantz also deserve special mention. They were intrigued by my early research and were active supporters. Moreover, their thoughtful questioning was often critical to the honing of the ideas expressed in this book.

To my three daughters, Kelli, Kim, and MacKenzie—the true wealth in my life—for their love and motivation to press forward. The future belongs to them and their generation.

To two very special ladies, Louise Sims and Alice Hopkins, who reached down and pulled me up during the many times I stumbled.

To my loving wife, Pat, who has been my sounding board for the last twenty years. Thanks to her tireless effort and support, I was able to put my best foot forward. Lord knows when this book would have been completed if it wasn't for her.

And the last word goes to my mother and mother-in-law, Mary Kimbro and Ruby McCauley. These are the rocks against which I've leaned. It's amazing how two black women with little formal education and less money can accomplish so much with their lives. I've sat at their feet and learned the great lessons of life. Their solution to any problem can be found in the Bible and hard work. This book is really about them.

Foreword

You are about to embark on a transformational experience. The information and ideas contained in this very special book will actually change your belief system. *Think and Grow Rich: A Black Choice* was written with the hope of giving you *another way* of looking at your world. It is a book filled with real-life, positive examples of high achievers. It is written in basic English and packed with emotion. You will see your reflection in many of the stories told.

The success stories in this book are actually every person's success story. They are founded in Universal Law and Principle, which shows no regard for color, race, or cultural differences. They work for everyone. However, there is one catch; they work only if you *work* them. You must believe and use the principles daily, not just every now and then. Just as food will nourish and strengthen your body only when eaten, the ideas and concepts shared in this book will work only when applied and practiced.

So, make a commitment that this will *not* be like so many

other projects you have begun and failed to complete. This time will be different. You are going to create a new and improved *you*. Let's give this project a name so it will have real meaning. Let's call it, ''Operation New Life.'' Can you think of a more worthwhile project? I know I can't. You deserve to be the best *you* possible.

Before you get started, a word of caution. This is not a ''read it once and put it on the shelf'' book. Read it before going to bed at night, read it as soon as you awake in the morning, take it to your place of business, on trips, to the bathroom, because *Think and Grow Rich: A Black Choice* was meant to be studied and put into practice, practice, practice. So, turn the page and get started on the greatest journey of your life, Operation New Life. I look forward to meeting the brand-new you.

Have a great life!

Aloha,
Wally Amos

Introduction

> "The noblest charity is to prevent a man from accepting charity; and the best alms is to show and enable a man to dispense with alms."
>
> —Talmudic philosopher

Black Americans who seek a way to abandon a mediocre life, a start on the grand highway to success—here is your road map!

This map is not new. It was developed just after the Civil War in the form of a lecture entitled "Acres of Diamonds" by a lawyer and newspaper editor named Russell H. Conwell. In 1881, Dr. Conwell also became a minister, and it was in this role that he developed his talk, which he delivered some 8000 times to audiences across the country. These appearances earned him nearly $8 million in lecture fees, which he used to found Temple University in Philadelphia, Pennsylvania, to serve "poor but deserving young men."

"Acres of Diamonds" was the true story of a poor farmer who settled in Africa and spent years struggling to raise his crops. His land was rocky and difficult to till. Disenfranchised with his circumstances, the farmer became increasingly fascinated by tales of "easy wealth" gained by men who had searched for and discovered diamonds in the countryside. He, too, wanted to be rich.

1

He grew tired of the endless labor, and impulsively sold his farm to search for diamonds. For the rest of his life he wandered the vast African continent searching for the gleaming gems. But the great discovery always eluded him. Finally, in a fit of despondency, broken financially, spiritually, and emotionally, he threw himself into a river and drowned.

Meanwhile, the man who had bought his farm found a rather large and unusual stone in a stream that cut through his property. It turned out to be a diamond of enormous value. Stunned by his newfound wealth, the farmer discovered that his land was virtually covered with such stones. *It was to become one of the world's richest diamond mines!*

Now, the first farmer had unknowingly owned acres of diamonds. He sold the property for practically nothing in order to look for riches elsewhere. If only he had taken the time to study and realize what diamonds looked like in their rough state, and had first thoroughly explored the land he had owned, he would have found the riches he sought—on the very land he had been living upon!

What so profoundly affected Dr. Conwell, and subsequently thousands of others who heard this lecture, was the fact that each of us, at any given moment, is standing in the middle of his or her *own acres of diamonds*. If only we acquire the wisdom and patience to intelligently and effectively examine our circumstances and to explore the work in which we are now engaged, we usually will find that it contains the riches we seek—whether they be material, spiritual, or both.

Before we go running off to what we think are greener pastures, let's make sure that our own is *not just as green, or perhaps even greener*! Oftentimes, while we're looking at other pastures, other people are busy looking at ours. There's nothing more pitiful than the person who wastes his or her life wandering from one thing to another, like the improvident seeker of diamonds, forever looking for the pot of gold at the end of the rainbow and never staying with one thing long enough to find it. For no matter what your goal may be, or whatever form your riches may take, you can be sure that your start on the road to its attainment can be found somewhere within your present surroundings.

Men and women who have become outstanding at their work are those who view their endeavors as an opportunity for growth and development. They have prepared themselves for the opportunities that surround them every day. James Brander Matthews, the nineteenth-century writer, observed, "Unless a man has trained himself for his chance, the chance will only make him look ridiculous. A great occasion is worth to a man exactly what his preparation enables him to make of it."

Preparation is the key. It means becoming so good, so competent at what you're doing, that you actually force the opportunity you seek to come your way. And come your way it will.

Today, Black America stands in the spotlight. Strong winds, strong tides, strong minds, and strong destinies are gathering to sweep the race into new directions, new actions, and new possibilities. Opportunities abound. The world waits to judge our valuation of ourselves, to see what we do with those opportunities that have escaped our grasp for so many years. The door has now opened, and the freedom to walk through it is ours.

But the freedom to do what? Freedom to define whatever you demand from life and what you expect to give life in return. Freedom is yours. You have the spiritual, legal, and social right to be or not to be. Only one out of every seventeen human beings on earth is blessed with this freedom that so many seem to take for granted. To progress and find your way to success is the debt you owe to life.

Freedom is yours. Though you may march in unison with your brother, each of you must step to your own cadence. You may reason together, but the product of that reasoning is a consortium of individual thought. You may love your fellow man, but you can neither breathe for him nor match the beat of his heart to your own.

This book is about Black America and success. But the concepts it articulates are applicable to all who dwell on this earth. Conscious power exists within the mind of everyone. Too often it goes unrecognized, but it is there. It is there to be developed and brought forth, like the great oak borne out of the acorn, or like the achiever who has risen above obstacles of purposelessness and low self-esteem. Within you lies a power which, when properly grasped and directed, can lift an entire race out of the rut of mediocrity, poverty, and failure, and onto the shores of fortune.

The key words in this context are ''grasped and directed.'' Let me offer an illustration. William Marsten, a prominent psychologist, authored a two-year study where he asked 3000 individuals the following: ''What have you to live for?'' What Dr. Marsten found was absolutely shocking. He discovered that 94 percent of those interviewed had no definite purpose. These were men and women who were simply enduring the present while they waited for the future. They waited for something to happen, waited for tomorrow, waited for the next year, waited for the their children to grow up and leave home, waited for someone to die. *Ninety-four percent—the overwhelming majority*—were men and women who were simply enduring the present, while they waited for more favorable circumstances.

This doesn't make sense when you're talking to free human beings who are living in the most exciting age in the history of mankind. We should realize that the only time that exists is the *here* and *now*. Yesterday is gone forever, and tomorrow never really comes. Those who wait for things to happen or for ''something to turn up'' never learn the rules of the most exciting and rewarding game on earth—the game of life!

Thomas Huxley, a nineteenth-century scientist and philosopher, noted the following:

Suppose it were perfectly certain that the life and fortune of each of us would some day depend upon our winning or losing a game of chess. Do you not think that we should all consider it to be our primary duty to learn at least the names of the pieces and how to position them on the chessboard? Yet, it is a plain and elementary truth that the life, the fortune, and the happiness of each of us depends upon our knowing something of the rules of a game more difficult, far more interesting and much more exciting than chess.

Here is a game that has been played for untold ages. Each of us is one of two players in a game of his or her own. The chessboard is our world; the pieces are the phenomena of the universe; the rules of the game are what we call the laws of nature. Now, the player on the other side—our opponent—is hidden from us. We realize that his play is always fair, just, and patient. But also we learn, to our cost, that he never overlooks a mistake or makes the smallest allowance for ignorance. He cannot favor anyone, but everyone has the same opportunity to win.

To the man who plays well, the highest stakes are paid with that sort of overflowing generosity with which the strong show delight in strength. And one who plays poorly is checkmated with haste but without remorse.

Huxley went on to say that those who take honors in nature's university, who learn the laws that govern men and things and obey them, are really the great and successful people in this world. The masses of mankind are the average who pick up just enough to get through without much discredit.

Yes, it is a plain and elementary truth that the life, the fortune, and the happiness of each of us depends on our knowing something of the rules of this game. It is a game that our Creator allows us to play just once, and there is no second chance should we play poorly.

It becomes important that we know the rules that will ultimately determine our success. Not just to know their meanings and what they do, but to make these principles a part of us—a habit that will lead us to do the right thing automatically, regardless of the circumstances. Then we will know that we need not wait for some distant opportunity to arrive. He who does can make no greater mistake. For no man or woman can become successful without enriching the lives of others; anyone who adds to prosperity must prosper in return.

The World Is Yours
When You Master the Secret

Napoleon Hill devoted his life to sharing the philosophy of individual achievement with millions of men and women. Born in poverty, Hill carved out a distinguished writing career, became a confidant of many of the most successful leaders of the twentieth century, and served as an adviser to presidents Woodrow Wilson and Franklin Delano Roosevelt.

As a novice reporter, Hill interviewed Andrew Carnegie, the multimillionaire steel magnate. During their three-hour meeting, Carnegie shared with Hill his grand idea: to develop and organize the world's first philosophy of individual achievement, based on the success principles that Carnegie had used to accumulate his vast fortune. Fast approaching the end of an illustrious career, Carnegie lamented, "It's a shame that each new generation must find the way to success by trial and error when the principles are really clear-cut."

After elaborating on his beliefs the tycoon put the question squarely to his young guest: "If you were given the opportunity to spend twenty years interviewing the most accomplished and wealthiest men and women of your day, probing their psyches thoroughly for the secrets to their success—would you undertake the venture?"

Without hesitation, the young journalist emphatically said, ''Yes!'' Napoleon Hill had seized his moment.

Unknown to Hill, Carnegie had allowed the reporter sixty seconds in which to make up his mind. In twenty-nine seconds Hill said that he would begin the job and complete it. Later Hill learned that the great industrialist had had a stopwatch in his hand, timing his answer. Had his deliberation exceeded the allotted minute, Hill would have lost his chance. Carnegie had learned from his observation of men that those who are slow to make up their minds *are equally as slow to carry out their decisions.*

Carnegie provided Hill with no subsidy for his effort, except to provide letters of introduction and pay his expenses while he interviewed men such as Henry Ford, Thomas Edison, John D. Rockefeller, John Wanamaker, F. W. Woolworth, and Alexander Graham Bell. Carnegie explained that he wished to make sure that Hill learned to apply the philosophy he was to organize—thus proving its soundness by its own accomplishments. In 1928, exactly twenty years after that fateful meeting, Hill published the highly influential book *Laws of Success*, in which he revealed all he had learned.

Nine years later Hill published *Think and Grow Rich*, a classic that sold more than ten million copies. Far from being a get-rich-quick manual, *Think and Grow Rich* distills the essence of the success system of those whom he had studied. At the book's core rests the conviction Hill absorbed from his mentor: *The individual must control his deepest perception of himself, lest he be overwhelmed by the forces of negativism and defeat in those around him.* In *Think and Grow Rich*, Hill demonstrated his genius for motivating others, which would become a hallmark of his subsequent books.

Black America Must Discover the Secret

Prior to his death in 1970, Hill wrote a manuscript specifically aimed at Black America. Unfortunately, the

manuscript was never published. However, it was pre-
served by the foundation that bears Hill's name, and made
available to me, a young, unknown black writer. The
crux of Hill's ideas are the underpinnings of this book.
It is my goal to capture Hill's motivating and inspirational style as I urge potential black achievers who possess the drive and initiative to uncover the secrets of
success and follow Hill's dictum to the letter. Today, at
this very moment, in every part of the country, there are
black men and women—as well as members of other minority groups—who wonder what they can do to realize
their goals and advance some shining ideal.

You and I are no exception. We have the same opportunities that all possess—regardless of race, creed, or social class—to succeed or fail in a land of unlimited riches.
Others before us have brought their desires and visions
to the doorstep of reality. Whether we do so, too, and
cross the threshold of achievement, depends totally on
one person—*the one whom each of us sees in the mirror.*

*Why do some men and women fail while others suc-
ceed?* Why do some wallow in the mire of poverty and
backwardness, while others enjoy success and prosperity? Why does one man live in a loving, caring home,
and another drag out a meager existence in a slum? And
why is one man popular and respected, and another disliked and ignored? This book will help clarify your
thinking as you search for answers.

Think and Grow Rich: A Black Choice began several
years before I came upon Hill's unpublished work on success. The underlying theme was etched into my subconscious during my many years of research while
interviewing dozens of the most powerful black men and
women in America. These high achievers offered me an
opportunity to observe them at close range. I saw them
reveal their traits, both good and bad; I discovered and
analyzed their accomplishments and setbacks, their successes and failures.

During my doctoral studies at Northwestern University

I learned that much of what is believed about race and ethnicity is based on repetition rather than fact. It would be a life's work to disentangle the myths, misconceptions, and half-truths that cloud the process of goal seeking as it pertains to the "ethnic" or "black" experience in America. What is often viewed as a unique and peculiar experience turns out to be not so unique as once imagined. The great mindless idea of our time is that success is only attainable by those of the "right" color, right background or class. *Why does one man fail while another succeeds?* This question is of tremendous concern to all mankind—especially those carving a tunnel of hope where no hope exists.

Understanding Black America

Black America requires special understanding. It embraces more than thirty million men, women, and children, and is becoming increasingly younger and more concentrated in urban areas. While it shares many of the concerns so common to American society as a whole—a decent education, a worthwhile career, an opportunity to build or share in an enterprise for one's future, the rearing of a strong and healthy family, and retirement in comfort and dignity—Black America has its own special set of concerns which exert a powerful influence in determining the quality of its life.

For instance, there are concerns about schools that do not teach but graduate functional illiterates; about employment, homelessness, and the tens of thousands of blacks who have never held a job; about the staggering increase of families headed by single women; about violent crimes where blacks are both the principal victims as well as the perpetrators.

But the idea of a monolithic Black America, if ever real, has become artificial since the civil rights movement. While it implies a unified community that defies today's adversity, the images presented by it are both jarring and inconsistent. On one hand, as of this writing, the *Cosby Show* is top-rated; Bryant Gumbel and Oprah Winfrey are among the most respected hosts of morning network news and talk programs; and an ever-growing number of blacks have grasped the keys to power in spectacular fashion. Dr. Clifton Wharton, for instance, saw race as no burden as he assumed his rightful place to head the nation's largest private pension fund. General Colin Powell, who, like Hannibal and Henry Flipper, paragons who had gone before him, beat back the odds to become America's first soldier. All her life Spelman College's Johnetta Cole had to elbow her way to the table. Now, she is a black woman marked for greatness. "Show me someone content with mediocrity," she says, "and I'll show you someone destined for failure." And Ron Brown, chairman of the National Democratic Party, is an agent of historic change. Throughout his life he had to sidestep barriers constructed to defeat him. "My goal," he says unapologetically, "is to make it more difficult for people to say 'but.'"

These men and women believed that life was meant to be more than a continuous struggle, a challenge to be met by working a little harder than was necessary, by carrying themselves one step further than what was required, and by proving—if proof was still necessary—that the actualized power of their potential was greater than any measure of racism which sought to restrain them.

According to the Bureau of Labor Statistics, the proportion of black professionals and managers has doubled since 1960; also, black poverty—as officially measured by the Joint Center of Political Studies—has declined by nearly one-half. Blacks as a whole have moved from a position of utter destitution—in terms of wealth, education, and human rights—to a place alongside their ethnic counterparts, though none have had to come from so far back to join the ranks.

On the other hand, however, some appalling trends still cloud these gains. Consider the following facts:

- According to the U. S. Census Bureau, the proportion of black children born out of wedlock in 1989 was nearly 60 percent. More than half of all black children are reared in fatherless homes; 31 percent of black Americans live in poverty.
- Forty-five percent of all black children live in families with incomes below the poverty line.
- The black unemployment rate is twice that of whites and Asians. For every black earning $36,000, there are twelve blacks living below the poverty line.
- The 8000 or so black Americans who lost their lives due to black-on-black violence in 1989 is equal to the number of black servicemen killed in action during the entire Vietnam conflict, according to the *Atlanta Journal & Constitution*. Black males, particularly, have edged precariously close to becoming an endangered species.
- More than 40 percent of inmates in federal and state prison are black. There are more black males in prison and correctional facilities than on college campuses.
- A Carnegie Foundation report states that the black high school dropout rate in many urban areas exceeds 40 percent. In some inner cities the rate is more than 50 percent.
- The President's National Commission for Excellence in Education reported that 44 percent of black seventeen-year-olds are functionally illiterate.

And consider the findings from a University of Chicago study as it was submitted to a government agency for public policy debate:

By the year 2000, seventy percent of all black men will be unemployed; seventy percent of all black children will be born into a household without a male; and

roughly one-third of all blacks will be members of a
permanent underclass.

Add to this an explosion of drug abuse and swollen
welfare rolls, and pretty soon the statistics become almost unmentionable. These conditions are both a waste
of human potential and a drain on our national economy.
Those who set social policy indulge themselves in a dem-
agogic game of finger-pointing. Liberals say, "Conservatives won't spend enough on social programs."
Conservatives reply, "We've already spent too much, and
the programs don't work." Many argue that government
is principally responsible. Though these responses possess some element of truth, they fall far short of providing real solutions.

In a very real sense, the civil rights struggle, envisaged
by its founders and millions of supporters, has won some
enormous battles. Blacks are no longer denied access to
the judicial process of impartial hearings, speedy trials,
and jury by peers. They are no longer denied access to
public schools and colleges due to race, nor are they denied access to the political arena. As of this writing,
blacks now serve as chief executive officers in the largest
of U.S. cities—New York, Los Angeles, Newark, Cleveland, Kansas City, New Orleans, Seattle, Baltimore, Detroit, Philadelphia, Atlanta—as well as in the state of
Virginia. On the national level, growing numbers of black
candidates add to their already impressive legions within
America's political and economic structures.

But life is not sociology. This was not the focus of Dr.
Hill's manuscript, and it will not be given consideration
here. Hill was deeply concerned with the "aim of the
common man." He committed the words of the great
American naturalist Henry David Thoreau to memory:

In the long run, men only hit at what they aim. Therefore, though they should fail immediately, it is best
they aim at something high.

The 500 or so achievers highlighted in Hill's Laws of Success represented but a small fraction of those whose personal success demonstrated the veracity of Hill's principles. As Hill asserted on numerous occasions:

> I have never known anyone who was inspired to use the secret who did not achieve noteworthy success in his calling. I have never known any person to distinguish himself or to accumulate riches of any consequence without possession of this secret. From these two facts I draw the conclusion that the secret is more important, as a part of the knowledge essential for self-determination, than any which is received through what is popularly known as education.

It was Hill's dream that Black America would discover the infinite possibilities that are available to *all* who inhabit this world. It was his hope and desire that the time-tested principles that he worked so hard to uncover would be available and practiced by anyone who wished to stamp their mark on society. Hill also stressed that anyone can reach a high level of personal achievement, and through individual initiative can motivate himself or herself to greatness. It boils down to the choices one is willing to make.

Is Racial Oppression and Discrimination an Insurmountable Obstacle?

As I pen my thoughts I can hear a chorus of *but*s. "*But* you don't understand the power of racism." "*But* you underestimate the three hundred years of psychic disrepair that has been heaped upon our people." You're wrong. I do understand. Am I saying that racial oppression no longer exists, that discrimination has vanished from the American landscape? *No!* Yes, racism and discrimination do exist, and they will probably remain as constants. But, and this is a big but, they should never be an excuse for your lack of developing. They should never be offered as a reason for your failure to dream, to strive, and to press forward. When you encounter injustices and social wrongs you must fight them tooth and nail, but you must never, never lose sight of the greater battle to develop as an individual.

The challenge for each black American—and it is a difficult one—is the same as it always has been: Not to go through life as a victim, but to live life victoriously! You need to meditate upon the words shared by the Reverend Dr. Johnnie Coleman, pastor of the Christ Universal Complex in Chicago, one of the nation's largest churches, who teaches, "You don't have to be sick or broke. You can go within and bring forth the power to change things." Or better yet, be still as you consider the thoughts expressed by Dr. Dorothy Height, president of the National Council of Negro Women, who, more than forty years ago, dared to ask the question *"What makes the great, great?"* Has she found the answer? I let you, the reader, decide. "Greatness is not measured by what a man or woman accomplishes," she says, "but by the opposition he or she has overcome to reach his goals."

Yes, even in 1991 America, it can still hurt to walk a mile in the shoes of a black American. But can racism or discrimination stop the man or woman on the move? As the illustrations in this book will attest, *never!*

A Promise to the Reader

For many years I searched for a clue that would foretell the future for any human being. Is there a clue—I wanted to know—that could predict a future of bright promises? Is there a key that would guarantee a person's becoming successful, if he only knew about it and knew how to use it? Well, there is such a key, *and I've found it!*

Why do some people succeed in life while others fail? I will share that answer with you. This answer, if you really understand it, will alter your life immediately. If you understand completely what I am about to tell you, from this moment on your life will never be the same. You will suddenly find that good luck just seems to be attracted to you. You'll find that the things you desire just seem to fall in line. And from now on you won't have the problems, the worries, or the anxiety that you may have carried like so much extra baggage. Doubt and fear will be things of the past. *For in this book lies the key to success, as well as the key to failure.*

A final word of warning before you digest the first chapter. Ignorance is no longer an adequate excuse for failure. Why? *Because virtually all limitation is self-imposed.* You will soon realize that *you*, the individual, are a minute expression of the Creator of all things, and as such, *you* have no limitations except those accepted in your own mind. Every man and woman has within himself or herself a sleeping giant. No one needs to be less than he or she is. There rests within each of us the power to become great—each in our own way.

Finding one's true self is the beginning of success. Simple as it sounds, many go through life without the vaguest notion of their true selves and the meaning of life. There are ingredients, like pieces of a puzzle, waiting to be placed by you into one breathtaking work of art. This process can and must be learned. It is your responsibility, in the final analysis, to overcome ignorance. This can only be accomplished if you remain receptive and teachable.

Special Instructions

As you read this book, read it as if I were a personal friend writing to you—*and you alone*. For this book is dedicated to you who seek the true riches of life. Read it again and again as you refresh your understanding of it. Underscore sentences, quotations, and words that are meaningful to you. Memorize self-motivators. Call on it often, as you will eventually read much between the lines. With each new reading you will see what lies behind each statement. Each of the following chapters contains a secret that is essential to your progress toward your goals and desires. And after you have digested all, understood all, comprehended all and put it all into action, make your choice. You will know, beyond a shadow of a doubt, that there is no reason for you to be held back any longer.

Through this book you will discover that success in life can be predicted with absolute certainty. You can have the desires of your heart—*all of them*. And you will have them if you make this manual a part of your way of thinking, a part of your way of life.

Let me paint a clearer picture. If I gave a blueprint to a skillful builder, do you think it will be a matter of chance or luck that he will complete the structure according to plan? Of course not. The builder merely starts at the beginning and follows the plan step by step to its completion. *Think and Grow Rich: A Black Choice* shares the same concept. *It is a blueprint for success.* If you follow the instructions outlined in this book, the results will be automatic. You'll suddenly realize that you are capable of achieving far more, doing far more, and having far more than you ever thought possible. And you will realize your potential simply by applying the secrets that lie within these pages.

Now the choice is yours. You can choose mediocrity and complacency, with its companion, failure—or you can choose success. *Which will you choose?* Take the first step. Turn the page . . .

1

Inner Space: The Final Frontier

"Wealth is the progressive mastery of matter by mind."

—R. Buckminster Fuller

"Poverty is a disease of the mind."

—S.B. Fuller

We have always been explorers. It is a part of our nature. Since we first evolved a million years or so ago in Africa, we have wandered and explored our way across the planet. Humans have explored every continent—from pole to pole, from Mount Everest to the Dead Sea. This exploratory urge has clear survival value and is not restricted to any one nation or ethnic group. It is an endowment that the human species has in common. But at just the time when the earth has become almost entirely explored, other worlds beckon.

"T minus two minutes and counting!"

The voice giving that command belongs to the test conductor in the firing room of NASA's Launch Control Center. He is completing the countdown for the "greatest" adventure in the history of civilization, the first manned lunar flight. "One small step for man, one giant leap for mankind."

It somehow seems difficult to believe that the Space Age is still in its infancy. Today, satellites routinely orbit the earth, relaying television programs from points all over the world, flashing warnings of developing storms, and surveying the planet's precious supply of natural resources. Robot spacecraft journey far into the solar system, transmitting unprecedented photographs of the once-mysterious faces of the moon, Jupiter, and Mars.

Man now talks almost matter-of-factly about the day when he will venture to other galaxies.

"T minus one minute and counting!" The voice crackles over one of the hundreds of communication circuits monitored by launch crew members.

Paracelsus, a sixteenth-century European philosopher, challenged our character when he wrote, "God did not create the planets and stars with the intention that they should dominate man, but that they, like other creatures, should obey and serve him." Yet historians will record that the opening of this era of infinite promise and potential occurred only in the middle of the twentieth century, when man first successfully launched a package of scientific instruments called *Sputnik 1*. The foundation for space exploration for the betterment of life on earth had been laid.

"T minus thirty seconds and counting!"

A button is pushed. An electronic sequencing springs into action. The rest of the countdown will be done automatically. If any trouble develops past this point, computers will electronically shut down the operation. Engineers and technicians will monitor the series of final events now taking place.

"T minus ten seconds and counting!"

Exploring outer space has been both a challenge and an obligation. Like runners exchanging a baton, scientists, engineers, and mathematicians employed the successes of past explorers to satisfy their hunger of discovering the universe and learning truths.

"T minus three . . . two . . . one! Lift-off!"

Rivers of flame gush down the scorched deflector and funnel out on both sides of the launching pad for several hundred feet. For nearly nine seconds the booster remains locked on its mobile launcher; the ground for miles rumbles and swells as if an earthquake were taking place. The rocket is finally freed. Slowly, ever so slowly, it begins to rise.

Mankind has now embarked on a new, cosmic stage of existence of terrestrial civilization. The message is clear—earth is seen not as our world, but as a part of a greater system of worlds that has now become accessible. It is thought that space exploration will have a profound effect upon life on earth. We have been informed that if man is wise enough to constructively apply this knowledge, the greater will be his opportunities. But what lies beyond this latest expedition into the outer regions of the universe? What will follow once the solar system's planets have been visited, first by robot spacecraft, then by man? What benefits will be reaped from the conquest of the endless seas of outer space—twenty years from now, thirty years, fifty years? Through the magic of satellites, will man have created a unified world? Will this improve human relations? Will famine wane? *Will this finally bring a halt to poverty, ignorance, illiteracy, war, or despair?*

The answer to these questions will not be found within the realm of some far-off sphere or galaxy unknown. Though man has traversed the earth, climbed its highest mountains, explored the depths of its oceans, harnessed electricity, uncovered the secrets of the atom, transmitted pictures and sound from continent to continent, healed with a pill, destroyed with an invisible beam, and now fired projectiles into outer space, the answers he seeks may be found much closer to home.

But something has gone amiss. The anticipation of progress has been supplanted by a foreboding of technological ruin. As I look into the eyes of my fellow man and ask myself what kind of future is being planned by those who have never explored outside of their seemingly limited domains, I realize they have been offered visions of a future that includes the inability to read, to compete, to anticipate events, to invent, or to think. There are those who sink into lethargy and economic decay as fear and ignorance conspire to destroy their opportunities.

Even as our investigation of the outer world has produced such startling results, we must now turn our attention inward to an investigation of ourselves. After many concerted, systematic, and historic missions to other worlds—including the reconnaissance of several planets witnessed in the night sky—*we must focus our being inward, at "inner space" and the conquering of our minds*.

The human mind is the last great unexplored continent on earth. It contains riches—material and spiritual—beyond our wildest dreams. However, like a fertile field, the mind will return anything that we plant.

Now you might say, "If that's true, why don't individuals use their minds more?" The answer is quite simple. Our mind comes to us as standard equipment at birth—it's free. Predictably, we place little or no value on that which is given to us for nothing. On the other hand, things that we pay money for, we value. But the paradox is closer to the truth. Everything that is *really* worthwhile in life comes to us free. Our minds, our souls, our bodies, our hopes, our dreams, our ambitions, our intelligence, our love of family—all these priceless possessions are *free*!

Ironically, things that cost us money can be replaced. A good man or woman can experience bankruptcy, but live to build another fortune. That can be done several times. Even if a home burns down, it can be rebuilt. But those things we get for nothing can never be replaced.

The mind isn't used because we take it for granted. It can do any task we assign to it, but regrettably, we use it for little jobs instead of big important ones. A 1970 Stanford University study proved that most of us are operating on less than five percent of our capacity. Though we are blessed with unlimited power, *we use only a fraction of it*. Unlimited wealth lies around us, but for numerous reasons, we don't grasp our share. With powers endowed to us by our Creator, we are content to continue in this daily grind—eating, sleeping, wandering—plodding through an existence less eventful than that of dumb animals, while all of nature, all of life, calls upon us to awaken from our slumber, to better ourselves.

But you are now entering a new age. An age when you will be your own master; when poverty, ignorance, and fear will no longer hold you captive. And where the very least among us can capture a place side by side with those who have attained greatness. The power to be whatever you wish, to obtain whatever you desire, to accomplish all that you can conceive, abides within the wellsprings of your being.

To those of you who do not know the resources of this innermost power, these will sound like rash statements. But science has proved beyond question that in the depths of everyone's consciousness are untapped deposits of ability, wisdom, greatness—and yes, riches.

Thousands of black Americans have applied this power for their own personal enrichment. For example, when Henry Flipper first took hold of this motivating force, he was a poor and friendless youth. Born in 1856 in Thomasville, Georgia, to ex-slaves, Flipper dreamed of a military career. Though victimized and discriminated against by an insensitive society, he achieved his goal and became the first of his race to graduate from the United States Military Academy at West Point.

Charles Clinton Spaulding took a small North Carolina insurance firm that was nearly bankrupted by a forty-dollar claim and built it into the largest black insurance company in the nation. Spaulding became acquainted with poverty at an early age. Born in North Carolina, and one of fourteen children, he grasped opportunity wherever and whenever he could seize it. With a vision of greater things to come, he saw education as his magic ladder to success. He rapidly absorbed all that he could, attacking his lessons with unprecedented vigor. To keep money in his pockets, he shined shoes, delivered gro-

ceries, sold newspapers, and picked tobacco into the
morning hours. By hard work he managed to graduate
from Durham's segregated public schools.

After graduation he worked as a stock boy in a nearby
general store. It appeared to Spaulding that he had risen
as far as he could go. But he had yet to recognize and
use his greatest asset—*the secret power within*. And then
it happened! Spaulding decided to apply himself to his
task at hand. He started work early, stayed late, and
worked tirelessly in between. His goal was to make his
employer the most profitable man in town. Spaulding
went the *extra mile* to please each customer, and soon
word spread. Under his leadership the small enterprise
prospered and Spaulding was promoted. And then came
the opportunity he had so diligently sought.

John Merrick, a barber who had no formal education,
and Aaron McDuffie Moore, a practicing physician, conceived the idea of a life insurance company that would
serve Durham's black community. It was a bold concept.
However, both men were actively employed and found it
difficult to promote their venture. What was needed, they
figured, was someone who was sharp and energetic, and
who could devote his time exclusively to the promotion
of their firm. Both had observed the hard-working clerk
in his duties at the general store and were impressed.
They approached the young man and offered him a position with substantially lower wages but brimming with
possibilities. With an eye toward the future, Spaulding
accepted.

Thanks to C. C. Spaulding's resourcefulness, missionary zeal, and "power within," the North Carolina Mutual Insurance Company became one of the shining
examples of black business.

Dr. Hugh Gloster, past president of Morehouse College, called on this power, too, as he responded to the
question, "What made [you] one of America's one hundred best college presidents?" He replied, "You must

establish your dreams and quietly move in the direction of attaining them."

To this great power and self-mastery, Althea Gibson owed her success. Born in 1927 to impoverished South Carolina sharecroppers, she started out under great difficulties. Hoping for better circumstances, her family moved to New York while Althea was still young. On New York's inner-city streets she was introduced to a game closely resembling tennis. Almost immediately she pictured a life beyond her humble beginnings. For the next decade her life consisted of "eating, sleeping, and playing tennis." Determined to mold herself into something special, and fueled by a burning desire, Althea Gibson became the first of her race to capture the prestigious Wimbledon Cup, symbolic of the game's best. *And what does she owe her success to?* Though initially shy and timid, and without adequate contacts or "proper" training, she put into action her one great power! This power remains ever present for all who dare to use it.

This same power had found its way into the mind of Frederick Douglass, the great abolitionist. Starting life against many great obstacles, Douglass nevertheless reached his goal. For years life seemed to turn a cold shoulder to his hopes of freedom. He was a slave who did not know his father and saw his mother rarely, when she could walk the twelve miles from a neighboring plantation to spend precious moments with her son. Douglass had little chance of learning; the unwritten codes of the "forbidden system" forbade slaves to read or write. But somehow, unnoticed by his oppressors, he managed to discern the rudiments of the alphabet from discarded newspapers. A seed was planted. And from this spark kindled an intellectual explosion! The truth was revealed to him when he "read" the Declaration of Independence. *In his mind he was always free!*

Douglass fled from slavery at twenty-one, went north and worked on a loading dock in Massachusetts. At Nantucket he was given an opportunity to address an anti-slavery meeting, and made such a favorable impression that he was sent by an abolitionist society to lecture throughout Europe. On one such tour he met a group of Englishmen who helped him purchase his freedom. During his repeated trials, Douglass relied on this omnipresent resource to accomplish his objectives. So persuasive was this ex-slave that he attracted a strong following and was selected for many influential public posts. Before his death his success was even felt in the commercial world, as he amassed a small fortune. For this reason Congress labeled him the "First Colored Man of the United States."

You should be moved by the preceding stories. No man or woman—however poor or indigent—need despair. There are riches for anyone who recognizes the power of the mind.

You Are a Mental Being

Think for a moment. Thoughts and ideas are actually living things. Thoughts produce tangible results and have a powerful, long-term effect on your life. Thinking is your greatest gift and is the most vital aspect of your being. The car you drive, the house in which you live, the chair upon which you rest, were first ideas in mind. Everything you see began as ideas in a mind. Your physical world is nothing more than the lingering evidence of that which has already taken place in your mind. It is merely an extension or outpicturing of your thoughts. Yours is a mental world.

"You are a mind with a body." That bit of wisdom comes from insurance magnate and philanthropist W. Clement Stone. And because you are a mind, you possess mystical powers, both known and unknown. This extraordinary power—mystical, as it has been rightly called—is both real and practical. It is wise to approach this concept in a spirit of awe, for it is the most profound subject of this book. Mental power is really no less than that which lies at the center of your being, and to discover this force is your birthright. It is your right and privilege to make use of it. Allow this power to work for you.

But where is this resource? Where may we find it? How is it brought into action? These answers are simple. This power is to be found within your own consciousness—*your ability to control your own thoughts!*

The power of thought may be likened to a rich garden. The soil may be converted, by organized effort and the Creator's beneficence, into a necessary food source. Or by neglect it may be allowed to produce useless weeds. The mind is eternally at work, building up or tearing down, bringing misery, unhappiness, and poverty, or joy, pleasure, and riches. *The mind is never idle.* It is the greatest of all human assets; yet, it is the least used and the most abused. Science has revealed many of nature's most astonishing secrets, but has overlooked the source of man's wealth—*the power of his own thoughts.*

Lying within your mind is a source of energy stronger and more potent than any explosive; unlimited and inexhaustible. You need only to make conscious contact with this force to set it working in your affairs. When you do, you will marvel at the following changes:

1. Mental and physical well-being
2. Success in your chosen field of endeavor
3. A sense of personal fulfillment

This is the key. The hidden cause of all things is the primal mind that lies behind creation, and it delivers our wishes to each of us, according to our thoughts. We are all guided by our own mind.

You must dare to investigate all the mental laws lying outside the realm of known physical processes—laws that have undoubtedly had, and will continue to have, an impact on your life. But beware, the very principle that

renders success is a two-edged sword. For the same principle that can lead a man or woman to a life of achievement, wealth, happiness, and the desires of his heart *can
also lead to a life of destitution and failure*. It's all in
how each uses it—for good or bad.

Mental Laws

What are mental laws? There are a few great truths that
govern all thinking, just as there are fundamental laws
that rule the physical universe. For example, a young
Isaac Newton, the seventeenth-century English mathe-
matician and philosopher, saw an apple fall from a tree
and switched on the power of his imagination. "Why
didn't the apple fall upward?" he thought. Newton spent
his life unfolding the keys to the physical universe.
Through his insight, mankind is able to understand the
physical laws of gravity and physics.

Mental laws, on the other hand, are just as broad as
physical laws. These spiritual principles exist on a grand
cosmic scale and rule over our mental well-being. All
that is good, all that is bountiful and worthwhile, emanates from the successful application of mental laws.
They are the very infrastructure of life.

The most significant quality of a mental law is that it
can neither be created nor altered. As one is blinded to
physical laws, mental laws are also undetectable to the
eye. We witness only their results—bearing proof of their
inevitable existence.

Not once, neither in grade school nor college, were we
ever instructed in the simple techniques of learning how
to apply mental laws; laws that have the power to overcome adversity, eliminate self-defeating habits, and increase our self-confidence. There are an infinite number
of mental laws, but fortunately we don't need a detailed
understanding of every principle of the universe to
achieve even the most grandiose of goals. However, there
are several key rules with which we must be totally fa-

miliar and use unfailingly as guides in all our dealings. They are:

What You Think Upon, Grows

This is the great idea that you will encounter again and again in your quest for personal fulfillment: You are a living magnet, constantly drawing to you the things, people, and circumstances that are in accord with your thoughts. In other words, you are where you are in experience, in relationships, even in financial conditions, because of what you are in thought.

Consequently, what you think about grows. William James, the Harvard psychologist, and someone who knew a great deal about achievement, said, "You are what you think about most of the time." Whatever you persistently allow to occupy your thoughts will magnify in your life. Whether the subject of your thoughts be good or bad, positive or negative, this law remains true.

The more you think about an affliction—disease, headache, or poor health—the worse it will become. The more you think of yourself as healthy and well, the more exuberant and vibrant your body will be.

The same is true concerning your finances. The more you think about lack, bad times, or scarcity, the more these circumstances will become manifest in your life. Conversely, by focusing on prosperity, abundance, and success, you will enable these riches to appear in your life. Good fortune nurtures good fortune. Learn to concentrate your thoughts on your definite major purpose. It is the starting point of all achievement.

Law of Cause and Effect

It is astounding and shocking to see the many thousands of people whose mental machinery keeps delivering to them the very effects they say they do not want. They bewail the idea that they are poor, but that doesn't make them richer. They complain about their aches and pains, but sickness lingers. They say that nobody likes them, which really means they care for no one. They aren't bold; they aren't aggressive; they aren't ambitious. They are the sum total of their thoughts and actions.

Cause and effect is a mental law that never fails. Day by day you write your own destiny. Thoughts are causes, and conditions in your life are effects. If you've ever wanted to know the status of your thoughts, you need only to look at your conditions.

One of the greatest messages ever given to mankind is written in the scriptures: "Whatsoever a man soweth, that shall he also reap." Translated, it means whatever you send out in word, thought, or deed will sooner or later return to you—and with astounding accuracy. In practical terms, if you crave friendship, *be a friend.* Do you want love? *Give love.* If you want the confidence of others, show confidence in others first and develop your own self-confidence as well.

Use or Lose

This law is apparent throughout all of life. Simply stated, *practice makes perfect.* This familiar proverb embodies one of the most important principles of human nature—to become proficient in any field you must practice. There is simply no achievement without practice, practice, and even more practice. An Olympic athlete will train for years just to be able to experience the thrill of a winning moment. Virtuoso musicians practice endlessly just to keep their skills at peak performance. The scientist who wins the Nobel Prize has experimented and refined his theories over the course of a career.

To achieve a standard of excellence, to accomplish anything extraordinary, means aiming high. It means being disciplined and willing to devote long hours to the task at hand. Intelligent practice is the price of proficiency; success is often a statistical event. Prosperity is a spiritual idea of excellence. And, like any form of excellence or superiority, it requires time and love and care. It is the secret of attainment.

Consider the following analogy. If someone were to place your leg in a cast for several months, by the time the cast was removed your leg would shrink or atrophy as compared to your other limb. Only months of regular exercise would restore the limb to normalcy. As you grow older and your life becomes more sedentary, you cease to use certain muscles. In due time a once-firm body can become soft and weak. Only regular and systematic use will prevent its deterioration.

Like physical effort, thought control is entirely a matter of intelligent practice. You must use your courage or it will desert you. You must use your determination or it will leave you. You must use your power of decision or soon you will find that you have none.

Law of Correspondence

Your thoughts are the prophets of the future. They can predict what to expect before it happens. Why? Because you are basically a thinker, a feeler, a dreamer. What you think, feel, and dream flows inward, then outward. The basic law is: *First within, then without.*

Could any genius ever achieve anything, could any inventor create anything, could anyone who accomplishes anything worthwhile attain it without first having thought about it deeply? Felt it? Been totally imbued with it, immersed in it? Every great victory demonstrates this process. Everything that happens to you in your external world happens because of what is occurring in your internal world.

There is a deeper significance in the statement made by psychologist William James. "You do not sing because you are happy; you are happy because you sing." It signifies that the way one feels can be determined to a large extent by the way one acts. It is an indication that we, as individuals, are not powerless to circumstances and can improve our lives. This is called the "law of correspondence"—your external world is nothing more than a mirror or reflection of your internal world.

Some readers will experience difficulty with this idea. If it seems impractical, examine your present circumstances from an objective point of view. First, decide what changes you wish to make in your life. Now, develop a habitual mental attitude that would correspond to the new circumstances which you wish to experience. It should become apparent that before any area of your life can improve, your mental attitude toward it must change first. This principle of attitude control is discussed in detail in a later chapter.

The law of correspondence makes it possible for you to change undesirable conditions and enables you to become the person you truly want to be. It requires nothing more than the ability to control your thoughts so they will correspond to the desired conditions and objectives that you have set for yourself. *If it is success that you seek, you must first develop a success consciousness.*

Law of Substitution

The only way to rid yourself of any negative thought is to substitute another one for it. You cannot dismiss a thought directly. You can do so only by substituting another thought for it. Why? Because your conscious mind can hold only one thought at a time.

If I were to say to you, "Dismiss any thoughts of lack or limitation," your mind would immediately center on that idea. When negative thoughts creep into your subconscious, immediately begin to replace them with those that are more positive. Though you may not be able to control all the circumstances that surface in your life, you are able, however, to control your response to those circumstances. You will find a direct relationship between your level of control and your ability to effectively use the law of substitution.

Law of Belief

How many times have you heard it said, "Just believe you can do it and you can!" Whatever the task, if it is undertaken in an air of positive expectancy, it can be done. This law states that anything you believe with feeling will become real in your life—whether it be a positive belief, such as a goal or a specific desire, or a negative belief, such as a self-limiting idea. The key to this law lies within the words *with feeling*.

Many times belief enables a person to accomplish what others consider impossible. The act of believing is the force or generating power that leads to realization. "Come on, fellows, we can beat them," shouts someone in command. That voicing of belief, challenging and electrifying, reverses the tide and rescues victory from the jaws of defeat—and all because some mighty believer knew that it could be done!

Belief is the key to the basic mind power that turns dreams into realities, the mental into the physical. The key to your riches and transformation for the better is a deeply ingrained belief.

Law of Attraction

Human nature assumes that opposites attract. Perhaps in the scientific realm they do. But not so with people. Actually, people are attracted to others like themselves. Individuals are drawn together because they recognize and appreciate certain common qualities in each other.

Those who criticize, find fault, and continually accentuate the negative attract similar people into their world. On the other hand, positive, life-affirming individuals attract like-minded people into their orbit. So, in effect, you create your own world through your thoughts about life in general and about yourself in particular. Those who are clear in their thinking and affirmative in their minds find self-fulfillment. They attract positive and constructive people like themselves, and prosper.

The mental force that controls the universe has been called many things—God, Jehovah, Mohammed—but the important thing is to know that it exists. The law of attraction has been likened to an enormous electromagnetic field, within a greater universal sphere, attracting others of the same source, kind, or quality.

For example, a highly magnetized piece of steel will attract and lift a piece of metal ten times its own weight. The same law applies within the world of human nature—the laws of attraction and repulsion operate electromagnetically. Out of this truth has grown the saying: *Success attracts more success, while failure attracts more failure.* A positive- or negative-minded individual will attract a person of the same attitude or outlook. Like always attracts like. It is important that you become magnetized with ambition.

Law of Compensation

The law of compensation can work for you or against you depending on the manner in which you guide it. It may take many years for punishment to follow transgression or for reward to follow virtue, but compensation always seeks its source.

An ancient Sanskrit text says, "Whatever you give to others, give with love and reverence. Gifts must be given in abundance, with joy, humility, and compassion." The Bible puts it this way: "As you give, so shall you receive."

Examine your attitudes toward giving. Never seek a trade-off—that subtle and sly thief that lies ready to rob you of the purity and joy of your giving. Be a joyful giver. Give help. Give energy. Give time. Give funds. Share ideas. Offer counsel to your friends if they desire it. *But give freely, with joy, and have no thought of a return.* If you give seeking or expecting a return, you are not giving, but investing. You are not releasing, but lending. Your real reward must come from the infinite source—the *law of compensation*.

The channels by which you may reach your goals are clear and straightforward. When your thoughts are clearly and confidently centered on a desired result, all that is good and right will be drawn to you by your own thinking. This is the omnipotent idea that you will undoubtedly encounter as you strive for all that life offers. You are a living magnet, constantly attracting the things, people, and circumstances that are in accord with your thoughts. You are where you are in experience, in relationships, and even in financial conditions, because of what you are in thought. I believe you have been drawn to this book by this powerful law. It could just be that *Think and Grow Rich: A Black Choice* is an idea whose time has come in your life.

Change Your Thoughts—Change Your Life!

Can you accept the dictum that you can think your way to success? In *Think and Grow Rich*, Napoleon Hill writes:

> You have absolute control over but one thing, and that is your thoughts. This is the most significant and inspiring of all facts known to man. It reflects man's divine nature. This divine prerogative is the sole means by which you may control your own destiny. If you fail to control your own mind, you may be sure you will control nothing else. If you must be careless with your possessions, let it be in connection with material things. Your mind is your spiritual estate! Protect and use it with the care to which divine royalty is entitled. You were given a willpower for this purpose.

The power of thought, depending on how it is used, is the most dangerous and the most beneficial force available to man. Through this power man has built great empires of civilization. Through the same power, other men have trampled down these empires like so many insignificant pieces of clay. By its application man rises to seize his opportunity. And through neglect or misuse of this same power, man has turned his back on opportunity, becoming a puppet of his environment, a slave to his circumstances.

Every creation of man, whether it be good or bad, is created first in a pattern of thought. All ideas, plans, and purposes are created in thought. As men search all their lives for worldly riches, they fail to realize that "the source" of all they would ever desire is already within their reach and under their control, awaiting only their recognition and use. Your only requirement for a productive, fulfilled life lies within the storehouse of your mind. *If you will change your thinking, you will change your life.*

From ancient times sages and seers have tried to understand the thought process and how it works. They sought to direct the mind through the spiritual disciplines of prayer, meditation, and psychic control. Sincere and dedicated spiritual researchers were impelled to communicate to others what they had learned about *infinite intelligence*, the way to work with one's mind and emotions to attain desired ends. Unfortunately, these efforts fell short for one good reason—they failed to apply the complete process that directs the creative subconscious.

Throughout all of history the great wise men, teachers, philosophers, and prophets have disagreed with each other on many different things. But on this one point they are in complete and unanimous agreement: *You are the sum total of your thoughts.*

"A man's life is what his thoughts make of it," said the Roman emperor and philosopher Marcus Aurelius.

The British writer and prime minister Benjamin Disraeli wrote, "Everything comes if a man will only wait. I've brought myself by long meditation to the conviction that a human being with a settled purpose must accomplish it, and that nothing can resist a will that will stake even existence for its fulfillment."

The nineteenth-century American essayist and poet Ralph Waldo Emerson added, "A man is what he thinks about all day long."

Shakespeare wrote, "There is nothing either good or bad, but thinking makes it so."

Harvard psychologist William James said in one of his emotionally charged lectures, "The greatest discovery of my generation is that human beings can alter their lives by altering their attitudes of mind. We need only to act as if the thing in question were real and it will become infallibly real by growing in such a connection in our life, that it WILL become real."

James further concluded that, "If you only care enough for a result you will almost certainly obtain it. If you wish to be rich, you will be rich; if you wish to be learned, you will be learned; if you wish to be good, you will be good."

And Ayn Rand, author and philosopher, emphasized, "Wealth is the product of man's capacity to think."

Man's essential characteristic is his rational faculty. His mind is his basic means of survival—his only means of obtaining that which he desires. Life for each of us is exactly as we construe it to be—according to the mental law under which we labor. All notions of theology or metaphysics are, for each of us, exactly as we sense them to be, for ideas that take root in our minds determine the scope and limitations of our well-being. This is the basis for the astonishing law of prosperity and success. Simply stated in three words: *Believe and succeed.*

Thinking along similar lines, Shakespeare put it this way: "Our doubts are traitors, and make us lose the good we oft might win, by fearing to attempt."

The English dramatist George Bernard Shaw reasoned,

"People are always blaming their circumstances for what they are. I don't believe in circumstances. The people who get on in this world are those who get up and look for the circumstances they want—and if they can't find them, they make them."

To many, mental power implies such chicanery as moving objects by sheer will. But the mentally adept person works on no one but himself. His is the eye through which all things are seen, and only insofar as he is able to influence his own perception is he able to influence his world.

In Spite of the Handicaps

Nothing can enslave an idea. An idea proceeds from an inner realm which is freedom itself. It is the offspring of the greatest power in the universe—*the mind*. Indeed, understanding the truth about your nature as mind-action can set you free from every negative concept, every enslaving belief or opinion. Ideas can move you forward to a higher quality of life, a new being, and a new awareness.

Decades ago Mary McLeod Bethune personally discovered that thoughts do become things. As one of America's most inspiring educators, she began her life's work by filling her mind with self-directed success affirmations. Though black, uneducated, and shackled by poverty, Mary Bethune took hold of one of the strongest principles behind personal development and applied it to reach her main objective. She desperately wanted to improve the lives of black children.

"There is hardly a reader," said Mary Bethune, "who will not be able to recall the early life of at least one man or woman whose childhood was spent in poverty, and who, in their youth, expressed a firm desire to secure a higher education."

Mary Bethune was one of seventeen children born to slave parents in a tiny cabin on a cotton farm near Mayesville, South Carolina. When she was eleven years old the board of missions of the Presbyterian Church opened a school near her hometown. Ecstatically, she was one of the first children to attend, walking nearly ten miles each day, lured by the promise of a quality education. Reflecting on her daughter's childhood, Mary's mother said, "We had to make some of the children go to school, but not Mary. She fell in love with that little schoolhouse."

Hard work and enthusiasm served her well. The following year, at the request of a wealthy Colorado dressmaker, Mary studied at the Scotia Seminary. Though initially shy and uncomfortable with her appearance, Mary met every slight and criticism with unfailing faith and soon won the hearts of her teachers and peers. As her formal instruction concluded, she received numerous scholarships that enabled her to continue her studies in Chicago.

At the end of a two-year term at the Moody Bible Institute, Mary hoped to see the fulfillment of a long-cherished dream to teach as a missionary in Africa. But bitter disappointment awaited her. She was told by the Presbyterian Board of Missions that because of her race, she need not apply, and was commissioned instead to Sumpter, South Carolina, and later to Daytona, Florida.

The setback would have ruined many a man—*but not Mary!* At that very instant fate was measuring her to play a larger role.

Mary arrived in Daytona with less than two dollars. She looked about her at the shambles of the black community. She saw the great need for someone to inspire her people. A desire had caught hold of her. She believed: *There is something infinitely better than making a living—it is making a noble life.* Undeterred by her limited means, *she knew that ideas were power!* She immediately made plans to build a school—complete with books, desks, and supplies. But without money it would not be easy.

Ever resourceful, Mary met the task head-on. In order

to raise the necessary funds to complete her mission, she worked unceasingly, day and night, and saved every dime. She lived on pennies a day while she baked pies and cakes and sold them on the streets of Daytona. "If there was ever a time when the Negro needed a boost, it is now," she told friends. In short order she overcame all obstacles.

At last her dream was fulfilled. The school she had hoped to establish for poor black children was complete. In the fall of 1904, in a tiny one-room schoolhouse, a beaming Mary Bethune—its only teacher—opened its doors and rang the school bell for the first time. Five little children stepped inside, and the Daytona Educational & Industrial Training School, as it was named, was founded.

Later, this school became Bethune Cookman College, and Mary Bethune transformed a world of ignorance and poverty into one of success, self-respect, and achievement for thousands of black men and women. Mary Bethune taught that the highest accomplishments are noble manhood and womanhood, and that achievement of true integrity and well-rounded character is in itself success. Before her death in 1955, she was an adviser to several U.S. presidents, and a counselor to all who would listen.

Mary Bethune's vision was part of the ongoing universal movement of thought power which anyone can grasp and use. It is only a matter of having a desire coupled with the right mental attitude, and applying these powers to good use in your life. By focusing on her goal and assuming full responsibility for her thoughts, Mary Bethune overcame setback and defeat and brought about an astonishing triumph in her affairs. Her rise to prominence is proof that if one has mental power, one can succeed without any other qualities.

"Conscious power," wrote James Lowell, a nineteenth-century American poet, "exists within the mind of everyone. Sometimes its existence is unrealized, but it is there. It is there to be developed and brought forth like the culturing of a beautiful flower. To allow it to remain dormant is to place one's self in obscurity, to trample on one's ambition, to smother one's faculties. To develop it is to individualize all that is best within you, and offer it to the world.''

Thoughts and ideas are living things. They produce results that can have powerful, long-term effects on your life and well-being. If you are not all that you would be, begin a thorough mental inventory to find whether your thoughts and feelings are aligned with your desires. Think and act as if you were prosperous—for this will be the first step toward a prosperity consciousness—and prosperity will come to you. Think and act as if you were healthy—for this will be the first step toward a health consciousness—and health will come to you. Think and act as if you are poor, and poverty will rule your day. It is up to each of us, individually, to make the decision as to what our thoughts will bring.

Wealth Is Nothing But Thought

The roots of riches all grow from the seeds of thought, seeds that only you can plant. In a justly ordered universe, individual responsibility is absolute. A man's weaknesses and strengths are his own, not another's; they are brought about by himself, not by another; and they can be altered only by himself, never by another. A man's condition is his own. His suffering, as his happiness, evolves from within. *As he thinks, so is he; as he continues to think, so he remains.*

As a reader of this book, I believe you have the human urge for the better things in life, a common desire of all people. You desire economic security. You may desire an outlet for your talents in order that you might enjoy creating your own riches. Some, however, seek the easy way to wealth, hoping to find it without rendering anything in return. Unfortunately, that too is a common desire. But it is a desire I shall hope to modify for your benefit.

From experience I've learned there is *no such thing as something for nothing*. Nature frowns on bargains; you must give an equivalent value for the object of your desire. There is only one sure way to riches, and hopefully you will have found that path before you complete this text.

Let it be known at the outset that when I speak of "riches," I have in mind all riches—not merely those represented by bank balances and material possessions. I have in mind the riches of liberty and freedom, which as Americans you enjoy more than any other people outside these distant shores. When I speak of riches, I refer to the abundant life which is available to *all* people of these United States, regardless of race and gender, and obtainable with a minimum amount of effort.

I sincerely hope that you will aim for your fair share, not only of the things that money can buy, but of the things money cannot buy. By riches I mean:

1. *Peace of Mind*
   Peace of mind is freedom from all negative emotions. Peace of mind is the absence of fear, anger, resentment, hatred, jealousy, and guilt. Peace of mind helps you live your life on your own terms, in the values of your choosing, so that every day your life grows richer and fuller.
2. *The Right Mental Attitude*
   All riches, of whatever nature, begin as a state of mind. Remember, that state of mind is the one and only asset over which you have complete and unchallenged control.
3. *Health and Energy*
   You cannot separate the body and the mind, for they are one. Anything that affects the health and vigor of the mind will affect the body. In turn, anything that affects the health of the body will affect the mind.

   Health and energy are the freedom from pain and disease; a sound mind plus a sound body. Health and energy begin with a "health consciousness." Your health is a priceless commodity.

4. *Loving Relationships*

Love is the great force that created the universe. Love is forever working in your life because it is the primal cause, the essence and nature of life. It is the creative force that propels all achievement, success, and ideas.

Love is the foundation of the golden rule: "Do unto others as you would have others do unto you." Love and affection constitute the finest remedies for the soul. You can always judge the quality of your life by the number of loving relationships you have entered into.

5. *Financial Freedom*

Financial freedom is not attained by the possession of money alone. It is attained by the service one renders. Useful service may be converted into all forms of human needs, with or without the use of money.

Those who are financially free have learned a central rule of riches: You may have all the money you desire—the only requirement is that you must *earn* it. Fully 80 percent of those with whom you come in contact think of money all the time without realizing the above maxim. The average man will tell you that he wants to *make* a million dollars, or that he wants to *make* a lot of money. He doesn't realize that the only people who *make* money are those who work in a mint. The successful must *earn* their wages or profits.

The wisdom surrounding money is strange: If you have enough of it, you hardly think about it; but if you lack it, you'll think of nothing else. Each of us must know that in order to enjoy peace of mind, loving relationships, and health and energy, we must be able to overcome any money problems.

6. *Worthy Goals and Ideals*

The greatest of all forms of happiness comes as the result of hope of achievement of some yet unattained desire. The German psychiatrist Victor Frankl called this state of mind "a feeling of meaning and purpose." It is a sense that your life has direction. Poor is the person who cannot look to the future with the hope that he will become the person he was meant to be, or with the belief that he will reach his objective.

7. *Sense of Personal Fulfillment*
   Only the man or woman who has found his true self can know himself, find his own best talent, and achieve his own high success.

Our automated society has come to expect path-breaking technological advances as routine and mundane. For instance, the transformation of the computer into a commodity appliance has liberated mankind from the tedious tasks of the past. Through this simplified machine, man has lengthened his life and improved its quality. The twentieth century has seen the world grow smaller but more efficient through an intricate web of microchips, threadlike wires, and lasers housed in a small metal box. How was this brought about? Easy. It existed in mind first. Yes, it's true: *Whatever the mind of man can conceive and believe, it can achieve. The mind is the first cause!*

When you come to grips with the enormous power at your disposal and earnestly put it to work, not only will you have dominion over this earth, as is your divine charge, but you will reach new heights and possibilities.

This power—*your inner spark*—comes as standard equipment. But it must be fanned into a flame of white-heat intensity before the mental processes will be transformed into physical manifestation. Success is not a product of fate, chance, or luck; it is the result of a burning desire that knows not defeat.

Prosperity Is Your Privilege!

Perhaps one of the greatest shocks I've ever received was the discovery that man's natural desire for prosperity was viewed as abnormal. Throughout my travels I've witnessed thousands of black Americans who've secretly wondered whether poverty is a spiritual virtue or a common vice. I stood by and watched as they struggled with internal conflicts over wealth resulting from years of self-inflicted mental wounds. If you've held this idea in the past, now would be a good time to rid yourself of this deadly thinking. Let me announce to all: *It is your right to be prosperous!*

Prosperity is the result of correct thoughts, an active way of thinking and living in accordance with spiritual principles. It borders on current hopes, faith, and desires. Prosperity is normal and is your natural heritage. Each of us is free to tap the infinite intelligence that makes prosperity possible. Rejoice in the idea of prosperity!

Poverty, on the other hand, is undesirable and unnecessary. Misery, debt, and lack are the direct result of a "poverty consciousness" and a "victim psychology" that springs from thoughts of limitation and fear. It is a form of living hell caused by man's blindness to the unlimited opportunities and abundance placed before him. In a country such as ours, where riches abound in every conceivable form, you should erase any thoughts that see virtue in either lack or want.

Thinking His Way to Success

When multimillionaire A. G. Gaston first decided to seek his fortune, he worked long and hard in Alabama's steel mills earning less than thirty cents an hour. Having devised a plan to increase his lot, Gaston and his father-in-law launched a string of funeral parlors which later grew into the Booker T. Washington Insurance Company. Their modest enterprise eventually became the hub of a network of businesses that would rocket Gaston's holdings to an estimated $40 million. His inspiring story and motivating philosophy are found in his autobiography, *Green Power: The Success Ways of Arthur G. Gaston.*

Gaston's riches were first embedded within the depths of his subconscious—what Napoleon Hill termed a "success consciousness." Gaston elaborated: "I gave serious consideration to what I was going to do with my life. I WANTED TO BE RICH—so I thought, 'How does a poor black man acquire wealth?' *Simple—by providing a useful service.*"

However, there was a time when Gaston had no service to provide and worked for less than two dollars a day. His childhood was punctuated with poverty. His father died when he was young, and his mother worked as a domestic to support her son. Because of their limited means, Gaston lived with his grandmother, who kept him fed and clothed. But it was these event-filled days at his grandmother's home that gave Gaston his greatest satisfaction, as well as his first business opportunity. A swing on his grandmother's porch became a favorite pastime among the neighborhood's children. For a modest fee of pennies, pins, and candy, Gaston's playmates could ride to their hearts' content. This was his first lesson in economics.

After completing the eighth grade and serving a stint in the Army, Gaston settled in Westfield, a sleepy-eyed southern town, where he worked for the county's principle employer, the Alabama Coal Iron and Steel Company. He remembers those long, hard days. "It was backbreaking labor for poverty wages. There had to be a better way to earn a living." Nonetheless, he managed to live on a small portion of his earnings and saved whatever he could. "Frugality is one of the essentials of success," he quipped. "It is the unwritten law of wealth."

This statement was a symbol of Gaston's idea. To supplement his tiny income he sold peanuts and loaned a portion of his earnings to less thrifty coworkers. Eventually the interest on these monies compounded and was used to start other businesses—motels, restaurants, nursing homes—and any enterprise that would render a service to a needy black population. To provide the necessary manpower for his ventures, Gaston created the Booker T. Washington Business College, which today is fully accredited and supplies highly trained graduates for various positions in business and government throughout the nation.

A. G. Gaston employed the secret to overcoming poverty and moving mountains. By directing and channeling his thoughts, Gaston realized his greatest gift—*thinking*! "There is a way to provide against the onslaught of poverty," he said. *"It is the recognition of the power of mind!"* Gaston substituted higher thoughts of abundance for his earlier restrictive thinking, which resulted in lack. Subsequently, he altered the direction of his life. A. G. Gaston knew that the most powerful forces in the universe are unseen—the silent forces of thought.

You Choose Your Thoughts

He grew up under the worst conditions, in a poor section of Detroit. He had little guidance except what he received from delinquent peers, who, like himself, avoided school and used crime to support drug habits. He was first arrested at age twelve—caught robbing a local grocery store. At fifteen he was again apprehended attempting another break-in. Later, as an adult, he was tried and convicted for his part in the armed robbery of a neighborhood bar.

While in jail, he was not a model prisoner. The moment he arrived at the State Prison of Southern Michigan, he vowed to himself that the facility was not strong enough to hold him and immediately made plans to escape. In fact, he was so hard-bitten, he was placed in solitary confinement three times during his stay. It was after his third stint in solitary that he received the advice that would later change his life. An inmate who had seen him play baseball in the prison yard admired his enormous gift. "You have talent," he told him, "a chance to make something of yourself. *Don't blow it.*"

The young man had heard it all before, but this time it seemed different. Some silent power within caused him to take a good look at his life. *He stepped back and took action!* He harnessed his aggressive behavior and adapted himself to prison rules. He became the most agreeable inmate at Southern Michigan. With this new resolution, his entire state of affairs began to reverse. Ron Leflore had finally mastered his greatest enemy—*himself.* Though incarcerated, he knew he was not powerless, and vowed to change his thoughts.

The change that Ron Leflore experienced came by reversing his attitude. He felt that his "old self" had died and a "new man" had moved in and taken charge. He began reading self-help and inspirational books. He looked for ways to make his prison stay as productive as possible. And this right mental attitude spilled over into other areas of his life.

After a goodwill tour of the prison and talent search by then Detroit Tiger manager Billy Martin, Leflore was offered a tryout. Impressed with his skill and ability, Martin signed the speedy inmate to a contract. Less than a year later LeFlore was a major leaguer playing center field for the Detroit Tigers!

Now, reflect for a moment. Here was a man at the bottom of the barrel—a convicted felon serving a lengthy prison sentence. But despite his wretched circumstances, he nevertheless managed to use his greatest gift. And more important, he decided to exercise it positively. Ron Leflore could have easily said, "I have no hope, no chance, no choice. I'm a convict—what can I possibly do?" But he didn't. What he did say was, "I do have power over my thoughts, and now I choose to change my thinking!"

From that moment Ron Leflore changed his life forever. He took a good look at the Ron Leflore of the past and resolved to avoid this same appearance in the future.

What is this power that Ron Leflore possessed? What miracle turned the tide in his favor? *It is the power of choice!*

As inhabitants of this earth, we all have the capacity to think, to express our ideas, and to *choose* our own thoughts. Here, according to the divine plan, we are given dominion. The creative process in life gives us the authority to direct the events that take place in our outer experiences. If we do not like the world that we have created for ourselves, or if we do not like our circumstances, we have been given the privilege of forging a new set of opportunities by choosing our thoughts.

The experiences of A. G. Gaston and Ron Leflore demonstrate that no one has to be a pawn of fate, to be tossed by the winds of chance. By taking responsibility for the quality of his thoughts, anyone can chart a course of planned achievement.

These stories prove once again that a man can change his world and alter his life by changing the quality of his thinking. They prove that by positively exercising the power of choice, men and women can lift themselves to significant accomplishments. There is no mystery about Gaston's and Leflore's rise to good fortune. Their success was captured by applying many of the principles outlined in this book.

Stop and think. You, too, have the right to use those same principles. *Now, what are you going to do with your right?*

Choice Is Not Dead

The world is full of people who believe that choice is dead and individual freedom is an idea of the past. These individuals would rather opt for the intangibles—luck, fate, or roll of the dice—as the determinators of success. It would be wise to abandon such thinking.

Historically, black Americans have caucused at great length over the subject of power—both its abuse and lack. Over the last fifty years power within Black America has come to mean control over one's destiny. "All power to the people!" to recall a past expression, called for the unification of black Americans to recognize a common heritage and move toward a common destiny.

"Black Power" is an intriguing slogan. It conjures up past struggles between a race and a nation groping to find common chords. It suggested dominance and retaliation by a black nation for centuries of oppression. It also implied emancipation and full participation in a culturally diverse society. However, both banners failed to uncover the one true power that every black American has—*the power of choice!*

At some point in life we Americans become keenly aware of the constant choices that present themselves—choices that will determine our destiny. It is as though at birth we were given two sealed envelopes, each containing explicit orders by which our lives would be governed. One envelope would contain a list of blessings we could enjoy if we recognized the power of our mind, take possession of it, and carefully direct it to the goals of our choosing. The other envelope would contain an equally representative list of penalties that we would pay if we failed to recognize this power and use it constructively.

Your thoughts are the only thing you control. Either you control them or you relinquish your greatest gift to others. Without control, the mind loses its effectiveness. With control and direction, it gains power. You will not have power until you organize your mind and keep it clear of disturbing influences. Use your mind to shape your destiny to fulfill whatever purposes in life you choose, and to avail yourself of all the riches that come in that sealed envelope marked "blessings."

Years ago Booker T. Washington penned the following

words. It would serve you well to commit his quote to memory: "The circumstances that surround a man's life are not important. How that man responds to those circumstances IS IMPORTANT. His response is the ultimate determining factor between success and failure."

Why So Many Continue to Fail

The reason why poverty still clutches the throats of so many in this land of abundance is because so many have yet to comprehend and apply the mental laws. Many, unfortunately, have not fully understood the premise: *First the dream, then reality.* By failing to direct their minds on that which *they desire*, and by allowing their thoughts to aimlessly drift to that which they *do not desire*, they've become like Job—"For the thing I greatly feared has come upon me."

Nor have the masses fully understood the law of cause and effect, or sowing and reaping. For their pain and anguish, their results are predictable. They must permanently lay to rest the damaging belief that it is possible to receive something for nothing. This simply cannot be done and runs contrary to the law of life! *At the counter of success, there are no bargains. A price must always be paid in advance, and in full.* For the individual who is willing to pay the price, his rewards will be greatly multiplied!

By overlooking the basic laws of riches, welfare continues to entrap successive generations of black Americans within the jaws of poverty. The focus is now, more than ever, on how one thinks and uses his unlimited potential to create the kind of existence he or she desires. Thought creates your inner world, and thought can eradicate your self-defeating creations.

Perhaps now would be a good time to ask the question: What are your thoughts? What are you currently thinking? Are you going to grasp the infinite possibilities that lie before you?

While some might say that it is too simplistic to suggest that thought controls everything, remember, your thoughts are the steering mechanism of your life. Constantly check your habits. Have you allowed your thinking to become clogged with the paralyzing visions of poverty, racism, anxiety, or fear? If so, change your mental pictures.

Set aside time each day for thinking, meditating, and concentrating your mind on your desires. You'll find that ideas are powerful and expand when reflected upon. The more you think, the more you will be able to see clearly. Subsequently, you will grow and develop as a person. Man never reaches heights above his level of thought. By engaging in thought-power control, not only will you transform your own life, you will begin to have an impact on those lives around you.

2

Imagination: Ideas in Action

"A man's mind, once stretched by a new idea, never regains its original dimensions."
—OLIVER WENDELL HOLMES

"To know is nothing at all, to imagine is everything!"
—ANATOLE FRANCE

"So God created man in His own image; in the image of God He created him."
—GENESIS 1:27

"I have a dream!"

"I have a dream today, that the brotherhood of man will become a reality in this day. I have a dream that my four little children will one day be judged not by the color of their skin, but by the content of their character. *I have a dream!"*

Many people think of Martin Luther King as a voice crying in the wilderness, a single man struggling against the attitudes of a nation. And it is true that as a black man he was in the minority. Black America did not hold the reins of power and had every reason to distrust those who did. Yet, when Dr. King preached those historic words, he spoke of the vision he had for his country. A vision that would inspire and spearhead victories against inequality and social injustice. By combining spiritual values and a deeply rooted belief in himself and the goodness of man, Dr. King infiltrated the consciousness of a nation and shook it at its roots, forging a racial bond. By sharing his dream, he gave democracy a new meaning and humanity a new life force.

There is an oft-repeated phrase with which you must become familiar. It is, "I can dream, can't I?" But this statement bears the tone of futility, as though the person asking it has little faith that his dreams will come true.

Actually, anyone who dares to dream and believe in his dreams is the creator, to a large extent, of his future. Though Dr. King's reality was a society of oppression and discrimination, his vision, ever so clear, was a world of love and mutual respect. It is debatable as to whether Dr. King was aware of life's simple dynamic: *Man can create anything that he can imagine.*

In his many lectures Napoleon Hill stated, "The imagination is the workshop of the soul wherein are shaped all plans for individual achievement. Man's greatest gift is his mind. It analyzes, compares, chooses. It creates, visualizes, foresees, and generates ideas. Imagination is your mind's exercise. It challenges and is the mirror of your soul."

Further, Hill said, "With the aid of his imagination, man has penetrated the stars, conquered the seas below and the air above, and created a simpler and easier quality of life by combining ideas and action. The imagination is the great workshop where the potentialities are practically unlimited."

If you have studied and fully digested the preceding lesson, you know that the materials out of which you transform your thoughts are assembled and combined in your imagination. In the previous chapter you were brought to the realization that life is collectivized thought. Now, by closely examining the power of creative thought, you will come to know that imagination is one of the most useful tools ever endowed to you by the Creator.

Ideas are the starting points of all success. It takes only one idea, followed by action, to create a fortune. By examining the following illustrations, you should develop a clearer understanding of what this process entails.

The Mighty Power of Imagination

Madame C. J. Walker engraved her name on the tablets of time by cultivating her imagination. At a time when the average black believed he was either too young or too old or ill-prepared to move beyond self-imposed limits, Madame Walker dreamed big dreams. Born in 1867 on a Louisiana farm in the vise of poverty, she was orphaned at seven. Sarah Breedlove, as she was then called, barely eked out an existence. Many days there simply wasn't enough to eat. In search of broader opportunities, she left her family's farm for life in the Mississippi delta.

Sarah settled into her new surroundings working wherever she could. As a domestic and washerwoman, she trudged countless miles through towns and back roads, lugging her laundry basket while she dreamed of better days. But neither lack of money nor influential friends would deter her from a date with destiny. Why? Because what she possessed was far more powerful than either—an unlimited imagination!

Like so many who have looked for success and found it, Sarah searched with her mind's eye. She gazed at her world, with its outward appearance of deprivation, hunger, and misery, with fresh eyes—*through her imagination*—and saw opportunities all about her. Her job as a domestic under a wealthy aristocratic family exposed her to the social graces of the upper class. As Sarah went about her daily chores, she was particularly mindful of the appearance and grooming habits of the well-to-do. She believed that all hair textures and skin tones were naturally beautiful. But she also believed that natural beauty needed enhancement to realize its full potential. She wanted to develop a product that would meet the specific needs of black Americans.

"What if someone could create a hair care system that

could straighten and soften coarse hair?'' she thought. Sarah's mind, now filled with a purpose, sensed an opportunity.

With a newfound goal and definite purpose, she worked hard and earnestly. Every waking moment outside of her duties as a domestic she spent concocting hair formulas and methods that would carry out her objective. Pushed by sheer desire, Sarah continued to toil into the early morning hours until an idea finally struck. With an initial investment of less than two dollars carefully saved from her meager earnings, she commissioned a metal worker to manufacture a special pressing comb. She later developed a procedure, combining her ''Walker'' comb and a special hair preparation, that would not only straighten coarse hair but give dull, dry-looking hair a soft and natural texture.

In 1905, Madame Walker, as she was now known, improved upon her original idea and developed a complete line of hair and beauty aids—which she initially sold door-to-door—transforming herself from laundress to hair care tycoon.

For millions of women, both black and white, her products were the answers to their prayers. Almost overnight she found herself in business, with assistants, agents, schools, and, eventually, a manufacturing company. Before her death in 1919, Madame Walker could count more than 2000 agents marketing an ever-expanding line of products, ringing up sales that made her America's first black female millionaire.

I wish to emphasize the part of the above story that most never mention—that Madame Walker's hair care system became a reality *in her imagination first*. Her proud manufacturing facility was built with brick and mortar and hard labor, as similar companies were built. These were paid for with the profits earned in much the same manner that profits for all companies are secured. But if you want the real story of Madame Walker's success, you must go back to that little country town where she worked as a domestic and laundress for pennies a day. It was here that she used the true materials to build a grand future—materials that were no more visible than the thoughts that she organized in her *imagination*!

"Dream," Jesse Jackson says. "Dream *big* dreams! Others may deprive you of your material wealth and cheat you in a thousand ways, but no man can deprive you of the control and use of your imagination. Men may deal with you unfairly, as men often do; they may deprive you of your liberty; but they cannot take from you the privilege of using your imagination. In your imagination *you always win*!"

His place in America is assured, but Jesse Jackson is not content to go down in the history books as the first black man to run seriously for the presidency—and lose. Although his imagination gained for him the opportunity that he wanted, he will dream again. Why? Because how else is a poor black child born to an unwed teenage mother going to rise to greatness? Only through imagination has Jesse Jackson come this far!

Do you want happiness? Do you want peace of mind? Do you want position, power, or riches? Then *imagine* them! How did the Almighty first create man? "In His image created He him." He imagined man in *His* mind.

"Imagination," Einstein said, "is more important than knowledge. For knowledge is limited, whereas imagination embraces the entire world, stimulating progress, giving birth to evolution." Popular folklore has it that Einstein's imagination, not his knowledge of physics and mathematics, led him to the theory of relativity. He understood the theory, the story goes, when he visualized himself riding a beam of starlight through space. When he imagined what would happen as he sat astride the beam of light, he was able to work out the mathematical formulas that proved his theory.

What is true for science holds equally true for other areas of our lives. If your imagination is the mirror of your soul, then you have the perfect right to stand before that mirror and see yourself as you wish to be. You have the right to see reflected in that magic mirror the home you intend to own, the business you intend to start, the company of which you intend to be president, the position in life you intend to occupy. *Your imagination belongs to you. Use it!*

Creative Dreaming

As individuals, we often engage in creative dreaming without even knowing it. For instance, when a hard-pressed family develops a plan to finance the education of their child; or when a teenager finds a way to salvage that old jalopy; or when an entrepreneur initiates steps to build a business—all are examples of the mind's unceasing ability to creatively dream. Practically speaking, creative imagination is the ability to bring about improvement within our lives.

Very few people have learned to use their imagination to its fullest potential. Society teaches us that it is not adult to fantasize. Too many of us have learned society's lesson so well that we never daydream; our imaginations rust away from lack of exercise. For some illogical reason, science, the arts, and literature have been dubbed as the only domain indicative of creative dreaming. Most associate creativity with an artistic painting or stirring poetry or a moving musical composition. While each painting, poem, or symphony is indeed evidence of the creative process, so too are all successes, no matter how great or small.

There is no need to shy from the word "creativity." Every moment you are creating. Each new word, each new thought, each action, changes your life. Regardless how you view creativity or the creative process, you will never be truly happy unless you are engaged in something creative. It is the dull routine, the humdrum, that makes work difficult and life uninteresting. When you are involved in the work of your choosing, there is always the possibility of doing it your own unique way, which means using God-given creativity. It is only through creative thoughts that you energize hidden talents which lie, too often, dormant within you.

Where Do Ideas Come From?

"Ideas are the most important things on earth," said the master motivator, Earl Nightingale. "Each of us has his own idea factory." But where do ideas come from? How do we attract great ideas, visions, dreams? Where do writers, scientists, and inventors acquire great ideas? How is it possible for a composer to hear in his mind an entire symphony as if it had already been written, yet it is entirely new to him? Why are some people more creative than others?

Each of us, at one time or another, must learn to rely upon the unseen source of all ideas, the universal subconscious mind to which we all have direct access. This universal subconscious mind has been referenced throughout all recorded history. It's been called the God-mind by wise men and philosophers alike.

Emerson referred to it as the "oversoul"—and said in an essay that "we lie in the lap of an immense intelligence, like a cork floating in a great ocean between the sky and the sea. When we experience this form of super-intelligence we realize that it comes from a source far beyond ourselves."

Napoleon Hill labeled this power "infinite intelligence," meaning, in essence, unlimited intelligence. "When ideas well up from deep within us," Hill wrote, "ideas that seemingly come out of nowhere, come through infinite intelligence."

Riches, you will find, often depend on this power. A single idea or spark can revolutionize your life. A single idea can lead you to great wealth, fame, or fortune—or it can bury you in despair. Srully Blotnick, an investment counselor, remarked, "The average person stumbles upon at least four ideas a year, any of which, if it were acted upon, might render vast wealth.'' Never before has mankind been so exposed to this phenomenon.

What Are the Characteristics of Infinite Intelligence?

Infinite intelligence is likened to the creative power which directs and governs the universe. This power has commonly been referred to as *The Universal Mind*, *The Great Unseen*, *The Divine Mind*, and by more orthodox religionists as *God*. In addition,

1. It is the source of all pure creativity. Innovation is invariably the result of infinite intelligence.
2. It is the source of all inspiration. Whenever you feel inspired or uplifted, chances are that infinite intelligence has been activated within you. It is the source of all intuition—the voice of infinite intelligence is the intuitive voice. It is the source of all hunches or gut feelings.
3. It functions as a part of our subconscious. Even as you sleep, infinite intelligence remains steadfast, activating new ideas, visions, and dreams.
4. It works best with clear, specific goals. The clearer and more specific the goal, the more rapidly infinite intelligence can develop the ideas you require.
5. It automatically and continuously solves every problem as you move toward your goal—as long as the goal is defined! This is the reason why people who start life from humble beginnings can arrive at positions of prominence and influence.
6. It grows in power as it is used and believed in.
7. It gives you the lessons you need in order to be successful. It is through infinite intelligence that you will obtain wisdom and insight.
8. It operates best with an attitude of confident expectation. This is the psychic fuel that feeds this principle.

9. It brings you the answer you require at the right time. The answers to your problems will always come when you need them the most. But a word of caution—when you receive your answers, you must take action immediately. Lost ideas may be difficult to recover. Write them down whenever they occur.

10. It makes all your words and actions and their effects fit a pattern consistent with your self-concept and your dominant goals. When you've tapped into this life force, you will find yourself saying the right words, to the right people, at the right time.

11. It responds to emotionalized commands—affirmations—whether they are positive or negative.

12. It brings into reality any thought, goal, plan, or idea held within your conscious mind. Infinite intelligence is capable of goal-oriented motivation and will release ideas for goal attainment.

From Slavery to Riches

When the subject of black economic development arises, Alonzo F. Herndon's name is on every tongue. Though he was born a slave in southern Georgia, Alonzo Herndon died a millionaire nearly three-quarters of a century later, perhaps the wealthiest black man of his time. How Herndon obtained his wealth is of great interest. He reached his goal by holding true to an intense belief in his ideas and his abilities. It was no surprise that he valued "creative thinking" as one of his most prized assets.

Herndon spoke discreetly about success. "Sometimes it's best," he said, "if a man just spends a moment or two thinking. It is one of the toughest things he will ever do, and that's probably why so few bother to do it."

Herndon mastered three of the most stubborn enemies of mankind and converted them into useful tools. These enemies were *ignorance*, *illiteracy*, and *poverty*. Any man who can stay the hands of these three antagonists—

and what is more, harness and use them to good account—is well worth close study.

Alonzo Herndon was seven years old when the Civil War ended. It was his first taste of freedom. He and his brother were raised by their mother in a one-room, dirt-floor log cabin. He was only a child when he got his first job, working for his grandfather in a lumberyard. From there he moved on to field hand, providing back-breaking labor on the farm of his former owner. For his efforts he was paid less than fifty dollars a year. To augment his painfully low wages, Herndon started a number of businesses on the side. He sold peanuts, molasses, and novelty items, but mostly he cut hair. His ventures rendered little in terms of monetary rewards, but the idea of working for himself gave him great satisfaction.

By the time Herndon had arrived in Atlanta, he had already shaped a career as a barber. Even as a farmhand in rural Georgia, he managed to cut hair in a rented space on Saturdays, in the black section of town. Atlanta in the early 1880s was a boomtown that seemed ripe for someone like Herndon with a head full of ideas.

Herndon made no bones about his desire to be rich. So it was little surprise when he launched "the finest barbershop in the world." And the world—let alone Atlanta—had never seen a barbershop as palatial or as opulent. In 1904, he opened a fancy establishment on Peachtree Street which was described at the time as "the most popular and most successful business of its type." Resplendent with exquisite fixtures and French provincial furnishings, "the emporium," as it was called, was equipped with twenty-three chairs, marble floors, bronze and crystal chandeliers, and a white steel ceiling. Surrounded by such luxuries, Herndon's elite clientele was pampered by six-foot-long bathtubs, highly skilled barbers, and bootblacks attending their every whim.

It was said that customers felt more important in Herndon's shop than in those of his white competitors. His was the only black enterprise on the city's busiest thoroughfare.

With his hair care business secure and earning handsome profits, Herndon was still dissatisfied. Why? He had already won his "rags-to-riches" race. He had convincingly acquired enough money to allow his family to live comfortably for their remaining years. *What was tugging at his subconscious?*

Since his childhood days in Walton County, Alonzo Herndon had always wanted to do things in a big way. (Even in his later years, he refused to apologize for his copious taste. "America is a capitalist country, and I am a capitalist," he told those close to him.) He was a man with a mission: to raise Black America from its economic stagnation. *But how?*

Herndon dabbled in real estate and was quite successful. He purchased properties throughout the city, and at one time owned an entire block of office buildings in the heart of Atlanta's business district. Before long he was a millionaire. Nevertheless, he was still looking for ways to expand his empire.

And because he searched it happened! Infinite intelligence had presented him with an enormous opportunity.

Almost by accident, Herndon came to the rescue of two local ministers whose enterprise was on the brink of bankruptcy. Georgia law had required that all mutual aid societies—insurance companies—deposit $5000 with state officials. Many black businesses, particularly those run by churches, could not foot the bill. Aware of their plight, Herndon purchased the church association for $160 and found himself in the insurance business. With no previous experience in insurance sales, Herndon applied the principles that led to his success in other areas.

The Atlanta Benevolent and Protective Association was launched in a one-room office on Auburn Avenue. The firm wrote policies for blacks when it was virtually impossible, because of presumed bad risks, for them to get insurance. Herndon, however, changed that. He began hiring black college graduates from Atlanta and Harvard universities, utilizing their eagerness and passing on his wisdom and sales savvy.

"Think of what this means," he told cynics who thought the idea of blacks becoming employers preposterous. "Just think—colored men and women offering employment to those of our own race!" Under his leadership the tiny company grew, expanding from one location in 1905, to 84 branch offices and 70,000 policyholders in 1911. He then changed the firm's name to the Atlanta Life Insurance Company and began offering all lines of insurance. Today, Atlanta Life has assets of more than $135 million and is the nation's second-largest black-owned insurance company.

The dramatic story of big business that you have just read is a perfect illustration of the method by which thinking can be transformed into riches.

What was this ex-slave-turned-millionaire's secret? Simple. Alonzo Herndon achieved his goals by putting his creative genius to work. Despite his lack of formal schooling and the handicaps of doing business in a deeply segregated society, Herndon placed great stock in his ability to dream, to imagine, and to dare. In 1913, Herndon told the faculty and students at Tuskegee Institute, where he served on its board, that "wealth and creativity go hand in hand. The black man must possess dreams and visions if he really desires to do anything in a big way."

Herndon knew of the power packed into the principle of imagination, and he made others aware of it also. When promising young students from neighboring black colleges came to his attention, he would invite them to his sumptuous mansion, and over dinner would encourage them to talk of visions, possibilities, and dreams.

Herndon, like so many creative thinkers, used a note pad and pencil as favorite working tools. When an idea occurred, he jotted it down. He, like other great men of accomplishment, engaged in thinking, planning, and meditation time.

You Will Never Know, Unless ...

Notice that the achievers above did not have success handed to them. At first the world was not particularly kind to Madame Walker or Alonzo Herndon. And yet, refusing to blame life for any shortcomings, each managed to carve out a successful career from the materials that life provided. The world was made better because they dreamed and translated their dreams into reality.

Life never leaves you stranded. If life hands you a problem, it also hands you the ability to overcome that problem. *Are you ever tempted to blame the world for your failures or shortcomings?* If so, I suggest you pause and reconsider. *Does the problem lie with the world, or with you?* Dare to *dream*!

You will never know what your capacity for achievement is until you learn how to mix your efforts with imagination. The products of your hands, *minus imagination*, will yield you but a small return, but those same hands, when properly guided by imagination, can be made to earn you all the material wealth you can handle.

Ideas are the most important things on earth. How many ideas or possibilities can you think of? How many ideas would surface if you would devote a few minutes each day to creative thinking? When you truly discover that success in all areas of life starts simply by employing the creative process that lies within, you can grasp a life of vast wealth. Research has shown that your ability to bring into action this deeper area of the mind will determine your level of success.

Napoleon Hill makes another profound observation. He wrote, "From the time of Socrates, the founder of ethical science, to the inventive Edison, Ford, and George Washington Carver, this little-understood area of mental activity has delivered the insight and know-how for al-

most every great achievement that makes possible and
sustains modern civilization as we know it.''

It Was Through a Dream . . .

It was through a dream that George Smith, though cursed
with poverty and illiteracy, built a successful oil business. Smith was born on the eve of the Great Depression
in Livingston, Texas. His father died when he was barely
a year old, leaving a wife and a handful of small children
to fend for themselves. Though an excellent student,
Smith was forced to quit school after the third grade to
help support his family. He cleaned yards, washed dishes,
and chopped cotton, all in an effort to feed his brothers
and sisters.

Smith left home for good at thirteen to work in the
Texas oil fields. Having learned just about everything
there was to know about oil pipes, he perfected a way to
reduce the amount of stress exerted on pipe joints. With
hardly any savings, he started a company—Smith Pipe &
Supply—that would earn more than $30 million in 1980.

It was through a vision that Samuel L. Gravely, the
son of a Pullman porter, climbed from an enlisted man
in the Naval Reserve to its first black admiral. In 1942,
Gravely was despondent when he was relegated to clean
the pool halls in the officer's lounge. But for the next
twenty-five years, armed with determination and the
dream of commanding his own ship, Gravely began his
long trek through the ranks.

And it was through a vision that Susan Taylor became
a precedent breaker, a proud black woman who refused
to be denied her true place. Hard work and discipline
have not frightened her one iota. She recognized early
on what it took to accomplish the goals she would set for
herself. Listen as she recalls her life-changing experience.

''One day, as I walked into a New York candy store,
I saw a magazine that changed the course of my life. As

I glanced at the newsstand, familiar faces of white fashion models and movie stars smiled from the magazine covers on the rack. But when I reached for my favorite magazine, I was pleasantly surprised to find *Essence*, a magazine specifically aimed at the black woman. The date of that first issue was May 1970, and the face on the cover was young and black—*like mine*.

"*Essence* had filled an obvious void. I bought a copy and read it from cover to cover before I even left the store."

In subsequent weeks Taylor became imbued with the idea that she was going to be a part of this new publication. But how?

"I wasn't concerned about how," she says. "The only thing that mattered was my decision to chase my dream and reach my goal." In 1981, eleven years later, with no contacts, minimal schooling, and no knowledge of the publishing industry, Taylor won out! She became editor-in-chief of the magazine she had vowed to become a part of.

She offers the following advice to readers in her monthly forum "In the Spirit": "Black man, black woman, remember, you have dominion. Each moment your thoughts, words, and actions either lean toward frustration or build new hopes and visions. Lift up your consciousness. Go on, dream big dreams, develop a plan for your future. And why not? *You built the pyramids, didn't you?*"

You, too, can convert your creative thinking and imagination into success, wealth, and happiness. You live in a strange and fast-paced world; each day your world is being altered by men and women who have learned how to unlock their inborn creativity.

Will you dare to dream? If your answer is yes, let the following steps be your guide.

Unlocking Your Inborn Creativity

Nothing is impossible for the man or woman with creative vision. He or she is the forerunner of civilization, the inspirer of individual achievement, the builder of empires. In today's society there is a place for every person who can render a useful service. The man or woman with creative vision will recognize these facts and profit by them. Those without creative vision will overlook them and complain of a lack of opportunity.

Wherever you find prosperity and leadership, you will find the individual who has mastered the following qualities.

1. *Relaxation*
   A relaxed body is a powerful body; a relaxed mind likewise is a powerful mind. If you are to be creative and receptive to new and bold ideas, then you must take time for these ideas to present themselves. Plan daily relaxation time; choose a favorite room or chair that will help set your mind at ease. As you learn to relax, you will receive "special instructions" (ideas that are handed to you through infinite intelligence) that will clear the path to your goals and objectives.

2. *Visualization*
   A composer thinks about music; an artist thinks about colors; a writer thinks about stories and words. If you will take one idea and visualize and emotionalize it, you will be astounded by the results.

3. *Affirmation*
   Strong, authoritative commands stated repeatedly will build new positive-habit patterns of thought.

4. *Take advantage of ideas as they come*
   Intuitive thoughts are fleeting, ephemeral, and transient. These thoughts run contrary to your habitual reasoning. Brief flashes of inspiration can occur without warning. Be prepared to record your ideas.

   Even during nonrelaxing moments, a creative person—one who has learned to listen with his "inner ear"—makes a point of always having a pad and pencil nearby. Many good ideas have been lost because of the inability to transfer them to paper.

5. *Evaluate your ideas*

Once you have finished brainstorming, become selective. Decide which ideas are sound and implementable. You will realize that each idea breeds additional ideas. A few moments of introspection will foster enough possibilities to last a lifetime.

When you learn the secret of unlocking your inborn creativity, your mind will begin to function in a natural, spontaneous manner. It will rid itself of any inhibitions, and effectiveness and energy will greatly increase. There are huge rewards to be gained by mastering the creative thought process.

Don't Limit Your Imagination

So many of the stories you have read and will read in this book demonstrate the power of ideas. Time after time, as I have studied the careers of successful men and women, I have discovered that each dates his or her own success from the day he began to open his imagination, never underestimating its power. A single idea or an unlimited imagination can launch you onto a bold new program, while providing a light on a once-darkened path.

As the physician, chemical engineer, and mission specialist of the 1991 shuttle *Discovery* flight, Mae C. Jemison has never been guided by the thoughts of others. One look at the background of America's first black woman astronaut illustrates the importance of her creative vision.

As a small child Mae Jemison wanted it all. She dreamed of a career in medicine and engineering. Reared in a loving family that stressed "why not" instead of "why," she gazed at the evening sky and envisioned life among the stars. With an unlimited imagination, she shared her dreams with all those who would listen.

"But a doctor and an astronaut?" her parents questioned.

"Why not?" she innocently responded. Even a supportive family knew the limits of her possibilities would be tested. Over the years the young girl's goals crystallized. She refused to be deterred by the obvious roadblocks—lack of money, few eye-catching references, and stiff competition from the country's most distinguished scholars. Mae chose to walk toward her dominant impulse.

After graduating from high school, Mae attended Stanford University, even after being warned of its highly competitive reputation. She felt this was just the scholarly environment she needed to pursue a degree in chemical engineering. As an underclassman, she ignored the insinuation that scientists and engineers were introverted and bookish. To ensure that she would not be isolated from campus life, she would experience as many activities as possible.

Though still an undergraduate, Mae taught classes on African culture and education to incoming freshman, and received a National Achievement Scholarship in the process. An accomplished dancer, she produced, directed, and choreographed dance and theater ensembles in her spare time. In addition to the rigors that a major in engineering demands, she also earned a degree in Afro-American studies.

In 1977, Mae graduated from Stanford and immediately applied to medical school. Cornell University made its pitch and she was sold. Her undergraduate training would serve her well as she settled into a bioengineering program—one of the nation's best. At Cornell, Mae would continue her breakneck pace, squeezing in a number of related activities into an already overloaded schedule.

Here she gained national exposure by presiding over

the medical school's student council, and was drawn to even more opportunities. An American Medical Student Association internship took her to Cuba; another fellowship sent her to rural Kenya, and from there she went to Thailand to work and study in a Cambodian refugee camp. All the while, she became infatuated with the health care systems of Third World nations.

Mae finished medical school with impressive credentials. Hoping to continue her training among less developed countries, she enlisted in the Peace Corps. Her initial assignments took her to Sierra Leone and Liberia, where she was responsible for developing health care programs for Peace Corps volunteers. At twenty-six, she was the youngest physician—not to mention black and female—to hold that post. When her tour was up, she flew back to the States. Little did she know that the chance of a lifetime awaited her.

By 1990, the National Aeronautics and Space Administration (NASA) began soliciting candidates for its shuttle program. When she learned of the openings, Mae was floored. Almost instinctively, she assembled the necessary documents and applied.

"Dreams do come true," she thought as the selection process commenced. And then she waited and waited. Nearly twenty years from the moment she dared to gaze into the sky and let her imagination roam free, she was about to make history. And she hit her mark. After being selected from a pool of more than 2000 applicants, *Dr. Mae Jemison was bound for outer space!*

Can you imagine the odds? What was her greatest asset? In her own words, she gives a clue. "People cannot let others limit their imagination or what it is they want to do or can do. Otherwise, we would never have discoveries or advance." This is a brilliant example of creative imagination at its best.

Many people who want to succeed have tasted failure. Unfortunately, their reasons for failing often point to something other than themselves:

"I'm black."

"I was raised in the projects. My father left home."

"I'm a dropout."

"I never had a chance. My parents used drugs."

What these individuals are really saying, in essence, is "I lack creative vision." They are blaming the world for their shortcomings, when, in actuality, their only real barrier rests with their inability to dream and envision success.

How often have we heard that blacks lack the discipline and wherewithal to pursue careers in the natural sciences? How many more young minds will fall prey to the fallacy that black students lack the capacities to score well on standardized tests or even to attend college? There is an important lesson to be learned in Mae's story: It is only when we actually begin to dream—*not as things are, but as they could be*—that we free ourselves of all self-imposed limits. When we recognize the vast talents that lie within us, we will then understand that we have the power to reach any goal.

Enhance Your Creativity Through Visualization

Long before ex-heavyweight boxing champion George Foreman reached his goal, an admirer sought the champ's key to success. Though Foreman's words were uttered in a spirit of jest, his words of inspiration found fertile soil in the young man's mind. "*If I see what I want real good in my mind,*" explained the champ, "I don't notice any pain in getting it."

There is no objective too important or too trivial for your mind to visualize. Much like boxing champion George Foreman, we soon realize that we can't achieve greatness in our outer world without first picturing it in our inner world—our minds. The simplest of actions takes on a new significance. We cannot reach for a pen, sit in a chair, or answer the telephone, without first (at least subconsciously) having a mental picture of such acts.

You can be anything you want to be, if you will only trust your imagination. Visualize your heart's desire; never allow the picture to distort or tarnish; keep it fresh, clear, and bright. Success will enter your life quietly and unobtrusively, without raucousness or fanfare, for it will follow the law that permeates the universe: *Everything begins in the mind.*

When you understand the relationship between imagination and visualization and the subconscious mind, you can see that the first step in the achievement of any purposeful goal is to create a picture of that which is desired. This picture is then placed in the subconscious mind and held there until the subconscious picks it up and translates it into its ultimate desired form.

"I Saw Myself a Recording Star!"

"You can't play the piano, and God knows you can't sing. You better learn how to weave chairs so you can support yourself!"

The words were tough advice from a teacher to her student. They were especially cruel to a youngster who liked to play the piano and sing. To a black child in the South, it should have been crushing. There was so little else for him to hope for.

When he was six years old, Ray Charles Robinson became totally blind. Doctors diagnosed his condition as "increased intraocular tension resulting from ocular disease." *Glaucoma!*

Ray's mother helplessly looked at the physicians, not wanting to believe. "Isn't there anything you can do? Wouldn't an operation help?"

"No," was the answer. "As of now, we know of no way to treat his condition."

Ray's eyesight did not go right away. It was more of a gradual closing in, as he puts it. One day he could see a mountain miles away; a month later that same mountain was only a fuzzy, hazy object in the distance. He went to his mother, rubbing his eyes, as she tried to find a doctor—any doctor. But it was 1936. And in the South there were few black specialists.

Though blind since six, he was not made to feel helpless. His mother would have no part in any self-pity. She told him, "You're blind, not stupid. You've lost your sight, not your mind." Ray has never forgotten her words.

Ray Charles couldn't see, but the love and faith of his parents made his life rich and rewarding. His mother refused to allow her son to succumb to his handicap. She emphasized that he could lead a productive and fulfilling life—despite his blindness. Through the encouragement of his mother, Ray Charles knew he had lost *only* his sight, *not* his power of visualization.

Ray was born normal and healthy in Albany, Georgia. His father was a repairman and his mother worked as a domestic. Not far from the little frame house where Ray and his family resided, there lived a boogie-woogie pianist named Wylie Pitman—"Mr. Pit," Ray called him.

"Whenever Mr. Pit would begin to play," Ray recalls, "I would stop what I was doing and run next door. I'd stand by the piano and pound on it with both hands."

Wylie Pitman, the man Ray credits for his success, willingly accepted the youngster's presence and taught him how to play. Mr. Pitman would listen to the loud, raucous noise, refusing to discourage his pupil. He would simply smile and say, "That's good—that's real good, sonny. But you've got to practice."

For nearly ten years Ray practiced every chance he got. But by then he was totally blind and in need of special care. Frightened, barefoot, and orphaned, Ray was sent to the Saint Augustine School for Deaf and Blind Children in Orlando, Florida. Life at St. Augustine's was inhibiting for the creative young boy. He sheltered himself from academic instruction and hid out in the school's music room. His only hope was to hang on to his mother's words: "You've lost your sight, not your mind."

Ray's talent for music began to flourish. At fifteen he quit school altogether to perform in small bands throughout the South. Far from an overnight success, he found the going tough. Nonetheless, his first job, providing background music at a local radio station, paid five dollars an hour. From there he joined another band—one of many—and lied about his age in order to obtain a union card. To keep abreast of new musical trends, he concentrated on the chords and melodies used by other piano players at the union hall. Later, he transcribed every note into Braille. It wasn't an easy process.

"Many times during auditions I was told that I couldn't carry a note with a bucket, and that I sure couldn't play the piano. As I look back over this period, I now realize that it was the best thing that ever happened to me.

"It was during these tough times that I developed a power that was to ultimately place me over the top—the power of visualization. Regardless of how bad things got on the outside, I kept a clear picture in my head of what I wanted to transpire. Through visualization I saw myself as a recording star!"

With his career on hold, Ray needed a break. He asked a friend and fellow band member, "What's the furthest point from Georgia?" Somewhat bewildered, his buddy replied, "I guess Washington."

"Then Washington it is," Ray exclaimed.

Based on faith and persistence, Ray borrowed $600 and boarded a bus for Seattle. He was seventeen years old. With a fresh start, he hired seven musicians and formed the "Ray Charles Group." Ray played the sax and piano, and doubled on vocals. The group became known as one of the best small jazz ensembles in the country. One year later Ray hit the big-time.

His record "I Got a Woman" helped him do what few musicians are able to do—create music that appeals to young and old, black and white, rich and poor. Because of his ability to successfully cross major boundaries, other musicians ungrudgingly use words like "genius" to describe him.

Ray went on to record best sellers like "Born to Lose," "Hallelujah, I Love Her So," and "Georgia on My Mind," the official song of the state that he left. Today, each record Ray Charles releases sells an average of 500,000 copies. Though sightless, he still *pictures his riches*, appearing before prestigious audiences and sell-out concert halls the world over.

The Substance of Things Hoped For

The substance of things hoped for is a real substance, formed from pictures in the mind as concrete and detailed as in the world itself. The evidence of things unseen, as with Ray Charles, is knowledge gleaned through the image-making power of imagination. It is impossible for us to act against our knowledge. For example, a man will not step in front of a speeding automobile for fear of injury, he will not swim in an ocean if he knows he will drown, and he will not venture forward if he believes he will fail. Success does not require a great amount of knowledge about anything, but it does call for the persistent use of whatever knowledge you may have.

No amount of persuasion can change a man's reaction to what he knows. But what he knows can be changed, and the most direct manner is to alter the images within his mind. If a man learns to clearly visualize his objective, this mental picture will ultimately become a reality in his life.

There are no limitations to the power of visualization, save those that the individual creates for himself or permits to be established by the influences outside of himself. Ray Charles visualized success regardless of countless setbacks and rejections. "I saw myself a recording star!" was not a baseless boast, but a preview of things to come.

The visual pictures that we possess lead us around by

our mental noses. This range of mental motion works just as quickly for what is considered evil as it does for what is considered good. For instance, if a person were to constantly visualize robbing the corner service station, almost automatically that individual will certainly find himself at that service station, gun in hand, prepared to empty the till. People who commit so-called crimes of passion often report that they were in the grip of a compulsion which they could neither control nor understand. Such compulsion proceeds out of our mental pictures. Images projected onto the movie screen of the mind take root in the motor impulses of the body, and each person is propelled into action by that which he or she has visualized.

A Future Hall-of-Famer

Walter Payton, future football Hall-of-Famer, was once asked, "How did you manage to gain more than 15,000 yards in your career and surpass nearly every seemingly impossible rushing mark in the process?" To this he crisply replied, "When I started out, I knew where I wanted to go and what I had to do to get there. I painted a vivid picture in my mind of all the goals I wanted to accomplish and simply set about the task of achieving them one by one."

Payton went on to say that he even "heard" the cheering crowds in great detail in his mind. He also pictured award ceremonies, complete with sportswriters and guests, and the style and brilliance of the Super Bowl championship ring that he would wear so proudly—*years before it ever occurred*!

The quality of your visualization in your inner world will determine how quickly you will manifest results in your outer world. Since most people are relatively unaware of the power of visualization, they give little consideration to what they actually envision.

Visualize the Things You Want

There are millions who believe they are doomed to poverty and failure because of some strange force over which they assume they have no control. Unknowingly, many create their own misfortune because of negative thought patterns, which are picked up by the subconscious and translated into its physical equivalent. Like the man or woman who has fervently visualized wealth and success and has attained it, so, too, has a portion of Black America approached the table of life famished—because their minds held pictures of poverty, lack, and failure.

By now you realize that thoughts are things that, when properly nourished and internalized, will become a reality in the world of form. If you envision yourself acquiring abundance, and if you keep this picture in your mind regardless of the obstacles you encounter, *then it must become manifest in your life.*

If you allow this picture to be the dominant image in your mental world:

- you will think successful thoughts and surround yourself with successful people who encourage your visions;
- you will save a part of your income and thereby pay yourself first, a crucial step in the acquisition of wealth;
- you will engage in a program of personal improvement and select your life's mission;
- you will seek the knowledge and expertise of those who have achieved success;
- and you will then succeed in spite of the difficulties!

Your entire life experience will revolve around an image of success based on your mental picture.

The reverse of this affirmation is equally as true. If you picture yourself poor, you will act out your poverty based upon that image. You will surround yourself with other like-minded people who lack the fundamental necessities and the wherewithal to succeed. You will relive past failures and speak of them as virtue. Yours will be a life haunted by missed opportunities and "what if's."

Follow These Rules

If your world is one of limitation and misery because you have not realized that you have within your power the ability to change your life, here is a concise set of rules for the process of visualization:

1. *Think constantly*, quietly, and persistently of that which you desire. Your thinking should have two qualities: *clearness and interest*.
2. *Relax*. Do not strain to obtain your ideas. Tension is inadvertently the cause of failure.
3. *See yourself already in possession of that which you desire*. Visualize and emotionalize your major purpose.

Imagine Success

The pattern of your thinking today is transforming your tomorrows. Once you comprehend this principle, you will think twice before indulging in any bouts of self-pity. You will actually stand in awe of the Law of Life: *You move in the direction of your dominant thought*. Drill into your being clear, concise, vivid mental pictures of that which you desire most. Let your imagination be a means of looking up, not down. Cast your sights toward the infinite possibilities ever present in your environment, for you are one with infinite intelligence. Through the power of creative imagination, there is no goal too great nor dream too high. Remember: *What the mind of man can conceive and believe, it can achieve*.

It was Thoreau who wrote, "If one advances confidently in the direction of his dreams and endeavors to

live the life he has *imagined*, he will meet success unexpected in common hours.''

"Great ideas," said Albert Camus, the twentieth-
century novelist and philosopher, "come into the world
as gently as doves. Perhaps then, if we listen attentively,
we shall hear, amid the uproar of empires and nations, a
faint flutter of wings, the gentle stirrings of life and
hope."

"A man may not achieve everything he has dreamed,"
wrote William James. "But he will never achieve anything great without having dreamed it first."

Do not hesitate to dream. Build your dreams, nurture
your dreams, lean on your dreams in times of difficulty;
but once having dreamed, believe in your dreams, visualize them as having already been fulfilled.

Be Idea Centered

In the proper sequence of the creative process, every need
or desire is first an idea before it is an object. The order
of life is "inner" before "outer." What is needed is the
right idea. Only then can you experience a natural fulfillment of the evolution of things.

Stay with the basic idea. Develop the idea. Produce
and project the idea. Then watch its outward manifestation in your life. The images we hold steadfastly in our
minds over the years are not illusions; they are patterns
by which we are able to mold our destinies.

All wishful thinkers boast of their grand plans, their
huge schemes and sure-fire bets that will produce their
fortunes. But they are only plans, no real programs, no
purpose. Ideas must be fostered, developed, *and then put
into action*. By themselves, ideas have no intrinsic
value—"they are a dime a dozen." They must be accom-
panied by action. Remember the old adage: The successful implementation of one good idea is worth more than
a thousand good ideas not acted upon. In this respect,
an idea becomes the first step in the success chain. It

takes a creative consciousness along with relentless action to breathe life into your dreams. This is the foundation of the grand plan governing the universe: *Ideas are created by infinite intelligence and manifested through you.*

3

Desire:
The Starting Point
of All Achievement

"Some of us seem to accept the fatalist position,
the fatalist attitude, that the Creator accorded to us
a certain position and condition, and therefore there
is no need trying to be otherwise."
—MARCUS GARVEY

"No one need fear death. We need fear only that we
may die without having known our greatest power."
—NORMAN COUSINS

In everyone's life there comes a time of ultimate challenge—a time when all our resources are tested. A time
when life seems unfair. A time when our faith, our values, our patience, our compassion, our ability to persist,
are all pushed to the limit and beyond. Some have used
such tests as opportunities for growth; others have turned
away and allowed these experiences to destroy their
hopes.

Have you ever wondered what comprises the critical
difference in the way we respond to life's challenges?
Society has been fascinated by what triggers us to behave
the way we do. We would all like to know what sets
certain men and women apart from their peers. You may
have heard the story of the dehydrated man in the desert,
who is weak, sun-worn, and exhausted, and after spotting an oasis miles away, summons unknown inner reserves in an effort to reach his goal.

Obviously, those who stamp their mark in this world are men and women who are motivated by the *desire to achieve*. Unless you *want to* taste the true riches of life—health, love, freedom, and prosperity—you will forever be among those who have *tried* but remained by the shoreline mired in their failure. You must desperately *want to* succeed. You must be consumed with an encompassing *burning desire* to reach a definite objective. You must be obsessed with an overwhelming urge to win.

When Julius Caesar landed his army in England, he was determined to take no chances of a possible retreat. He wanted to show his troops that their invasion meant victory or death. So he burned his ships before their eyes. His objective was *not a hope or a wish*, but a pulsating desire that transcended everything else!

"That day we sailed westward, which was our course," were the legendary words that Columbus jotted in his journal day after day. Hope might rise and fall, terror and dismay may seize the crew, but Columbus, undaunted and resolute, pushed due west, and nightly added to his record.

Napoleon knew there were plenty of great men in France. However, his adversaries failed to recognize the might of his steadfast desire that was to ultimately shape a new and glorious Europe. "It is impossible," said a staff officer when Napoleon gave orders for a daring plan. "Impossible?" replied the great commander. "Impossible is the adjective of fools!"

Many leaders in their march into greatness have burned their bridges behind them. Cut off from all sources of retreat, they left their troops with one choice—either win or perish! A burning desire is the real source of genius.

We face life with only two options: *Either move or be moved*. The battle-tested and determined individual will stand out from the crowd.

The Man Who Desired to Be Rich

Hailing from humbling beginnings, S. B. Fuller was once identified as one of the wealthiest black men in America. In his long life, Fuller owned businesses throughout the country. A fearless believer in individual initiative, he denounced welfare as the enemy of motivation. Fuller dedicated his life to achieving his dreams and helping others realize theirs. He lived by the phrase: "Nothing comes from doing nothing."

Fuller was born in Ouachita Parish, Louisiana, in 1905, the oldest of eight children raised by tenant farmers. He was driving mules at age nine, and quit school after the sixth grade. By the time he was seventeen, his father had left and his family had moved to Memphis.

For the next several years he struggled to make ends meet. As he drifted from job to job, something was gnawing inside. "Why are some people wealthy and others poor?" he constantly thought. Unexpectedly, he found the answer in his mother's dying words.

"We shouldn't be poor, S.B.," the frail black woman said on her deathbed. "And don't let me ever hear you say it's God's will. We're poor only because Father has never developed the desire for anything else." It was his mother, among all other influences, who refused to accept this hand-to-mouth existence, though it was all she had ever known. Fuller's dying mother knew there was something drastically wrong with the idea that her family, *living in a land of plenty*, was barely getting by. In a split moment in time her son became the sounding board and the recipient of her years of wisdom.

The few words passed on to him became deeply ingrained in his mind. Almost immediately they changed his life. Fuller *wanted* to become rich, and his goal soon became an obsession.

There's an important rule that governs the principle of desire. The rule states: You can be, have, or do anything that you want—if only you *want* it hard enough! In other words, you must eagerly long for something—not a mere wishing or wanting, but a *fierce, eager, consuming hunger that knows no defeat and demands satisfaction.*

Just as the great oak, as an embryo, sleeps within the acorn, success begins in the form of an *intense desire.* Out of a strong desire grow the motivating forces that cause men to embrace hopes, initiate plans, develop courage, and stimulate their minds to action in pursuit of a definite plan or purpose. There is nothing behind desire except the impulse through which it may be transformed into action. Anyone who is capable of stimulating his or her own mind to produce intense desire is capable also of the achievement of that desire.

Though no one in his family wanted to be wealthy, Fuller conditioned his mind with such intensity that he was compelled into action. The attainment of his goal became his sole driving force.

After hitchhiking to Chicago in 1928, Fuller held a variety of jobs—but mostly he sold. He sold life insurance until he discovered he could earn more money peddling soap. Said Fuller, "A local magazine printed the names of Chicago's highest paid executives. In 1934, the president of Metropolitan Life earned $50,000. On the other hand, the president of Lever Brothers—a soap company—made nine times as much. At that point, I quit selling insurance and started selling soap."

So intense was Fuller's desire that he took his last few dollars, purchased a case of soap, and began selling toiletries door to door, in Depression-laden Chicago.

He sold soap for pennies a cake and pitched his products for as long as people would listen. "Repetition is the mother of knowledge," he quipped. In 1935, Fuller boasted he would one day own his initial supplier, Boyer National Laboratories, who many times refused to give him credit. A decade later he made good on his promise and bought the struggling company. During his years as a salesman and entrepreneur, Fuller gained the respect and admiration of his peers. By setting aside nearly every penny he had earned, he managed to save $25,000, which he used as a springboard to buy other businesses and expand his empire.

What was Fuller's secret? What power, known or unknown, allowed him to leave the masses of the impoverished and join the ranks of the wealthy *in the teeth of a depression?* Listen as he unveils the key: "I knew exactly what I wanted. *I had to be a millionaire!*"

With only a sixth-grade education, Fuller began reading for self-development. "When you know that you don't know, you've got to read." His favorite books were the Bible, Robert Collier's *Secret of the Ages*, and Napoleon Hill's *Think and Grow Rich*. One day Fuller read a single fact that changed his outlook: Of the 4043 millionaires in America then, 3954 had not finished high school. This helped fuel his desire—"If they can do it, so can I!"

Within five years Fuller had dozens of salespeople and a small factory. He had bought real estate, a drug company, a department store, a string of theaters, and two black newspapers. And yes, he had become a millionaire.

It is important to note that S. B. Fuller started life with few advantages. However, he chose a goal and armed himself with an intense desire and set out to reach it. There is an immense difference between the chances of the man who begins with a thorough understanding of himself, with a resolution to win at all costs, and the individual who sets out with no particular purpose or ambition, and no firm determination that he will reach his objective.

There is all the difference in the world between the prospects of the man who has committed himself to his life's purpose without reservation, has burned all bridges behind him and has taken a secret oath to succeed, has vowed to see his proposition through to the end, no matter what sacrifices he must make or how long it may take, and the man who wavers and goes about his objective halfheartedly.

Not everyone would care to be an S. B. Fuller or any of the other achievers highlighted in this book. Not everyone would choose to pay the price of success. To many, the riches of life are different. But the choice remains yours, and yours alone. The principle through which S. B. Fuller got his millions *is still alive! It is available to you.* Whether success to you means material rewards, as it did to this penniless, uneducated black man, or advancing in your chosen field—whatever it is that you choose *will only come through intense desire.*

Complacency is the enemy of achievement. It makes all the difference in the world whether you undertake a proposition to win—with clenched teeth and a resolute will—having prepared for it thoroughly, and determined at the very outset to hit your mark, or whether you begin your task with indecision and indifference. It is widely believed that the man who has the fortitude and the right mental attitude will, sooner or later, reach his objective.

Now, have you knocked on the door named Desire? Will you accept the torch of opportunity this great nation has to offer? Are you willing to study the principles spelled out in *Think and Grow Rich: A Black Choice*? If you answer yes, chances are this lesson is for you.

The Power of Desire and Motives

Basic motives, moved to action, are all prefaced by the desire for a specific objective. Men and women of ordinary ability become pillars of strength when aroused by desire, stimulated by action. Bring a person face to face with the possibility of death, and, amazingly, he or she will exhibit all kinds of physical strength and prowess. The following story clearly illustrates this point.

An old African sage, wise and influential, lived on the side of a mountain near a lake. It was common practice for the people of the village to seek his advice. The old man spent many hours sitting in front of his small hut, where he rocked in a crude rocking chair made of branches and twigs. Hour after hour he sat and rocked as he thought.

One day he noticed a young African warrior walking on the path toward his hut. The young man walked up the hill and stood erect before the sage. "What can I do for you?" the old man said.

The warrior replied, "I was told by those in the village that you are very wise. They said that you can give me the secret of happiness and success."

The old man listened, then gazed at the ground for several moments. He rose to his feet, took the boy by the hand, and led him down the path back toward the lake. Not a word was spoken. The young warrior was obviously bewildered, but the sage kept walking. Soon they approached the lake, but did not stop. Out into the water the old man led the boy. The farther they walked, the higher the water advanced. The water rose from the boy's knees to his waist, then to his chin, but the old man said nothing and kept moving deeper and deeper. Finally the lad was completely submerged. At this point the wise man stopped for a moment, turned the boy around, and led him out of the lake and up the path back to the hut. Still not a word was spoken. The old African sat again in his creaky chair and rocked to and fro.

After several thought-provoking minutes, he looked into the boy's questioning eyes and asked, "Young man, when you were in the lake, underwater, what was it you desired most?"

Openly excited, the boy replied, "Why, you old fool, I wanted to breathe!"

Then the sage spoke these words: "My son, when you want happiness and success in life as badly as you wanted to breathe, you will have found the secret."

This tale provides an excellent analogy. *What is it that you desire more than anything else?* When you pursue your objective with the same state of mind so clearly described in the above tale, then you will reach your goal!

The desire for financial gain often lifts men and women of average ability into positions of great power. The desire for fame and fortune is easily discernible as the chief motivating force of leaders in every walk of life.

Look around at the successful men and women in any line of work and you will see embedded a deeply developed desire. Their white-heat intensity and fierce craving would tolerate nothing less than the attainment of their major purpose. Many people go through life looking for favorable "breaks." *Perhaps the biggest break anyone could ever receive is to decide exactly what it is he or she wants and then become obsessed with obtaining it.* Study the key ingredients in the following success stories. By now you should be in a position to extract principles from specific illustrations so that you can relate, assimilate, and apply them.

Wally Amos was not always famous, but he possessed the *desire* to attract both fame and fortune. As a young boy he lived with his aunt in New York, who introduced him to her special chocolate chip recipe. With little direction, he dropped out of high school and joined the Air Force. Four years later he returned to New York and worked in a department store. A positive outlook and hard work helped him advance from stock clerk to supply manager. Amos carried the same skills over to the William Morris Agency, where he worked as a talent agent. But Amos demanded more from life. So, in 1975, infused with spirit, enthusiasm, and *desire*, and possessing neither a high school diploma nor sufficient capital, the "Famous Amos Chocolate Chip Cookie" story began. The company that bears his name has since expanded throughout the nation and is now a well-known recipe for success.

Edward W. Brooke *desired* a seat in Congress. In spite of his glaring differences—a Protestant in a predominately Catholic district, and a Republican in heavily

Democratic Boston—Brooke nevertheless became, in 1966, the first and only black since 1881 to win membership in the United States Senate.

Several years ago George Halsey tried desperately to supplement his income. His salary as an insurance claims adjuster barely covered his family's living expenses. So when a young Amway distributor in Greensboro, North Carolina, convinced him to become involved, Halsey already possessed a fervent *desire* to succeed. "Amway provided me with an opportunity and a product," said the super salesman. "But George Halsey provided the rest."

And what was the rest? Some of the ingredients you've heard before: hard work, persistence, determination. But the most important was *desire*. Without a burning desire, Halsey would not have reached his goal. Oblivious to anything but success, Halsey marched door to door selling cleaning products that enabled him to retire as a young man with millions.

Leontyne Price was filled with the desire to sing in the great opera halls of the world. At age five she received a toy piano for Christmas. Several years later her mother took her to see Marian Anderson, the first black soloist to sing at New York's Metropolitan Opera House, who electrified her audience with a pulse-pounding performance. It was a magic moment. A single spark mushroomed into flames. Leontyne would later tell her mother, "I know my life's purpose. *I want to sing!*"

This exposure furnished Leontyne with a musical sense of direction that would propel her from rural Mississippi to the Met. And neither the lack of money, training, nor contacts would bind her. The seventh black artist to make a Metropolitan Opera debut, she was the first to achieve worldwide status as "prima donna assoluta." In a career spanning more than a quarter-century, Leontyne Price has garnered many honors, including eighteen Grammy awards and the Presidential Medal of Freedom. To this day she proclaims, "I love nothing more than to hear my own voice. It's a personal adoration. Singing is the most important thing!''

Gwendolyn Brooks cannot recall when she did not want to be a poet. Suffused with an intense desire, Brooks became the first of her race to be awarded the Pulitzer Prize. At fifteen, already an accomplished author, she wrote to her idol, James Weldon Johnson, who inspired her immensely. ''He was quite kind,'' Brooks remembers. ''He returned my poems with editorial comments and little assurances. He praised my talents and hoped that I would continue to write. Though my parents were delighted with this sort of attention, I would have gone on writing no matter what anyone said. I had to be a poet!''

Her first book, *A Street in Bronzeville*, published in 1945, was a huge success. She went on to earn many awards, including the Pulitzer Prize in 1950. In 1968, Gwendolyn Brooks was named poet laureate of the State of Illinois.

Thurgood Marshall, though barred from many law schools because of his race, focused exclusively on making an impact in the courtrooms of America. After graduating with honors from a Baltimore, Maryland, high school, Marshall attended Lincoln University in Pennsylvania, earning his tuition as a grocery store clerk and waiter. Despite a constricting schedule, he still found the time to join the school's debating team, fine-tuning the skills that would serve him well as one of the nation's top lawyers. In 1933, after earning a law degree from Howard University, he was admitted to the Maryland state bar. He quickly developed a reputation for civil rights cases and was in high demand.

In 1954, Marshall was ushered onto center stage while acting as special counsel for the National Association for the Advancement of Colored People (NAACP). He argued successfully before the Supreme Court that racial segregation in the public schools was unconstitutional. In addition to this precedent-setting case, he presented

32 other cases before the nation's highest court—*winning 29 of them*! In 1967, then-President Lyndon B. Johnson elevated Marshall to Supreme Court justice—the first black to hold such a position.

The son of a waiter, he nearly single-handedly forced a nation to come to grips with its commitment to freedom. In a rare interview he told a reporter that "blacks must earn their way to higher achievement." And how does one earn anything? *Through perseverance, hard work, and desire.*

To those familiar with track and field, her name is synonymous with speed. In the 1988 Olympics in Seoul, Korea, she won three gold medals, earning the title of the "world's fastest woman." With her cover girl looks, her style and grace, her name has also become synonymous with success. All of her life Florence Griffith Joyner simply has desired to be the best.

But it hasn't been easy. As a seven-year-old reared in the projects of Watts, California, Florence competed with ten older siblings. To divert her from the temptations of the streets—drugs, crime, and gangs—her mother enrolled her in a summer youth program. It was Florence's first exposure to organized sports, and the attraction to the track events seemed natural. Florence quickly found that she could beat most boys in 100- and 200-meter sprints with little effort or training.

But that changed by 1984. Crestfallen and demoralized, Florence used a second-place finish in the 200 meters in the 1984 Olympics as a springboard to a stronger effort. "Second place wasn't good enough," she said without blinking an eye. "I had decided that I was going for three gold medals in the 'eighty-eight games, and I knew what it would take to reach my goal."

What did it take? Let's count the cost. It took discipline, determination, and sheer *desire* as she meticulously adhered to a rigorous training regimen. Every morning she would run at sunrise before going to work at a neighboring bank. Her afternoons were filled with even more sprints followed by stretching, strength exercises, and weight training. And if that wasn't enough, when funds got low she squeezed more hours into an already hectic schedule by moonlighting as a cosmetologist at area beauty salons. Day after day, month after month, she maintained this grueling routine, *for four years!*

Was it worth the effort? No question. At the Seoul Olympics it all came together as "Flo Jo," as she is affectionately called, turned in three breathtaking performances by breezing to easy victories in the 100- and 200-meter dashes, as well as the 100-meter relay—setting world records in each.

"The ladder of success is never crowded at the top," she says ecstatically. "To be a winner in any field takes hard work, discipline, and desire."

In 1933, H. Naylor Fitzhugh became one of the first black Americans to be awarded a master's degree in business administration from Harvard University. A year later he joined the faculty of Howard University, and for more than thirty years has mentored hundreds of black business students. Revered by corporate America as a marketing genius, Fitzhugh has had enough accomplishments in his lifetime for two or three similarly gifted men.

The bedrock of Fitzhugh's personal credo was instilled during his childhood. He was raised by parents who imparted an unwavering aim for success. "Though my father never completed grammar school," Fitzhugh said, "he made me *want to* succeed. No matter what the undertaking—whether it was collecting newspapers, hauling coal, or pursuing graduate studies at Harvard—I *had to* perform!" It was this "want to" and "had to" that has paid great dividends throughout his life.

In 1960, during spring training in St. Petersburg, Florida, Bill White was fed up with the unwritten rule that forced black baseball players to find housing among local black families, while their white teammates enjoyed luxury hotels. Disregarding the risk that came with being outspoken, he stood up in the Cardinal clubhouse and vehemently protested to St. Louis management the discriminatory practices. As a result, the team moved its training facilities to an adjacent city. Forty-three years after Jackie Robinson broke baseball's color line, Bill White again overcame years of mounting frustration when he was named the sport's National League president.

Was it a definite purpose or a personal goal? Probably not. I make note of this example for other reasons. Though White did not seek the position, former baseball commissioner Peter Ueberroth emphatically stated, "Bill White was hired because he was the best man for the job. Throughout his career, Bill always desired to be the best!"

In this race for success, you should be encouraged to know that our changing world is demanding new services, new methods, and new leaders. In order to fulfill this demand for new and better ideas, you must possess a definite purpose—knowing exactly what it is you want—and a burning desire to possess it.

Marva Collins simply desired to teach. She began where she stood to put her dream into action. Soon after she founded Chicago's Westside Preparatory School in 1975, her ability to transform children who were labeled as retarded, troublesome, and truant into shining scholars made her a national celebrity. The media referred to her as a "miracle worker," and "superteacher." But she is neither. In her own words Marva promises her students, "I will not let you fail!"

Because of her success, she was offered the opportunity to head many influential organizations—including U.S. Secretary of Education, superintendent of Los Angeles schools, and Chicago school board member—but turned them all down. Why? Because Marva simply *desired* to teach. And because of this insatiable desire, her accomplishments captured recognition from such institutions as the National Educational Association and the American Academy of Achievement, as well as other prestigious organizations. Marva Collins has demonstrated to an intellectually starving generation what reading can do, what love can do, but most importantly, what reading *and* love can do.

If you are to achieve riches in your life like those mentioned above, plant a strong unquenchable desire into the fiber of your being. What other force on earth but desire could do as much?

Millions of people struggle all the days of their lives with no stronger motive than to acquire the bare necessities—food, shelter, and clothing. Now and then someone will step out of the crowd and demand of himself and of the world more than a mere living. He motivates himself with desire and achieves fulfillment through action.

What is it that you desire? What is it that will make you stand boldly and firmly, crying out, "This I will have—it is my destiny, and I am going to possess it!" As Robert Collier, author of *Secret of the Ages*, has stipulated:

Unless you want a certain thing "the worst way" and manifest that desire in the shape of a strong, impelling force, you will have no will with which to accomplish anything. You must not only "want" to do a thing, or to possess a thing, but you must "want to" hard. You must want it as the hungry man wants bread, as the choking man wants air. And if you will but arouse in yourself this fierce, ardent, insatiable desire, you will set in operation one of Nature's most potent mental forces.

The Miracle of Motivation

Disraeli once wrote, "Action may not always bring happiness, but there is no happiness without action." Neither does action bring satisfaction—even in those instances where action does not bring happiness. Basically, you are presented with three decisions in life: Whom are you going to spend your life with? How are you going to spend your life? What are you going to live your life for? The answers to these questions will provide you with the key to the riches you seek. You will either drive yourself or be driven—motivation will be the difference.

The word "motive" is defined as "that within the individual that incites him or her to *act*." It is the inner urge that produces specific results that can be learned and developed. In order for motivation to be effective, driving you toward your desire, it must be internalized. Until the incentive has been interpreted and accepted, motivation has no real power.

Every thought you think, every act you take, can be traced back to some definite motive or combination of motives. No one ever does anything without having been motivated to do so. You will need to develop a strong, positive approach to self-motivation if you are to be successful in your quest for achievement. There are nine basic motives to which everyone responds, and which influence practically every human thought or deed. The nine motives are:

> Love
> Financial Gain
> Self-Preservation
> Sex
> Power and Fame
> Freedom
> Creativity
> Anger and Revenge
> Fear

Within this framework you will find the roots of everything you do or refrain from doing. Though love and fear are poles apart, they remain the strongest of all our motives.

"The Children Know That Somebody Loves Them"

Sitting in an old rocker on the third floor of a Harlem brownstone, Clara "Mother" Hale cradles a three-month-old infant who has already fought a battle that has defeated many adults—drug addiction. Born prematurely to a mother who herself was an addict, the tiny baby once exhibited all the symptoms of heroin dependency. The small, frail-looking black woman remembers the day the child was brought to the center.

"He was always shaking, scratching himself, and crying," says Mother Hale, as she is affectionately called. "We had to keep him covered up because he was always cold."

The baby is just one of more than 600 children, black, white, and Hispanic, between the ages of two weeks and three years, who have overcome drug addiction through the care offered by the Hale House. Located in a four-story converted apartment building on Harlem's west side, in the midst of the New York drug trade, the center was conceived by Clara Hale in 1969. The cure she continually employes is not based on miracles or medicine, but on the healing power of love and positive reinforcement. With soft, tender eyes, she says, "The children know that somebody loves them."

Born in Philadelphia, Clara Hale acknowledges that the loving care she received from her own mother provided the foundation for her work. At age twenty-seven, Mother Hale found herself a widow with three small children of her own to support. Searching for ways to raise her family, she began caring for her neighbors' children. Her home-based business was successful except for one minor flaw. Many of the children became so attached to Mother Hale that they didn't want to go to their homes at the end of the day. Consequently, many of them boarded with her during the week and visited their parents on the weekends. Over the next thirty years Clara Hale raised more than forty foster children in that five-room brownstone on 146th Street. The majority went on to lead successful lives.

"I have cared for more than six hundred addicted babies since we opened the center," she says softly. "I hold them and rock them. They love you to tell them how great they are, how good they are. Somehow, even at a young age, they understand that.

"I tell my children being black does not stop you. You can stand on the corner and say, 'Well, white people kept me back, and I can't do this.' Not so. *You can have anything you want if you make up your mind and you want it bad enough.*"

As the founder and guiding spirit of this program, Clara Hale was cited as a "True American Hero" by then-President Ronald Reagan in his 1985 State of the Union address. Hundreds of infants and children have returned to health and to their rehabilitated parents after living and being loved under her gentle care.

Love is man's greatest experience. It brings one into communication with that infinite source of all creation. Love makes all mankind akin. It clears out selfishness, greed, jealousy, hate, and envy. True wealth will never be found where love does not abide. The love to which I refer is the love typified by the Master, when he said, "And now abideth faith, hope, love, these three; but the greatest of these is love." Love, courtesy, and friendship are three priceless assets that cannot be purchased or bargained for. They must be given away before they become valid.

Love is the one factor that draws a clear line between man and all other creatures on earth. It is the one factor that determines for each of us the space we will occupy in the hearts of our fellowmen. It is the solid foundation upon which all of humanity is based. You can judge how well you are succeeding in this game of life by the number and quality of loving relationships you have engaged in. If a man is truly great, if he is worth his salt, he will love all mankind. *There is only one thing that will attract love, and that is love.*

This love is the same love exhibited by Clara Hale and all those who have attained riches. It is the love that is the "life-giving" force, the spring of all action, a motive that triggers desire. It is the outward expression of the spiritual nature of man.

The great minds of every age have recognized love as the eternal elixir that binds the heart-wounds of mankind and makes men their brothers' keepers. Emerson held a vision of this kind of love when he wrote: "The magnanimous know very well that they who give time, or money, or shelter, to the stranger—so it be done for love, and not for ostentation—do, as it were, put God under obligation to them, so perfect are the compensations of the universe. In some way the time they seem to lose is redeemed, and the pains they take, remunerate themselves. These men fan the flame of human love and raise the standard of civic virtue among mankind."

The Opposite of Love Is Fear—the Great Paralyzer

What is more pitiful than a healthy, able-bodied, educated young man or woman whining about the hard times or the lack of opportunity in this land that is so packed with opportunities? In what other country, or at what other time in human history, were the times better or the chances for success greater?

Hundreds of thousands, young and old alike, try to excuse themselves for their failure to achieve by saying that society or "the system" or racism is the cause for their lack of accomplishment. Chances are that the great numbers are bound and gagged by their own minds, held captive by the *fear of failure*. John H. Johnson, founder of Johnson Publications, describes this state of affairs best:

Most people don't really believe in success. They feel helpless before they even begin. "Whitey's" not keeping blacks down. He's not keeping us from jobs or education. We have the power to make it in this society, and so we can't blame the system for everything. It is the fear of failure that gets into the way.

Fear, the most powerful of negative motives, mirrors love, but in reverse. Instead of appealing to the constructive or life-giving forces, it appeals to the force of destruction. It becomes a god in itself, demanding endless painful sacrifices. People rarely admit that their lives of bitter privation may be founded on nothing more than constant fear—and yet it happens all around them.

But not all fear is negative. Though man controls his own thinking, the Creator provided that he be capable of fear, because justified fear is a part of self-preservation. For example, one who meets a lion on a jungle path and has neither a weapon nor a means of defense is well-advised to be fearful and to take measures toward his self-preservation. Likewise, the child who is taught to exercise caution before crossing a street is alerted to danger. In both circumstances fear is positive.

However, self-made fears can be the most damaging. Psychologists have discovered that we are equipped with only two fears at birth—the fear of falling and the fear of loud noises. But man, nonetheless, remains paralyzed by many other forms of fear, among which the fear of failure emerges most prominent. Other forms of fear are:

Fear of Poverty: The fear of poverty is the most destructive of all the basic fears. Nothing brings man so much suffering and humiliation as poverty. Only those who have experienced lack and misery can understand its full meaning. This fear rears its ugly head within the generations of individuals who have known nothing but poverty. Fearing poverty, and with good reason, these people allow their wits to dull and cancel all initiative and desire. In the greatest nation in the world, a nation throbbing with opportunity, millions settle down to live in want. If you resent poverty and are determined to be rid of it, search and beware for the signs of this fear.

Fear of Criticism: Have you any idea what the fear of criticism does to an individual? The fear of what people will say or think keeps many from developing and presenting ideas that would give them independence if acted upon. A person who is filled with this fear will shun his ideas lest he be rebuffed. Consequently, he loses his great gifts of imagination and creativity. The story of personal achievement is the story of those who refused to give in to the "unqualified they" and remained true to their hearts and their own uncompromising minds. We should be our most severe critic, honestly and objectively examining our own actions. What, then, can we fear in the criticism of others?

Fear of Dying: For thousands of years men and women have been asking the question "Where did I come from, and where am I going?" Heaven or Hell? Paradise or damnation? Birth and death are necessary components of the overall plan of the universe, but people are nevertheless afraid of the afterlife. Recognize that eternity is not something that comes after death, but is a representation of time—*limitless.* Heaven and Hell are not locations, but states of mind. Eternal life is the quality of life, well-ordered, stable, confident, and not a quantifiable description of our current being. Just the mere thought of it all coming to an end is enough to send thousands into a frenzy of the fear of dying. Though no one knows what lies beyond death's impenetrable door, there is nothing to fear from a circumstance that you cannot control.

Being in full possession of your mind, you can free yourself of any and all fears. Granted, fear is a motive that can sufficiently arouse you to act and obtain that which you desire. But as you properly relate to life, you'll find that you no longer need such fears.

Your mind has limitless power to make your desires come true. To bring a beneficial desire to reality, your mind must first function unhampered. The fears mentioned above have crippled the most highly developed minds and have dashed the hopes of the strongest desires.

Fueling Desire—
How to Stay Motivated All the Time

Remember, anything you fear and dwell upon will manifest in your life: *poverty, ill health, criticism,* or *love.* There is nothing more important than learning the art of keeping your mind focused upon the things, conditions, and circumstances of life that you really want. Here are ten essential elements that will fuel your motivation.

1. Develop the right mental attitude.
2. Aspire to something greater than yourself. Develop a "magnificent obsession."
3. Possess a futuristic outlook; take the long-range view. Release the past.
4. Develop deep personal integrity. Be someone you can admire.
5. Accept total personal responsibility. Remain in complete control at all times. Do not be manipulated by people or events. Operate on a personal timetable.
6. Edify and affirm others. Remember, nothing is greater than love.
7. Be grateful, not critical. Develop a gratitude attitude.
8. Select your friends with care. Minimize people dependency. If you dominate your associates, there is no way for you to expand or grow.
9. Do it now! Decide what habits or changes you wish to alter in your life; make those changes and never let an exception occur.
10. Look for mentors. Mentors who "are larger than life" expand us, mentors in different fields broaden us, and deceased mentors inspire us.

None of these ten elements regarding motivation calls for any formal education or great sacrifice. Each can be verified for its soundness by anyone who understands the power of self-motivation as it relates to achieving a worthy goal.

A Worthy Destination

It is almost impossible to pick up a newspaper without reading of someone who has achieved great success. Almost invariably, these profiles include the overcoming of what at one time appeared to be virtually insurmountable odds. For example, the boy whose legs were terribly burned, and who seemed destined to face life as a cripple, becomes one of the world's outstanding runners; the poor, fatherless child who amasses a fortune; the youth with a disabling speech impediment and poor self-image who becomes one of the nation's most prolific public speakers. Every day a new and dramatic story appears. This is the same tale of obstacles overcome and outstanding success achieved.

But how are these feats accomplished? These individuals are faced with great barriers, and seemingly are blessed with few resources. Nevertheless, they overcome their obstacles and rise above their difficulties. *How did they do it?* But it's more than a matter of how—you must ask the question "Why did they do it?" If fully understood, the answer will bring you the riches you desire.

Simply put, they had a goal. That is, they had fixed in their minds a point they *had* to reach. Something that was more important—*far more important*—than the effort and time that had to be expended; a dream seen only in the mind and felt only in the heart, that was too big to be denied. A dream that appeared before their eyes when they awakened in the morning, and was glued to their lips as they dropped off to sleep at night.

This grand vision, this surging dynamic that is invisible to all the world except the person who holds it, is responsible for every great advance of mankind. It is the cause for everything we see in the world around us. Every manifestation in the world is a dream come true. It is a goal reached. It is the skyscraper, the bridge spanning the river, a shuttle to outer space; it is the little corner grocery store; it is the lovely home in the suburbs; it is the young man or woman receiving a diploma, a mother holding a baby in her arms; a golf handicap, a job promotion come true—you name it.

Do you know what this means to you and me? Once the point is understood, life becomes easier, more fun, far more exciting and incalculably more rewarding. Let me explain.

In order to fully understand this idea, you must realize what lies at the very core of achievement. One of the most comprehensive definitions of success was offered by radio announcer and worldly philosopher Earl Nightingale. More than twenty years ago Nightingale stated that "success is the progressive realization of a worthy ideal." If you think about it for a moment, you'll realize just how perfect his definition is. *Success is the progressive realization of a worthy ideal.*

What does this mean? It means that any person engaged in achieving anything that he or she considers a worthy ideal is successful. At the same time, it means that anyone not so engaged must be moving toward the opposite of success—*failure.* Anyone possessing a dream in his heart which he or she has established as a worthy goal, and who is moving toward the attainment of that dream, is successful. It has nothing to do with money necessarily, unless that happens to be the goal. And each of us must decide for himself or herself what our goal is.

Successful is the person who says "I'm going to become this" and works toward that goal. A success is the schoolteacher who's teaching school because that's what he or she *wanted* to do. A success is a woman who is a wife and mother because she *wanted* to become a wife and mother, and is doing a good job of it. A success is the man who operates a corner gas station because that is his dream—that's what he *wanted* to do. A success is the successful salesman who *wanted* to become a top-notch salesman and grow and build with his or her organization. A success is anyone who has a deliberately predetermined goal because that's what he decided upon—deliberately. With such a simple and clear definition as this, you might think that everyone is successful. Everyone should be. Unfortunately, however, it has been estimated *that only five percent are.*

The Top Five Percent

To further his argument, Nightingale also developed what he called the "top five percent theory," which was equally as insightful. In practical terms, his theory is more fact than conjecture. Nightingale explains:

> If you approach one hundred men and women of equal education, equal skills, equal background at age twenty-five, and ask if they would like to be wealthy, in the field of their choice, you'll notice a sparkle in their eyes, an eagerness toward life, and a keenness in their manner—*for they truly WISH to be rich.*
>
> Now project these same individuals forty years into the future—allowing for time, growth, experience, and opportunity. At the end of those forty years—with the chance to be great in the field of their choice, in *THE RICHEST NATION on the face of the earth—ONLY ONE will be rich!* Four will be financially independent; thirty will be dead; and sixty-five will be forced to rely on any number of government programs in order to survive the remaining years of their lives.

Think for a moment of those whom you pass on the street, no matter how large or small the city, no matter its location, and regardless of the race or creed of its inhabitants—only five out of one hundred people will achieve their financial goals. *Only 5 percent!*

And what of the other 95 percent? Unfortunately, they just drift along, hoping and wishing that something positive will "turn up," or at least that nothing negative will. These are able-bodied men and women who've allowed the winds of circumstance to blow them in any direction.

Why, in this land of plenty, is there such a disheartening ending to so many lives? What has happened to the sparkle in their eyes and their eagerness toward life? What became of their hopes, their dreams, and their plans?

Rollo May, the distinguished psychiatrist and author of *Man's Search for Himself*, explains the psychological origin of this question. May regretfully says, "Man simply conforms. Many people feel they are powerless to do anything effective with their lives. It takes courage to break out of the settled mold, but most find conformity more comfortable. This is why the opposite of courage in our society is not cowardice—it's conformity."

One thing you must put aside in order to fulfill your destiny is conformity. We all conform in hundreds of ways. Even those of us who feel we have traveled on our own separate paths, who have lived more or less as free and independent spirits, are conformists to some extent. But you must realize the ways in which you should not conform. You should not lead your life according to the dictates and mandates of others. Conforming to the whims and standards of others is insidious and dangerous. There is a human tendency, no doubt acquired and strengthened in childhood, to believe that whatever people in significant numbers are doing must be correct or so many would not be doing it.

We live in a society in which popularity is confused with superiority or excellence. For example, the most popular consumer brands are not necessarily the best consumer brands. American-made cars and clothing are heavily advertised and therefore are most popular. But the truth of the matter is, the great majority of people seldom enjoy the best of anything—clothes, cars, cuisine, or life-style. *The best is never the most popular.*

You must find your own unique pathway in the world; the masses, or majority, never do. Until you set the tone for your existence, *you will follow others, who are, in turn, following you.* As you continue your trek to greatness you must remember this: If you do the exact opposite of what everyone else is doing, you'll probably avoid one of life's most costly mistakes.

Goals

Now, why don't more people set goals? This question has been raised and argued for decades. Basically, there are four reasons:

- A failure to realize the importance of goals
- An inability to set goals
- A fear of rejection
- A fear of failure

Dr. Benjamin E. Mays, scholar, educator, and president emeritus of Morehouse College, put it more succinctly:

It must be borne in the mind that the tragedy of life doesn't lie in not reaching your goal. The tragedy lies in having no goal to reach. It isn't calamity to die with dreams unfulfilled, but it is a calamity not to dream. It is not a disaster to be unable to capture your ideal, but it is a disaster to have no ideal to capture. It is not a disgrace not to reach the stars, but it is a disgrace to have no stars to reach for. Not failure, but low aim is sin.

If you were to compare human beings with ships, the following scenario might prove a revealing analogy. It has been estimated by researchers that nearly 95 percent of the current population can be compared to a ship without a rudder, subject to every shift of wind and tide. They are helplessly adrift. And while they fondly hope that they will one day venture into a rich and prosperous port, you and I know that for every narrow harbor entrance there's a thousand miles of rocky coastline. Their chances of just drifting into a safe port are 1000 to 1 against them. However, the 5 percent who have taken the time and discipline to decide on a destination and chart a course sail straight and far across the deep oceans of the world, reaching one port after another, and accomplishing more in a few short years than the majority will accomplish in a lifetime.

If you should visit a ship in port, climb to the navigation bridge and ask the captain his next port of call, he will answer you in one sentence. Every person should be able to do the same. Unless you can say in one concise, well-defined sentence what your goal or definite purpose happens to be, chances are good that you have never clearly defined your goal. The ship's captain cannot see his destination for fully 99 percent of his journey— but he knows what it is, where it is, and that he will reach it if he keeps doing certain things a certain way, each day.

When you ask most people what it is they seek, they'll respond in vague, unrealistic terms. They may say "happiness," or "good health," or "money." These are not goals, they're simply conditions desired by everyone. When we speak of goals, we mean, *What is it that you want?*—you, as an individual. What is it that you would like to have or be? If you can tell me what you want, I can tell you how to get it, as long as it's worthy, doesn't violate the laws of your fellowman, and is within the realm of human accomplishment.

Progressing successfully through a lifetime should be a matter of routinely setting and achieving goals, one after another, each a little better than the former. Just as a ship sails to only one port at a time, set your first port of call. When you've reached your goal—and reach it you will—you can then set a new goal, and then another. By following this meaningful and common-sense approach to life, you will be successful and accomplish more in a few short years than the great majority do in a lifetime.

Walk to the Beat of a Different Drummer

Henry David Thoreau wrote, "If a man does not keep pace with his companions, perhaps it is because he hears a different drummer."

While most of us are not as insightful as Thoreau, each of us is unique. I may not be able to do what you do, or vice versa, but each of us has the ability to choose his particular way and style of life. You may choose to stay with the crowd that is content with mediocrity—those who say "it can't be done" or "no one in the past has ever done it"—or you can follow the desires of your heart.

You are free to strike off in a new, personally chosen direction, unencumbered by the prejudices and opinions of others. There is a Chinese proverb that drives home this point: "A man who says it cannot be done should not interrupt the man doing it." There will always be those who are ready to speak persuasively about the utter impossibilities of your achievement, or the minuscule chances of your success as you venture forth. Consider their words, if you must, then proceed to go your own way. Listen instead to the inner rhythms of the music within your soul.

How's Your Aim?

Realizing that without a goal we are unsuccessful, and realizing, too, that with a goal we will have direction and purpose, and that our goal will be reached, we begin to understand that the setting of a clearly defined objective is the most important step that we could possibly take.

Aristotle, the great philosopher, was asked one day by a young citizen, "How do you get to Mount Olympus?" To which Aristotle promptly replied, "By simply ensuring that each step you take is toward Mount Olympus."

Mahatma Gandhi once instructed a fellow Hindu leader during their quest for Indian independence not to lose sight of his destination. "There will be many turnings along the way," Gandhi said. "It will be easy to get lost on attractive bypaths that lead nowhere. Resist deflections."

It has been a constant source of bewilderment to watch the overwhelming majority of people drift aimlessly through life, without the slightest conception of the work for which they are best suited, and with no idea of even the need for a definite objective toward which to strive. This, indeed, is one of the tragedies of civilization. Clinical psychologist Harry E. Gunn, an expert in career counseling, notes that nearly 60 percent of all Americans say they are unhappy with their careers, and that they would rather be in a different field of work. Napoleon Hill quotes an even higher figure. Hill insists that "ninety-eight out of every one hundred people working for wages today are in the positions they hold because they lacked definiteness of purpose to plan a specific course of action."

Toward this end, goal-setting is the master skill. It is a quality without which no one can attain riches or outstanding success. The man or woman on the move is the person who is intensely goal-oriented. The man or woman who sets a goal is the mover and shaker in every area of human endeavor. It is through the practice of goal-setting that one can compensate for life's shortcomings, whether those shortcomings be real—lack of money, limited schooling, or poor self-image—or imagined. The setting of goals, and strict adherence to them, will cause the window of opportunity to open in your life.

How to Set Goals

Every successful individual follows, in one form or another, the same goal-setting techniques. Some follow it diligently. Those who stand at the threshold of achievement have utilized goal-setting on a routine basis. You must do the same. Follow these instructions to the letter; comply with them in good faith, and remember that by doing so you are duplicating the procedure used by many of the greatest leaders this nation has ever produced.

With pad and pencil, settle into a place where you feel comfortable—a favorite desk or chair—somewhere you feel creative. Plan to spend the next sixty minutes defining exactly what it is you expect to be, to do, or to create. It could very well be the most valuable sixty minutes of your life.

- First, write down a clear, concise statement of what you want most in life. This could be reaching a certain salary level, gaining a promotion in your present line of work, or starting your own business. Write what you wish, but you must be specific.
- Second, outline your plan of achieving this major goal. The plan need not be long; in fact, the opposite is probably true. The shorter your plan, the more likely it is to focus on major issues. Just as a ship can reach only one port at a time, you can achieve only one goal at a time. Most of the confusion and indecision found within the majority of people can be traced to one of two obvious sources: either they haven't decided on a specific goal, or they have dispersed their efforts, and as a result, accomplish very little at all.
- Third, set a definite timetable for achieving your goal. Remember, major goals are seldom reached in giant steps. Your plan should include all interim steps necessary to reach the top.
- Fourth, memorize your chief aim and your plan. Repeat them several times a day—almost like a prayer—ending

with an expression of gratitude for having received what your plan calls for. By so doing, you will be forcing your major purpose into your subconscious mind, from which will come the steps you need, as you need them, for its accomplishment.

Most importantly, put your plan into *action*! Plans and goals are vital—essential, really—but they are wasted without action. You must take the necessary steps to implement your plans.

How One Man Used This Goal-Setting System

Thousands of people have applied this goal-setting system for their own enrichment. Legend has it that this is the same system used by scientist and inventor George Washington Carver, who has been labeled the greatest agricultural scientist this country has ever produced. Carver, a former slave, is credited with single-handedly transforming the pattern of agriculture throughout the South.

"When I was a child, my owner saw what he considered to be a good business deal and immediately accepted," Dr. Carver often told visitors to his Tuskegee, Alabama, laboratory. "He traded me off for a horse.

"That may have been the best thing that ever happened to me, for in my new environment I managed to get much more schooling than I otherwise would have had. Maybe it was that trade that helped to prepare me to spend years studying sweet potatoes, peanuts, and soybeans."

George Washington Carver was born in 1864 to slave parents on the Diamond Grove, Missouri, farm of Moses Carver, whose name he bore. Carver's earliest recollections were the death of his father and the kidnapping of himself and his mother by slave traders in the last year of the Civil War. Though his mother was never heard from again, a racehorse valued at $300 was given in exchange for him. He was returned to Missouri to his master's plantation.

Five years later, when freed by the Thirteenth Amendment, Carver faced all the disadvantages associated with poverty, race, and ignorance. He was thirteen years old. With an insatiable thirst for knowledge but no school to quench it, he borrowed an old spelling book and, in effect, became his own teacher. For nine years he worked as a servant, laboring by day and studying by night, until he was financially able to attend Iowa State College. After graduating in 1894 with both bachelor's and master's degrees, he joined the school's faculty, specializing in agricultural research.

Carver's students loved him. His wide knowledge of soils, minerals, birds, and flowers, and his love of nature made study under him a pleasure. In his greenhouse he experimented with many types of plant-crossings and grafting, and became known as the "plant doctor." His botanical exploits were soon discovered by Booker T. Washington, who called Carver to his life's work at Tuskegee Institute. The institute's 2000-acre farm was in wretched condition. Much of the land had been depleted by years of growing cotton. Crop rotation to replenish essential minerals was unknown at the time; in an endless cycle, farmers simply cleared excess timberland and let the barren soil erode. Without vegetation, more and more topsoil washed away.

Carver's methods were simple. He set out to achieve one goal: *to improve the conditions of the soil.* He knew that peanut and sweet potato plants drew their nourishment from the atmosphere and that they replaced nitrogen and other essential minerals that would fertilize the land. Unfortunately, there was no market for these products. Peanuts were considered useless.

But Carver began to change things. He made flour, alcohol, vinegar, rubber, shoe blacking, and syrup from sweet potatoes; and dyes, stains, cheese, Worcestershire sauce, margarine, paints, facial cream, and a preparation used in the fight against infantile paralysis from peanuts. In all, he made 118 different items from sweet potatoes and found more than 300 uses for the peanut.

By the time the United Peanut Association of America held its annual convention in Montgomery, Alabama, in 1919, peanuts were second only to cotton as a cash crop. Although it comprised an $80 million industry, most of the peanut farmers didn't know that Carver had brought them prosperity. To them he was just an eccentric old colored man who dabbled with plants. Nonetheless, one of the group insisted that they should learn as much as they could about their product. They invited Carver to attend their meeting to discuss his experiments. However, when he arrived at the hotel the bellman wouldn't let him in because he was black. But Carver was accustomed to such indignities. He had come to the South to help a struggling country confront its agricultural problems. He promised himself he would bring credit to his race regardless of the sacrifices and personal humiliation.

The peanut growers were so impressed with his discoveries that one association member invited him to Washington, D.C., to address Congress. Carver rode the train all night, sitting upright on a wooden bench in a segregated car designated "colored only," to have the opportunity to present his findings to Congress.

It was during this congressional testimony that Carver gave a clue as to his ability to uncover nature's secrets. He said:

Life requires thorough preparation. We must rid ourselves of the idea that there's a short-cut to achievement; we must understand that education, after all, is nothing more than seeking and understanding the relations of one thing to another. First you must get an idea about a given thing; then you must attempt to determine its cause.

Carver used this system again and again to unlock nature's secrets. Many times he could be found in his laboratory concentrating on *a single idea*, determined to reach his goal, before he would move on to his next objective.

The goal-setting process that allowed George Washington Carver to ignore discrimination and work tirelessly toward the attainment of his goals earned him the respect of many of the great men of his day. For example, Thomas Edison sent an assistant to Tuskegee to persuade Carver to work in Edison's laboratories at a six-figure salary. Other offers followed. Henry Ford, Joseph Stalin, and Mahatma Gandhi considered Carver the world's greatest scientist, and each tried to lure him away. But his answer was always the same. He declined the offers, content to make his mark at Tuskegee.

Emulate Dr. Carver. First, focus on a dream, an idea, a goal—then concentrate your thoughts as often as possible on that particular objective. Create a mental image of your goal already having been attained. Be specific, don't generalize. If it is money that you desire—establish in your mind the exact amount. It is not sufficient merely to say "I want plenty of money." Be definite as to the amount, and set a time limit for earning it. If your goal is a beautiful home, get a picture of the exact home you wish to own, even if you have to pay an architect to draw the plans. Be very careful about what you set your mind and heart upon. For if you want it strongly enough, you'll get it.

I have spent a major portion of my life trying to figure out what separates the "haves" from the "have nots." Not just in a financial sense, although that's certainly an important part of success, but in all phases. I started searching for the answer while completing my doctoral requirements at Northwestern University. The answer I was looking for was the secret to achievement—the secret of success. Finally, I realized that in the hundreds of lives I studied, in the countless books I read, a plain and simple truth had been staring me in the face all along. It is simply: *You become what you think about.*

You are, at this very moment, nothing more than the sum total of your thoughts. Similarly, you will be next year or even five years from now what you think about from this point onward. That's why establishing a goal is so vital to your success. Unless you think about the thing you wish to accomplish, your thinking will be erratic, confused—jumping from one whim to another—with the result of achieving nothing, arriving nowhere. By thinking every morning, each evening, and as many times during the day about the single most important goal you've set for yourself, you'll actually begin moving toward it.

Concentrating your thoughts is like taking a river that is twisting and turning, meandering throughout the countryside, and putting it into a straight, smooth channel. Now it has power, direction, and speed. It is the same with your mind. Once you know where you're going, you'll know exactly why you get out of bed in the morning; you'll know why you're working and what you are working toward; and you'll know why it's important to do the very best work of which you are capable. You'll know why it's essential that you cut yourself away from the big, sluggish river of people who are drifting without purpose and direction, and cut the channel straight and clear to the dream that lies within your heart.

The requirements for goal-setting are simple:

1. Goals must be conceivable, capable of being put into words.
2. Goals must be believable, within the realm of possibilities.
3. Goals must be achievable, doable within your given strengths and abilities.
4. Goals must be desirable, something you desperately want to accomplish.
5. Goals must be just out of reach, but within your grasp. Aim high!

6. Goals must be measurable. What gets measured, gets done.
7. Establish timetables for the completion of all goals. If you are unable to reach your goal in a specified time frame, simply reset the goal.
8. Create a workable master plan. Describe precisely what you intend to give in return for the realization of that which you desire. Remember, there is no such thing as something for nothing. Describe clearly the plan through which you intend to reach your objective. Success demands a price that must be paid in advance, in full.
9. Put your goals into action every day.

These instructions call for no effort that you can't easily put forth. They make no demands on your time or ability with which the average person could not comply. Decide now what it is you want from life and what you plan to give in return. Decide where you are going and how you are going to get there. *And then start from where you are. Get into action!*

There is no road to riches but through a clear, strong purpose. Nothing can take its place. A purpose underlies character, culture, position, attainment of every sort. Decide on your goal; insist upon it. If the thing you wish to do is right, and you believe in it, go ahead and do it! Chase your dream, and never mind what "they" say if you meet with temporary defeat. There is a difference between wishing for a thing and being ready to receive it. No one is ready for a thing until he believes he can acquire it. The state of mind must be belief, not a mere hope or wish. There is nothing, right or wrong, that belief plus burning desire cannot bring to pass.

For the next thirty days review the goals that you specified in step 1 of the goal-setting process. Read your goals every morning, evening, and as many times during the day as you can. Force your goals into your subconscious mind; see yourself as already having attained them. Do this without fail *every day* for thirty days, and it will become a habit—a habit that will lead you from one success to another, all the days of your life. For this is the lodestone of riches: *You are now, and you will become in the future, what you think about.*

4

Faith: The Prerequisite to Power

"The wise man must be wise before, not after, the
event."

—EPICHARMUS

"Faith is the substance of things hoped for, the
evidence of things not seen."

—HEBREWS 11:1

"But first, you must believe."

—PETER PAN

Is there a force, a power, a science—call it what you
will—which few people understand and even fewer use,
to overcome difficulties and achieve outstanding success?
I firmly believe there is, and this lesson will explain it,
so you may use it for the attainment of your chief aim.

Great men and women have never found the easy road
to triumph. It is always the same old route—by way of
hard work and plenty of *applied faith*. Let me tell you
of the power of applied faith.

At one time in his life, eighteen cents and two cans of
sardines were the only thing that stood between him and
starvation. He moved from one cheap Greenwich Village
apartment to another—simply because he couldn't pay
the rent. Twenty years of his life had already been spent
in the military. While serving as a cook in the Coast
Guard, he used nights and free time to write letters for
fellow enlistees to their wives and girlfriends back home.
Men who were either illiterate or found it too difficult to

express themselves—at least on paper—became routine customers.

It was during this time that he, too, fell in love—with writing. He didn't know it then, but his literary talents would eventually carry him to fame and fortune. But his success was anything but instant. Like so many things in his life, writing did not come easy. Creativity and composition were brutally difficult barriers. He labored seven nights a week for eight years before he sold his first article. When he retired from the Coast Guard, he dedicated himself full-time to his writing. Though his income was paltry and erratic, his bills never failed to arrive on time. He was offered several nine-to-five jobs, but refused them all. Why? "Because I'm a writer!" he said. "I've got to keep writing."

Determined to scratch out a living in the literary field, he came up with an idea—a book which as originally planned would take no more than three years to write.

Actually, the project took twelve years, leaving him on the brink of bankruptcy—both financially and spiritually. For these twelve years he spent every waking moment either writing or researching. He devoted more than 6500 hours in 57 libraries on what seemed to be an endless search. His airfares alone, commuting between the United States, London, and the west coast of Africa, totaled more than $30,000. Nine years after starting this complicated task, he found himself $100,000 in debt, depressed, and contemplating suicide.

While preparing an editorial assignment on a private yacht of a friend, he figured the only solution to his problems was for him to simply throw himself overboard and end it all.

But something stopped him! At his lowest point of despair, after hundreds of setbacks that penetrated the depths of his soul, while constantly surrounded and harassed by unsympathetic family and friends, he met his greatest source of power—*applied faith!*

"Recognizing, perhaps for the first time in my life,"

he said, "the amazing power of an enduring faith, I carefully surveyed my bleak circumstances to determine just how much of this form of riches I possessed. The assessment was both revealing and gratifying." In his own words, these are the thoughts of a man who discovered how to condition his mind for the expression of faith. Something rose up within greater than himself. Believing his book would be of enormous value, he dismissed all notions of ending his life.

Roots, the book that made Alex Haley a millionaire, traced the story of the author's family beginning in Africa in 1750 and ending 117 years later in Henning, Tennessee. This monumental 885-page best-seller had the largest printing for a hardcover book in U.S. publishing history. Since 1977—*for his faith*—Haley has been honored by more than 400 different countries, institutions, and organizations. *For his faith*, Haley has become one of the most celebrated writers ever, winning a Pulitzer Prize in the process. For his faith, *Roots*, the television series, broke all viewing records and seized nine Emmys, becoming the highest rated television show ever.

What was Alex Haley's response to his newfound success? He declared, "The only way to succeed is through hard, hard, hard work and plenty of faith."

The person who succeeds in life is one who is convinced that faith is necessary to make contact with infinite intelligence, the source of all power. Believing is the beginning of faith. When the force of faith is unleashed, power becomes unlimited and possibilities are without end. The magnificent power of faith is yours to control through your own undeniable, inalienable privilege of thought. Faith is a state of mind that has been labeled by Napoleon Hill as the "mainspring of the soul," through which your aims, desires, and goals may be translated into their physical equivalent. When you truly believe and comprehend this attribute—putting it into action—you may then control or at least be able to adjust to every setback or negative experience in your life. Faith is a means by which you can put yourself in a frame of mind to tune in and draw upon the power that controls the entire universe.

I have related Alex Haley's story to emphasize the manner in which one may clear his mind, even in the midst of chaos and insurmountable difficulties, and prepare it for the expression of faith. Stated in his own words, you have the story of a man who discovered how to condition his mind for this expression. And what a dramatic story it is! Dramatic because of its simplicity.

Faith is the prerequisite to positive power; it gives perspective, accurate analysis, and the ability to forge ahead. For the individual seeking to develop a powerful, persuasive personality, there is no substitute for honest self-evaluation and faith.

Think of someone you know who always seems to be convinced that he or she will succeed. That person is one who understands faith and knows the power that it transmits. Seemingly, nothing can destroy the determination of a person who thinks, believes, and possesses a faith strong enough to move mountains.

Every man or woman must have faith to achieve. No one can aspire without it. The Creator has not likened us to His image with aspirations and longings for heights to which we cannot climb. *Have faith.* Life should be lived in earnest. It is no idle game, no farce to amuse and be forgotten. You cannot have too much of that yearning one calls aspiration without an ample supply of applied faith. Have faith in yourself, have faith in the Creator.

As the rational person knows, there has to be a plan and a power controlling the universe. You must realize that you, the individual, are a minute expression of infinite intelligence, and as such, there are no limitations except those accepted in your own mind. As the carpenter from the plains of Galilee said, "According to your faith, so be it unto you."

When you find things in your life that you feel need changing, summon this principle. By increasing your level of faith, you will gain new strength and a new belief in yourself. Set in motion the words of Booker T. Washington, the Wizard of Tuskegee, who urged black Americans to "start where you are with what you have, knowing that what you have is plenty enough." If you *believe* that you can take the first step, that very thought resonating within your being will give you the power to take the next, and so on.

Fortunate is the man or woman who has had the gentle guidance of parents, guardians, or mentors who instilled in him or her in the early formative years the principle of faith. The following example points up the influence of such training.

Belief—the Stepping-stone to Faith!

When she was five years old, Bonnie's right leg was amputated just above the knee—a blunt and painful remedy for a birth defect that had stunted the growth of her leg. When doctors in a Los Angeles hospital performed the surgery, her right leg reached only the knee of the left. The amputation was only the first in a series of surgical procedures that would be performed over a six-month period.

For reasons that remain a medical mystery, Bonnie St. John's right leg was missing a growth center at birth, resulting in a shortened femur. Until the surgery, she had spent her childhood wearing a bulky leg brace and orthopedic shoes. It was hoped that a prosthesis would free her from any limitations. Everyone knew Bonnie would not walk, run, or play like normal children. Everyone that is, except her mother.

"I just chose to ignore her handicap," insisted Ruby St. John. "I didn't focus on it. Rather, I asked our doctor just how much Bonnie could do with one leg. His reply was, As much as she believes she can do. So, I told my husband, that's what we're going to do—we'll let Bonnie decide what her limits are."

Breaking through the mental barriers proved to be a formidable obstacle for the young girl. For nearly a decade after the amputation, Bonnie shut herself away, refusing to venture any farther than her bedroom door. Only on occasion did she peer through her window at the children playing outside—the same children who in the past teased her and poked fun and called her "Wooden Leg."

Beliefs and limits can sometimes become roadblocks. Many people think of themselves in terms of what they *can't do* rather than what they *can do*. Bonnie knew what she couldn't do; she faced it every morning when she strapped on her prosthesis. But in her mind she was looking for something she could do. When a friend took her on a ski trip, she found her niche.

Bonnie was fifteen when she first stood on skis. It was an experience to remember. "It was a disaster," she recalled. "I was numb with cold, and I kept falling down." But the sport added a new dimension to her life. She became aware of the relationship between mind and body and the power of the belief system. After all, skiing with two legs required some skill, but skiing with one leg required faith. With practice and pluck on the slopes, she became more self-confident as well as proficient.

In the summer of 1981, Bonnie left home to study at Cornell University in upstate New York. It was there that she decided to try out for the U.S. Handicapped Olympic Ski Team. Such a goal might be dismissed as misguided dreaming for someone who had skied for only two years, not to mention an amputee. But a steadfast determination and iron will convinced Bonnie that her goal was possible. Soon she enrolled in the Burke Mountain Academy, a ski school that gave in-depth instruction to a select group of Olympic hopefuls. Bonnie was the first handicapped racer to ever be considered by the school.

For the next six months Bonnie had a thousand reasons to quit. For starters, she began her training by falling off a skateboard and breaking her *left leg*, leaving her totally incapacitated. Once recovered, she hiked and cycled every hill, participated in all drills, and competed in non-handicapped events. She even raised money by working part-time as a waitress to finance her tuition. By the time Bonnie left Burke Academy, she was one of its best skiers.

In April 1983, Bonnie's dream became a reality—she was named to the U.S. Handicapped Olympic Ski Team. In January she competed at the 1984 Winter Games in Innsbruck, Austria, *capturing a silver and two bronze medals!*

Bonnie's belief system has spilled over into other areas of her life. A Cornell and Harvard graduate with a 4.0 grade-point average, she was rewarded with a Rhodes Scholarship. Today, she is nearing the completion of a Ph.D. in economics at Oxford University. Bonnie St. John is a perfect example that anything within the realm of human understanding is possible for the *believer*.

Now, what do you believe?

I have made myself familiar with the lives of outstanding black men and women; I have met and interviewed many high achievers; and I have often wondered just what it was that took them over the top. I have seen coaches take apparently inferior teams and infuse them with that "something," a force that drove them to victory. I have seen average individuals in the depths of despair and anguish do an abrupt about-face, reaching heights unknown.

Apparently, I was born with an insatiable curiosity, for I have always had a yearning to seek explanations and answers. My inquisitiveness has brought me face to face with many peak performers, led me to many peculiar cases, and has directed me to read every book I could muster on the subject of achievement, psychology, and metaphysics. Gradually I discovered that there is a golden thread that runs through these teachings and makes them work for those who sincerely accept and apply them. This thread can be named in a single word—*belief.*

Belief is the same element or factor that causes people

to be cured through mental healing, enables others to climb the ladder of success, and produces phenomenal results for all who accept it. Why belief is a miracle worker is something that cannot be satisfactorily explained; but have no doubt about it, there's genuine magic in believing.

I have counseled individuals who've said, "There is a position I desire very much, but I could never fill it." Initially, I often agreed with them, that they could never acquire a certain position as they are now—but it is totally self-defeating to believe that they must remain that way. No one is unchangeable. One must *believe* in his power of accomplishment! This is not so much faith in yourself as faith in your potential. Without it, many of your goals and desires will remain beyond your reach.

Success-oriented individuals enjoy continued success because they expect or anticipate success in advance. But the majority, plagued by long strings of repeated failures, are unabashedly accustomed to failure and expect no more out of life. The aphorism, "As a man thinketh in his heart, so is he," not only embraces the whole of man's being, but reaches out to every condition and circumstance of his life. You've learned by now that a man or woman is what he or she thinks—his or her character becomes the total of all his thoughts. Now, take this concept one step further and condition your mind. As the Master stated, "If thou canst believe, all things are possible to him that believeth."

The one way to separate yourself from the mass of humanity and climb out of complacency is to hitch your wagon to the star of some strong purpose or chief aim and *believe!*

Here is a basic faith statement: *To do something— anything—you must first believe it can be done.* Believing something can be done triggers the mind into motion to do just that—find a way to do that which you desire. Mind you, things do not occur because of special magical powers, but because people believe so intensely that they become affected by words and actions. In plain terms, your life is what you believe. If, for example, you believe in scarcity, think about it regularly, and make it the focus of your conversations, I am sure you will see your fair share of poverty in your life. On the other hand, if you believe in happiness and abundance, think of these attributes and act on your belief in them, there's a good chance that you will manifest wealth, supply, and opportunity.

Modern philosophy asserts that if you have confidence in your abilities—believing in yourself—you can accomplish those things that might have been inadvertently labeled impossible. Belief is the prerequisite that improvement is possible in spite of outward appearances. Believe in yourself. Have faith in your abilities. With a sound self-confidence you can, and will, reach your goal.

Push Aside All Self-Limiting Beliefs

Somewhere in your makeup lies dormant the seed of achievement which, if aroused and placed into action, would carry you to great success. Most of us feel that we are capable of more than we've shown, but we don't take the necessary steps to change our circumstances. This is life's paradox. Many apparently well-educated men and women in their respective fields will, in their broad ignorance, condemn the idea of thought power and make no effort to apply its teachings. And yet each of them, if successful, has consciously made use of it. There are those who will believe only what they wish to believe or what fits into their scheme of beliefs, summarily rejecting anything to the contrary, lessening all that they could possibly become in the process.

Every man-made creation starts with seeds of thought. The idea is then germinated with action to form its physical equivalent. All that we savor or avoid is eventually transformed through this process. But beware. When you live exclusively in form—the physical senses—you live in a world of limitations. Think of all the limits that are placed on your form. You can lift only so much weight. You can run only so fast. You can work only so hard. Limits are all in the dimension of form.

Now consider the part of you without physical limits, the dimension of thought. There are no limits to your ability to think. If you can imagine yourself doing anything or achieving anything, then you can attain the physical equivalent.

In this context, the power of belief is dialectical; it can work against you as well as for you. It can defeat you as well as place you on the pedestal of success. If you are currently burdened by any self-limiting beliefs, resolve to dispose of them immediately.

In 1963, Bob Hayes, called by sportswriters "The World's Fastest Human," reached a top speed of 28 miles per hour during a 100-yard race—then the fastest speed recorded by man. "Will anyone run faster?" the experts thought. Today, no one really knows how fast a man or woman can run because we are not certain what limits the performance of runners. Most theories center around the physical—the idea of energy being released from the leg muscles. Energy released in this fashion is a chemical process triggered by an electrical impulse from the brain. Seemingly, the faster the pulse from the brain, the faster energy is released and the greater the power of the runner. For more than 3000 years, in the history of the sport, no one has ever run as fast as Bob Hayes. However, the only limits to this breakthrough were established by *Bob Hayes's beliefs*—not by impulses from his brain.

Before they can predict the ultimate limits of the human body, theorists must first account for "other factors" involved in the steady improvement of achievement. For example, in 1968, Bob Beamon stood motionless after jumping 29 feet, 2½ inches—nearly two feet farther than anyone had ever jumped before. While he was aided ever so slightly by the lower air resistance due to Mexico City's high altitude, there was no denying the magnitude of his feat. Beamon had gone so far beyond what was then considered the limit of human abilities that sports physiologist Ernst Jokl called his performance a "mutation." When questioned about his record-breaking leap, Beamon ecstatically said, "I believed I could do it!"

In 1933, aware of the limitations that ignorance imposed, Charles Drew, who ranked within the top five of his medical school class, was awarded two prestigious fellowships. The fellowships allowed him to continue his studies in a field that was to have a profound impact in the medical profession. Drew continued his research at Columbia University, where, seven years later, he published his thesis, "Banked Blood," in which he uncovered new approaches to the uses of plasma preservation, transportation, and subsequent transfusion. It was considered the final word on blood preservation and was translated into numerous languages.

Unbelievable? Well, for some it was. For you see, medical authorities during the time adopted a policy of blood segregation—that is, the collecting, storing, and separate administration of blood drawn from different races. Drew knew there was no scientific evidence for the continuation of such a dangerously wasteful procedure. His research concluded that there was no racial difference in human blood, and that plasma was to be classified by *types, not race of donor*. Again, another self-limiting belief proved believable. Need we hear more?

Calvin Peete was twenty-three years old when he first handled a golf club. By the standards of this demanding and precise sport, he was labeled an *old man*, though he earnestly declared, "I never considered myself too old for this sport. I just enjoyed playing the game." *Peete never took a lesson.* As a result, he just hit ball after ball—sometimes a thousand at a time—fine-tuning his game and analyzing every stroke.

It is the natural reflex for all golfers to label this as impossible. Why? Because every professional golfer has had plenty of lessons—thousands of hours of individualized instruction in every phase of the game. Nobody approaches this sport without the rigorous assessment of a seasoned professional who can correct undetected flaws. Not so with Calvin Peete. To compound his general lateness, when he was eleven years old Peete fell from a tree on his grandmother's farm in Mississippi, breaking his left elbow in three different places. To this day he cannot straighten his left arm completely. Nonetheless, unfazed, Peete simply learned to play golf his way.

At thirty-two, he left the amateur ranks, finally qualifying for the Tour's professional circuit in 1975. Since 1982, he has won more major tournaments—eleven—and more money—$1.6 million—than most other golfers on the U.S. Tour. Today, Calvin Peete is the most unlikely champion in professional sports—a black man with a bent arm who has mastered a game where everyone else seems to be both young and well-tutored.

Consider the things in your life that you currently deem impossible. *What are your self-limiting beliefs?* Whatever they are, they can only be dismissed by applied faith.

A better job? A business deal entitling you to a handsome commission? A major promotion? A college education? Whatever it is that you desire but think unreachable will undoubtedly remain so unless you change your thought process. Are you ready to reach your destiny and climb the mountain of success? Do you have the audacity to step out from the crowd and capture what life really holds for you? If so, there's little you cannot accomplish if you unleash your faith.

Being truthful to ourselves means taking the responsibility for making the best use of what we have. *And what do we have?* We have our underutilized minds, our abilities, our talents and time, all waiting to be thrust into action by the guiding spirit of faith. These are our possessions, which comprise an immense amount of wealth that belongs to each of us. And it is the investment of our wealth that will determine our rate of return.

But we must express these powers through the principle of faith.

You may compare the average human being, filled with fear, with no faith at all, to the horse or elephant that meekly does what it is directed to do. It is completely unaware of its own strength. It does not know how easily it could do whatever it desires. Much in the same way, millions of human beings live in tiny self-imposed prisons of their own fashioning, completely unaware of their powers to be *free*—to do what they'd most love to do— and in so doing, to reap a harvest beyond their wildest imaginations. If only they'd recognize this power of faith, they would not be slaves to any circumstance.

As long as you consider that which you desire impossible, your subconscious mind will go to great lengths to convince you why the task *is impossible*! By allowing your mental processes to take such command, you will be forever paralyzed by unnecessary barriers.

Believe Me—You've Got What It Takes!

Never consider that you do not possess the ability to obtain all that you wish. A man who succeeds in life must not only know where he is going, but must settle within his mind, with an unshakable faith, that he is indeed capable of reaching any port no matter how rough the sea or how distant the destination. Realizing this, he can remove any outside influence that may attempt to discourage him. Applied faith is the voice of authority speaking to all those who will prevail, no matter the odds or difficulties.

Believe it can be done; that is basic to creative thinking. First, eliminate the word "impossible" from your vocabulary. "Impossible" is a word tainted with connotations of failure. Second, when confronted with a seemingly insurmountable task, commit your thoughts to paper. Write all the reasons why your goal or objective *can be* accomplished; be detailed and specific. Many of us relinquish our desires prematurely, simply because we've concentrated on why we can't accomplish more with our lives, when the only thing worthy of our mental concentration is *why we can*. Become receptive to new approaches. Welcome new ideas. Focus on achieving and attaining more with your life. Creative solutions will come. Some of your answers may entail better planning and organization of your task, or breaking away from the routine. And third, be courageous enough to venture forward to your goal.

You'll find the solution for reaching your goal will present itself. *Every adversity carries with it the seed of an equivalent or a greater benefit.* Repeated victories over your problems are the rungs on your ladder of success. And with each victory you grow in wisdom, stature, and experience. You become a better, bigger, more successful person each time you meet and overcome an obstacle. As you eagerly accept the opportunity to do more, your level of complacency will slowly dissipate.

What Faith Can Do

This entire principle of faith is based on a single premise: *Faith only enters the mind that has been properly prepared for it.* The Creator has provided every individual with complete, unchallengeable control over his mind. You, in turn, can make the contact with your inner being either positive or negative. As human beings, we are the only creatures on earth who can appropriate the power of the mind and direct it to ends of our own choosing. No other creature can do so.

As humans, if we can direct the power of our minds to the ends of our own choosing, can we not therefore conclude that success, or riches, are absolutely assured us? We have only to *apply this faith* in our minds toward the achievement of our objectives.

If you ever wished evidence of the power of faith, study the achievements of men and women who have applied it. At the top of the list comes the Nazarene. The basis of Christianity is faith. You can grasp this solid truth by gaining a thorough understanding of the most fundamental biblical teachings and those who have applied its philosophy in their lives.

With Good Looks, Hard Work, and Faith in God

Silence spread through the convention hall as each finalist was announced. The hush of the crowd grew more intense. And then a voice pierced the quiet over the public address system.

"Fourth runner-up, Miss Ohio!"

The applause was followed by a deafening silence. "And third runner-up, Miss Illinois!" The noise grew to fever pitch as it anticipated the next winner.

"And second runner-up, Miss Colorado!"

Now, hearts began to pound, pulses escalated. The anticipation was overwhelming. Time stood motionless as the seconds seemed like eternity. As the two finalists stood center stage, both within a hair of achieving their lifelong dreams, one in particular reflected on her road less traveled.

It took seven hard years and eleven attempts in competitions held in two different states before Debbye Turner made it to the Miss America pageant. In 1988, after her third failure in the Miss Arkansas pageant, Debbye and her father had a long talk. Although he never told her to quit, even he was beginning to stagger from the number of heart-wrenching defeats. Surrounded by confusion and dejection, and left stunned and lonely by the repeated setbacks, her mind gravitated to the following thoughts: "Faith is the starting point of all achievement. It's the basis for all miracles, and the only antidote for failure."

Long before midnight she kneeled by her bed and prayed. Not for the completion of her goal. But for the *faith* to continue her journey!

Determined and focused, Debbye redoubled her efforts

to compete again. In 1989, she was living and attending
school in Missouri. Believing she had a fair chance of
winning the state's pageant, she entered the contest and
captured the top prize. As "Miss Missouri," she then
competed against 51 equally successful and talented
young women, all with their hearts set on winning the
title "Miss America." But now all of that was behind
her. Her mind once again came full-circle back to the
matter at hand.

The emcee slowly approaches the mike and tears open
the next envelope. After a painstakingly long pause, he
finally ends the suspense. "And first runner-up—Miss
Maryland! *The new, 1990 Miss America—Miss Missouri—Debbye Turner!"*

It was a long and difficult road. After the competition
concluded and the audience filed from the convention
center, Turner fielded hundreds of questions during the
ensuing press conference. It was here that she gave a clue
to her extra added edge. It may interest you to hear it in
her own words:

"Over the years I've experienced my share of rejection. I was continuously told that the odds were against
me. My musical ability was questioned. No other contestant had ever played the marimba and won. And besides, I was black.

"Sure, the natural tendency would have been to quit,
but I had total faith in God, and I believed that He takes
a personal interest in my life."

Debbye went on to perform beautifully, and she won
over the judges. When crowned in September 1989, Debbye Turner became the first Miss Missouri to win since
the pageant began in 1921. She also became the third
black contestant to wear the Miss America crown.

All those who hunger for the riches that life has to offer
must have faith. A man without faith is a man without
hope. Faith is born within the hearts of those believing
in strong convictions and higher powers. There is tremendous power in faith. It is through faith that you'll

arrive at the destination you've so chosen. It is through faith that you'll break the bonds of poverty, *because poverty confines no man who has faith*. It is through faith that you will eliminate fear. Fear is faith in reverse gear. Though fear is real—it is one of the strongest forces known—faith is stronger! Faith always overcomes fear.

Faith is trust and believing without proof. It is never static, but like life, it is constantly in motion. Faith can live only so long as it is being used. Every time you master failure, your faith becomes stronger and you are better prepared to meet your next obstacle. Faith applied—put to work—is the beginning of all self-confidence, all self-reliance. It is the moving spirit of personal initiative and enthusiasm. Until you learn the basic fundamentals of applied faith, your accomplishments will be few. *Faith can move mountains!*

The Fundamentals of Faith

The fundamentals of faith begin with a burning desire for a specific purpose and a reason for that purpose. As an illustration, consider for a moment the reason why you are reading this book. The object is, quite naturally, to acquire the ability to transfer thought into action, and action into physical realities.

In general, the fundamentals of faith are these:

Positive Mental Attitude. The removal of all negative emotions such as fear, hatred, jealousy, and greed is an outgrowth of our understanding of self-worth. Anyone who has advanced mankind through innovation or improved service has usually done so without the approval of so-called progressive men. Edison's light bulb and the Wright brothers' conquering of the skies are worthy examples. A constant struggle, a ceaseless battle to bring success from inhospitable surroundings, is the price of all great achievement. However, careful inventory of your past defeats and failures will demonstrate that all difficult experiences *do carry the seed of an equivalent or a greater benefit.* Go back into your past and analyze the times you tasted defeat; chances are that if you would have withstood defeat long enough for your wounds to heal, you would have been able to find the seed of an equivalent benefit. Search diligently for that seed, and sooner or later you'll find it.

The Power of Prayer. Most people who believe in a Higher Power believe in prayer. It is through prayer that we commune with the infinite. It is through prayer that we align ourselves with universal principles which, if we obey and comprehend, we can consciously use to further our ideals. Debbye Turner is a splendid example of this spiritual idea in action. Every man or woman is his own savior because each has his own direct approach—if he so chooses to abide in Him. Through prayer, each of us has the power of faith, though few of us consciously use it. One does not possess this power over and above another, or to a lesser or greater degree; it is a part of our divine heritage.

Heavyweight boxing champion Joe Frazier once remarked, "As important as roadwork is prayer."

The business tycoon S. B. Fuller, in his quest for his definite purpose, once told a writer, "I had exhausted every source of credit I knew. It was in the solitude of my room where I knelt down and prayed. My answer came within the next day."

A man who later became president of Liberia, William Tubman, said this about prayer: "When God has put a dream in your heart, He means to help you fulfill it. To gain His help you must ask for it . . . and this asking is prayer."

Armed only with his immovable faith and in the ultimate victory of his cause, a diminutive, Gandhi-like figure has emerged as the most visible and most outspoken critic for social change in South Africa's brutal rule over

26 million blacks. He is the Most Reverend Desmond Tutu, Anglican Archbishop of Cape Town and 1984 Nobel Peace Prize laureate. Even in the face of constant government harassment, he has refused to be silent. "The worst thing they can do to me," he says, "is kill me—and death is not the end for someone who has faith."

Look about you and you will find that the world's most successful people are those who readily apply faith through their capacity for prayer.

Self-suggestion. How many times have you heard it said, "Just believe you can do it and you can!" Many stories have been told of the great reserves of the subconscious mind, how under its direction and by imparting its enormous strength, frail men and women have been able to perform feats far beyond their normal powers. It is the act of believing that is the starting force or generating action that leads great men and women to accomplishment. "Come on, men, we can beat them," shouts someone in command. Whether in a game, or on a battlefield, or in the strife of life, that sudden voicing of belief, challenging and electrifying, reverses the tide. "I can do it . . . I can do it . . . *I can do it!*"

Similarly, a man engaged in concentrated effort often talks to the man within. This "self-talk" or "self-suggestion," as it has been called, is completely self-contained. Self-talk is often the power that inspires the machinery of achievement into operation, and causes the subconscious mind to begin its creative work. It is the repetition of words or phrases that transforms faith into belief, and finally into accomplishment. Autosuggestion can take the form of thinking, seeing, hearing, feeling, tasting, and smelling through the power of your imagination.

"Be the best! Be the best!" were the hypnotic words of faith that packed pride, a sense of mission and achievement, into the rich and rewarding life of Dr. Ronald McNair, *Challenger* astronaut.

Edwin Moses, one-time world-record-holder in the 400-meter hurdles, utilized self-talk during his training sessions for the 1984 Summer Olympic games. By affirming his statement of faith and positive expectancy—''I'm the best, I'm the best!''—he captured national acclaim as the gold medalist in this event.

"If You Can Keep Your Head When All About You . . ."

During 1968, his first year with professional football's Oakland Raiders, Art Shell had memorized a poem—Rudyard Kipling's ''If'':

> *If you can keep your head when all about you*
> *Are losing theirs and blaming it on you;*
> *If you can trust yourself when all men doubt you*
> *But make allowance for their doubting too . . .*

Shy and soft-spoken, but not easily intimidated, even as a rookie offensive lineman Art Shell shared a private dream with his teammate Gene Upshaw of someday becoming an NFL head coach. At six feet, five inches, and weighing more than 300 pounds, Shell could shock opponents with his size alone. But he was a gentle giant. Moreover, he was an intelligent player who fastidiously scribbled detailed notes in his playbook. In team meetings he always asked probing questions regarding strategy. Night after night he studied game films at home. He made it his business to learn what each offensive player's assignment was on every play.

During the off-seasons Shell volunteered as a line coach with area colleges. He worked at this every year until he retired in 1982. In an illustrious fifteen-year career—all with the Raiders—he had played in the Pro Bowl eight times, anchored an offensive line that took his team to two Super Bowl titles, and in 1989 was inducted into Pro

Football's Hall of Fame. Nonetheless, at forty-two, with his playing days behind, Art Shell wondered if he would ever get an opportunity to coach on the professional level. He pondered his future and quietly recited the poem he had learned twenty-one years ago. The answer to his question would come sooner than he thought.

> . . . *If you can force your heart and nerve and sinew*
> *To serve your turn long after they are gone,*
> *And so hold on when there is nothing in you*
> *Except the Will which says to them: "Hold on!"* . . .

In 1982, Shell was offered the job as Raider offensive line coach, working under then–head coach Mike Shanahan. Shell eagerly took on his new responsibilities and did everything he could to foster a winning image. But Shanahan had his problems. He had coached the Raiders to an 8–12 record in less than two seasons, becoming the first coach in twenty-seven years to leave the franchise with a losing record. With the program in disarray and Al Davis, the Raiders' owner, dissatisfied with the direction of the club, Shanahan was dismissed. In a major turn of events, Davis then selected Shell to direct the team.

For Art Shell, and a race of people, the historic event came October 3, 1989. The NFL had its first black head football coach.

> . . . *If you can fill the unforgiving minute*
> *With sixty seconds' worth of distance run,*
> *Yours is the Earth and everything that's in it,*
> *And—which is more—you'll be a Man, my son!*

Some say that success is timing; some say it's destiny or pluck. But for twenty-one years it was *autosuggestion* that had inwardly directed Art Shell. For his entire football career he had used that poem as a point of reference.

These are fundamentals of major importance that prepare the mind for the expression of faith. The man who has faith in himself brings under control and direction those powers of his subconscious. He also inspires a similar feeling in the minds and hearts of others with whom he comes in contact. A study of achievers will disclose the proof that those who "arrive" or "do things" are marked by a deep intuitive faith in themselves. These individuals overcome temporary defeat and use their failures as stepping-stones to ultimate victory. They are the living expression of Henley's "Invictus"—they, indeed, are the masters of their fate, the captains of their souls!

Unfortunately and unnecessarily, there are far too many who live dissatisfied lives. Counted within these ranks are black Americans too many to number. Every crowded project or public housing tenement harbors the lives of those who drift through life without a major purpose or goal, who don't apply the power of this principle of faith. These lives are wrecked by the aimless expenditure of time companioned with a litany of self-limiting and negative beliefs.

Every day there are those who lose faith in themselves and then blame their loss on others. This is one of man's greatest faults, to blame his family or his spouse for his laziness and his failures, when his own inability to coordinate his activities and *direct his mind* to ends of his own choice lies within himself.

Listen to the words of one inner-city resident describe a life full of despair: "We got civil rights, we got welfare. But look around here," he says as he kicks a pile of empty beer cans littering the sidewalk. "When I was growing up in Mississippi, we were poor, all right, but we didn't have madness. Now we're just stuck here in this ghetto, watching Oprah Winfrey on TV and listening to gunshots at night."

What has gone wrong for the five million black Americans still trapped in festering inner-city ghettos? Why do one-third of all black families remain mired in poverty? Why is the jobless rate for black teenagers nearly 40 percent? Why are 60 percent of all black children born out of wedlock? And why has the American ghetto become a self-perpetuating nightmare of fatherless children, welfare dependency, crime, gangs, drugs, and despair? The answer is clear. Does discrimination play a part? Certainly. How about the lack of a quality education? That, too, has done its fair share of damage. But the real cause remains hidden from view. These depressed souls have never taken hold of the power that lies within their grasp—*applied faith!*

Go back through the pages of time and you will observe that the story of civilization's unfolding leads invariably to the works of men and women who cracked open the door to achievement, using applied faith as the master key. Observe, too, that great achievements are always born of hardships and struggle and barriers that seem insurmountable—obstacles that yield to nothing but an indomitable will are overcome by an abiding faith.

You Must Make the First Move

There is a legend of a man who was lost in the desert, dying of thirst. He dragged himself on until he came to an abandoned house. Outside of the dilapidated, windowless, weather-beaten shack was a pump. "Water, at last!" he thought. He stumbled forward and began pumping furiously, but nothing came out of the well.

As his heart raced he noticed a small jug with a cork at the top and a note scribbled on the side: "You have to prime the pump with water, my friend. P.S. And fill the jug again before you leave." He pulled out the cork and saw that the jug was full of water.

He weighed his options. Should he pour the water down the pump? What if it didn't work? All of the water would be gone. If he drank the water from the jug, he could be sure he wouldn't die of thirst. But to pour it down the rusty pump on the flimsy instructions written on the outside of the jug?

Sweating profusely, he listened to his heart and chose

the risky decision. He proceeded to pour the entire jug of water down the rusty old pump and furiously pumped up and down. Sure enough, the water gushed out! He had all he needed to drink. With a thankful heart he turned his thoughts upward. He filled the jug again, corked it, and added his own testimony to the words on the bottle: *Believe me, it really works. BUT YOU MUST HAVE FAITH!*

The people who really succeed are those who dare to risk, who challenge the status quo and push themselves beyond their normal limits. No person ever fully discovers and develops all the potential within himself until he expresses his faith.

How One Woman Tapped the Power Within

As a fitting climax to this chapter, study the story of a woman who carefully took stock of her abilities and circumstances, and who took matters into her own hands and shaped a glorious future. Explore her secret of success; look deeply into every word. If you can do this, if you can lay your finger on the key principle that took her to the top in her profession, you can equal her achievements in almost any calling for which you are suited.

"My grandmother epitomized the person who constantly searched inside for strength," said Barbara Gardner Proctor. "Though she was deeply religious, she never asked the Lord to do anything she could do herself. And she taught me many values, foremost of which was *to simply keep the faith!*"

Barbara Gardner Proctor was born in a forgotten, small North Carolina town choked with poverty. The house where she lived had neither running water nor electricity. She never knew her father. Her mother, whose sights were focused elsewhere, left the raising of her child to her mother, Barbara's grandmother. A dynamic woman with a strong but tender hand, Coralee Baxter would share years of wisdom with her granddaughter.

"She was loving and affectionate; beyond that, she was strong-willed and courageous," says Proctor. "She had plenty of dignity, pride, and was inner directed. My grandmother never misunderstood or misjudged me. But most important, under her influence I learned that unfavorable circumstances, for the most part, are temporary, and they can be changed simply by keeping the faith." Adhering to her grandmother's wisdom, Barbara Proctor would change her life.

In her grandmother, Barbara had a most enthusiastic champion who would urge her to attempt great things. Miss Baxter's beliefs in personal excellence caused her granddaughter to view her life and surroundings in an entirely different light.

Always an excellent student, Barbara received a scholarship to small Talladega College in Alabama, where she majored in both English and psychology. Through hard work and determination, she graduated in three years. Because she had a head start on her future, campus life seemed snail-paced compared to the lure of the big city. So she packed her belongings, bid her classmates farewell, and headed for Chicago, where she searched for opportunities.

Her search did not come easy. Barbara would spend the next three years careening from job to job—from freelance writer to disc jockey to girl Friday—looking for anything to hold her interest and give way to a career.

Her wandering came to a halt when she was contacted by a local advertising agency that needed the services of a young, energetic copywriter. Barbara knew very little about advertising, but was willing to give it a try. And besides, based on her talents and creativity, she thought she might be able to tackle the job and make a name for herself. She joined the small but reputable firm and pushed forward.

Her instincts were right. The advertising business intrigued her. She was attracted to the industry by a convergence of factors—products, personalities, creativity, and constant change—all squeezed into fast-paced deadlines. Writing ad copy can be tough, but to this self-starter, it came naturally. Barbara put her skills to good use. She turned her imagination loose as her employer assigned her to work on high-level accounts such as General Motors, Procter & Gamble, and Coca-Cola. In five years she worked for three different agencies, learning the business from the ground up. By 1969, she was earning more than $40,000 a year and her future never looked brighter.

"I was a hot property," she mused. She became the first black advertising executive in Chicago.

But rougher waters loomed ahead. It was the 1970s, a time of increasing social consciousness and awareness. Everything and everybody appeared to be making a statement. Advertising became receptive to the images of the day, and Barbara Proctor seemed especially in tune with the times. Uneasy with the long-term impact of her company's ads, she refused to work on several socially unpopular ad campaigns and was charged with insubordination. Regrettably, one thing led to another and she was eventually fired.

Out of work and with few options for the future, she began to question her life's direction. Her grandmother's teachings began to cross her mind as she looked for another career. After months of soul searching, Barbara came to the realization many entrepreneurs have: *There's room for only one dream in any organization—and from this moment on that dream will be mine.* She desperately wanted to be her own boss.

Having mastered her trade, Barbara was convinced the time was right for an ad agency that addressed the needs of the black consumer. She studied the spending habits of black Americans and knew that manufacturers could not afford to overlook this expanding market.

"Black consumers are different from white consumers," she explained. "They have different tastes, different preferences, and much more brand loyalty." With proposals in hand, Barbara presented her ideas to the top ad agencies in Chicago, but received no takers.

Unemployed and with dwindling funds, she decided to start her own firm. She approached area banks and similar lending institutions, but encountered only more frustration. Her difficulties increased as potential money sources closed their doors while creditors closed in. Down to a few dollars, she sat numb and motionless in her Chicago apartment, fearing the worst. Emotionally spent, she asked for divine guidance.

"In my hour of need," she recalled, "I found my greatest strength to be my grandmother's values. 'Keep the faith,' she told me. 'Keep the faith' regardless of the appearance of things. Over and over I recited those three words—*keep the faith*—until my answer came."

Short on collateral, but long on faith and hope, Barbara applied for a loan from the Small Business Administration. Since she hoped to start a service business and had no collateral, she normally would have had little chance to acquire such a loan. But with *faith*, the tide shifted. She audaciously persuaded a loan officer to ask the heads of three of Chicago's leading advertising agencies what salary they would pay her if she were an employee. The answers came back: $65,000; $80,000; and $110,000 respectively. In a whirlwind twenty-four-hour period, Barbara Proctor obtained an $80,000 loan—enough to keep her fledgling agency going until she landed her first two accounts, Jewel Foods and Sears, Roebuck and Company.

Twenty years later Chicago's Proctor & Gardner Advertising has become a small but respected firm, with an estimated $15 million in annual billings. The company's original two clients are still on her client list, which also includes G. Heileman Brewing, Alberto-Culver, and Kraft Foods.

Many years ago Coralee Baxter told her granddaughter of her priceless gift. She also taught her to apply this lifesaving principle throughout her life. Some people seem to use this power instinctively. Others have yet to learn it. And still others—the vast majority of us—have never really begun to use this tremendous power at all. The principle that I am trying to emphasize is the *power of faith*. The moment you apply the power of faith in your life is the moment you will begin to step ahead of the crowd.

Two facts stand out in Barbara Proctor's rise to prominence. First, the circumstances in which she found herself as a child might have discouraged the average man or woman from pursuing his or her dreams at all. And second, through faith she was able to withstand the challenges of a major crisis.

There is nothing new about the principle of faith. It may be applied by anyone who makes use of desire and belief as strongly and intensely as Barbara Proctor did. One of faith's stranger features is that it generally appears because of some emergency that forces men and women to look beyond the power of ordinary thought for the solution to their problems. It is during these emergencies that we draw upon that secret power from within which knows no resistance great enough to defeat it.

The scriptures say, ''According to your faith be it unto you.'' Remember, no more effort is required to aim high in life, to demand abundance and prosperity, than is required to accept misery and deprivation. Search until you find the secret power that dwells within, and when you find it, as you most assuredly will, you will have discovered your true self—that person who you were meant to be.

5

"By All Means—Persist!"

"Well, son, I'll tell you:
Life for me ain't been no crystal stair . . .
So boy, don't you turn back . . .
Don't you fall now—
For I'se still climbin',
And life for me ain't been no crystal stair."
                              —LANGSTON HUGHES

"Never, never, never give up!"
                              —WINSTON CHURCHILL

"Nothing takes the place of persistence."
                              —CALVIN COOLIDGE

Emerson said, "Nature provides the exercise, the challenges for the development of the person. All development is the result of effort. And this effort is what strengthens the person." Life favors those who are able to stick with things when the going gets tough, because it does get tough at times. That is a part of life's challenge.

Life will always be a challenge. Understand that you are not alone in facing the hurdles that life presents. To live is to live in a state of challenge. Look at the lives of many great achievers. Beethoven lost his hearing *before* he composed many of the masterpieces for which he is remembered. John Milton wrote *Paradise Lost* while totally blind. Abraham Lincoln was forced to borrow money for train fare to his own inauguration. And after years of searching for meaningful employment, a resolute and lean Albert Einstein formulated his seminal theory of relativity while working as a clerk in a patent office. Need you hear more?

Poor, black, and seemingly without hope—her father peddled coal and ice in the streets of Philadelphia to pay for her music lessons—Marian Anderson still became America's most famous contralto. Dr. Selma Burke, a black woman whose depiction of Franklin D. Roosevelt appeared on freshly minted dimes, and founder of art institutes throughout the nation, received her doctorate from Livingstone College in 1970. *She was seventy years old!* The indomitable nine-year-old Darlwin Carlisle, who was trapped in an attic in an abandoned Gary, Indiana, building without heat, food, or water in the middle of winter, hung on for several days until a construction worker heard her cries for help. Though doctors amputated her legs in order to save her life, she has confronted her obstacles with irrepressible resolve. *Is there anything that she cannot do?* "No!" she proudly proclaims. And Vincent "Bo" Jackson, a product of a fatherless home in Bessemer, Alabama, whose childhood was a depressing portrayal of poverty and disappointment, made it to the doorsteps of Auburn University to become a latter-day Jim Thorpe. *Just show him the game he can't play!* He won the coveted Heisman Trophy in 1985, symbolic of college football's best, turned next to pro baseball with the Kansas City Royals, and then to pro football with the Los Angeles Raiders. No athlete of recent times has had such a triumphant run in two major leagues.

There has never been a successful or creatively gifted person who hasn't known failure, frustration, or tough times. Times when money was scarce or nonexistent; times when he or she seemed out of touch with the rest of humanity; times when fresh ideas and inspiration didn't flow; and times when physical or emotional handicaps seemed insurmountable.

The hallmark of success is the ability to ride out these

moments and still prevail. Frustration and disappointment, even sorrow, can lead to joy and prosperity. Often, those who overcome the fiercest difficulties are the men and women who ultimately achieve the greatest triumphs and inspire us the most.

In this lesson, I wish to discuss a principle that never fails. By adhering to this rule you will add quality and richness to your life, eventually drawing you to the shores you seek. Without this characteristic, you can never fully enjoy riches of any kind—spiritual or material. With this principle, others will stand and view your efforts and accomplishments in awe. This element will also produce peace of mind that will never waver. The principle I speak of is persistence.

Persistence means conviction, enthusiasm, perseverance, and courage in the face of obstructions. *Above all, it means never stopping, never giving up, and never giving in!*

The power of persistence is characteristic of all men and women who have achieved greatness. It is not so much brilliancy of intellect, talent, or resources as it is persistency of effort and constancy of purpose that draws greatness to the individual. Those who succeed in life are the men and women who keep their shoulders to the wheel, who do not believe themselves overly talented, but who realize that if they are ever to accomplish anything of value, they must do so by a determined and persistent effort.

The Stoic philosopher Epictetus observed, "It is not the things themselves that disturb men, but their judgment about these things." Life is a continual pattern of growth and refinement, challenge and obstacles. It has a way of sifting out the weak, the lazy, and the uninspired—those who are not able or refuse to stand on their own two feet in the best, as well as the worst, of times.

Think about what happens when a master craftsman forges a steel blade. First, he chooses the strongest, most durable, and resilient steel possible. Then the metal is put through a refining fire and is heated and tested repeatedly until it is as solid and resistant as possible. Finally, the blade is honed and sharpened to its finest point of precision.

The challenges that you will face are akin to this process. The hard-charging individual understands that there will always be difficulties to conquer. The achiever faces these challenges squarely and is strong enough, resourceful enough, and resilient enough to prevent them from becoming pitfalls. The type of inner stamina this requires is what I mean by persistence. *It is the stuff achievement is made of.*

How This Author Discovered the Power of Persistence

Persistency of purpose is power. It creates confidence in others; society believes in the determined person. When he undertakes anything, his battle is half over. Why? Because those who know him realize that he will not stop short of his objective. He will indeed accomplish all he sets out to do. His detractors have long since understood that it is useless to oppose a man who will use his stumbling blocks as stepping-stones; who is not afraid of defeat; and who never, in spite of exclusion or criticism, shrinks from his task.

The persistent man or woman never stops to consider the costs. Whether his major purpose leads through mountains, over land, or across oceans, he or she *must* reach his or her goal—all other considerations are secondary to this dominant purpose. For it matters not how bright the student, how clever the innovator, or how lofty the ideal, no person of ambition will ever succeed if lacking this essential trait. Many men and women who might have made brilliant doctors, lawyers, teachers, or well-paid executives have unfortunately fallen short of their goals simply because they failed to arouse new effort at each new obstacle.

Napoleon Hill says of persistence, "There may be no

heroic connotation to the word 'persistence,' but the quality is to the character of man what carbon is to steel.''

I, personally, went through an experience that not only confirms Hill's words, but provided me with an example which I can present to those who would convert their ability to persevere into a constructive interlude of great benefit to themselves. Let me share my story with you.

When I had set about the task of writing a book on our forgotten heroes—those men and women who had built many of America's most successful black businesses—I compiled a list of 35 black entrepreneurs whom I would interview within a twelve-month period in an attempt to uncover their secrets to success. Some were young, some were old, some were more well-known than others, but all were successful within their own line of business.

During the months in which the material for this project was being gathered and prepared, the manuscript progressed as planned, except for one major hitch—I was unable to obtain a favorable commitment to interview Mr. Earl Graves, publisher and founder of *Black Enterprise* magazine.

Just imagine, a book centering on the successes and failures of black men and women in American enterprise not including Earl Graves! The entire project would have been completely remiss without the thoughts of this entrepreneurial giant. Graves is a role model in the classic American mold. A local boy who made good, the embodiment of the work ethic. As I contemplated his life, the impact of his personality and philosophy, I knew that I *had* to meet and interview him. I put my request in writing, prepared a questionnaire with a cover letter outlining my intentions, and immediately mailed the package to his New York headquarters.

As I started my series of interviews, I received a letter postmarked New York. It was from Earl G. Graves, Ltd., the parent company to *Black Enterprise* magazine. It simply stated that I was "to be commended for such a noble effort," but—*and that was a big but!*—Mr. Graves,

due to a constricting schedule, would unfortunately have
to be excluded from the study. It was signed by his vice-
president for corporate affairs. *I was devastated!* I immediately phoned his office in New York from my Atlanta,
Georgia, home in an effort to convince either him or his
staff of his much-needed input. I was unsuccessful.

Month after month I repeated this same ritual—I called
and sent off additional letters. They were always met with
"He's too busy," or "Mr. Graves is flattered by your
request, but . . ." I seemed to be getting many different
versions of the word no. No matter how despondent I
got, subconsciously something told me to keep going.

"Stay with it," I would say to myself, week in and
week out. "Stay with it," I would tell myself subconsciously as I reviewed my notes from interviews with
everyone on my initial list—except Earl Graves. "Stay
with it," I thought as I went through my daily routine as
a sales representative for a major pharmaceutical firm.
"Stay with it," as I coaxed back deadlines from would-
be publishers. *Just stay with it.*

I hadn't realized that eighteen months had passed since
my first encounter with his office. In all honesty, I had
nearly relinquished any hope of ever meeting or interviewing the man. I unfortunately had to face the idea of
writing a book on the state of black business with only
passing comments by an individual who had done so
much in this arena. It wouldn't have been much of a
study, but nevertheless, with my hopes frayed and sag-
ging, I had resigned myself to that fate.

Experience has taught me that a man is never quite so
near to success as when that which he calls failure has
nearly overtaken him. For it is on occasions of this sort
that he is forced to *think*. If he thinks accurately and with
persistence, he discovers that so-called failure is usually
nothing more than a signal to rearm himself with a new
plan or purpose. Most real failures are due to limitations
that men set up in their own minds. If they had the courage to go one step further, they might discover the key

to the door of all they desire. I searched vainly for a solution to my dilemma.

The Answer Finally Arrives!

I had found the key! I suddenly realized in my despair that maybe, just maybe, there was a way for me to succeed in my mission. I remembered a conversation that I had years ago with a friend of my parents who had met Graves. Not having communicated with this individual for a number of years, I obtained his phone number from operator assistance and spoke with him at his New Jersey home. In our conversation, he vaguely remembered our talk, but he informed me that he was invited to the silver wedding anniversary of Mr. and Mrs. Earl Graves, to be held the coming weekend, at their Connecticut home.

This was my chance, and I planned to seize it. In my haste, I had briefly told him of my desire, and asked him a huge favor. *Could he possibly hand deliver a letter addressed to Mr. Graves—either before or after the ceremony—from me?* After a brief pause, he consented. Now I had to send my contact the letter via special delivery for Graves to receive it the coming Saturday. My hopes were resurrected.

As I prepared this correspondence, I thought of those powerful words that were leading me to the successful completion of my objective. I reflected on the many times I had muttered to myself, "Stay with it!" I tell you of this experience simply because the world is full of those who tried to get out of the doldrums and, meeting with difficulty and repeated turndowns, retreated back to the crowd. *Nothing takes the place of persistence.* I'd realized that staying with it had paid off, just like it always does.

To my good fortune, Earl Graves was given my letter as planned, shortly after his anniversary ceremony. Within a few days I received a phone call, ironically from the same vice-president who had delivered disappointing news eighteen months prior. But this time she was calling to arrange a mutually beneficial time for an interview. Her exact words were "Mr. Graves would be most delighted to talk with you."

It was during my meeting with Graves that I uncovered the power of this principle that could only have been revealed in this fashion. As I waited in the foyer of his company's headquarters on New York's Fifth Avenue, I sensed success. Neatly displayed throughout the hallway were plaques, mementos, awards, and framed clippings highlighting Graves's twenty years of achievement. My unashamed gazing was interrupted by his personal secretary.

"Mr. Graves will now see you," she said, and I was led to his office.

Though I had interrupted his dictation to a staffer, Graves seemed unconcerned. He caught one glimpse of me, complete with briefcase and questionnaire, dropped his notes, and extended his hand in an expression of warmth and hospitality. Then came those words, which I shall never forget: "Young man, you are to be commended for your persistence. If you are not in sales, you should be!"

Stay with it! Persistence is another form of faith. There is a place for anyone who will persevere; there is success lurking in everything we do. In every conflict there are few people who exhibit staying power, and this staying power nearly always represents the difference between prosperity and the settle-for life-style. Boldness of spirit and tenacity of purpose accompany those whose acts are in accord with greatness. *A man or woman who refuses to quit, who keeps going in the face of defeat, who does his best against superior forces, strikes within us a sympathetic chord.*

Opposition comes to the man who aspires. He does not turn away from the challenge, nor assault or deny its appearance. Though the ostrich hides its head from impending danger, and the possum topples over and plays dead, the inspired individual neither turns away nor ceases in his efforts. Patiently, with a persistence that never tires, he examines his own mind to determine how his understanding is blocked from the true perception of the encountered obstacle. He will grow because he must, and when his period of growth is over, he will find himself beyond his stumbling block. Looking back along the path he has traveled, he will not even find his obstacle, for what he didn't know seems simple when understanding has been achieved.

We are all aware that life at times is not easy, that the lessons it teaches are often learned through pain and tension. In addition, we realize that those who aspire for the brass ring will encounter obstacles. This is a tribute to courage and perseverance. But greater than courage is persistence—the willingness to stand and keep trying.

By persistence, the patient positioning of determined lives, barred doors eventually open and stone walls crumble; the drop of water gently wears away the granite; the tender flower emerges through the concrete and lifts its petals toward the sun. *By persistence*, the great pyramids of Egypt were built, offering civilization a springboard to even greater knowledge. *By persistence*, African missionaries were able to survive long, trying periods before ever obtaining a convert.

By persistence, Ira Aldridge, Black America's first internationally known actor, swallowed his pride and endured many unobtrusive years in Europe and Russia, often performing without compensation, before hitting his stride in the United States.

By persistence, Dr. Benjamin E. Mays, educator, philosopher, and author of numerous books and scholarly articles, was able to pursue his college studies after graduating from high school, a grown man of *twenty-two*!

By persistence, Charlayne Hunter-Gault achieved her dominant purpose of obtaining a degree in journalism. This well-known news reporter of the *MacNeil/Lehrer News Hour* risked life and limb in 1961 by enrolling as the first black female at the University of Georgia. Her pioneering determination and persistence was rewarded in 1986, the twenty-fifth year after her arrival on the campus, when her alma mater bestowed her with television's highest honor—the George Foster Peabody Broadcasting Award!

By persistence, Beverly Johnson, the strikingly attractive New York model, challenged the fashion industry, which ignored the natural beauty of black women. "You're not qualified to model," agencies and designers rebuffed. But after scanning countless fashion magazines and pounding against many doors, Johnson declared, "If those girls can do it, so can I." Over the years, her face has lured advertisers and consumers alike, while her good looks have graced the covers of the most widely read newspapers and magazines. What kept Beverly Johnson going through the early years of disappointment? *A large dose of persistence.*

It was through persistence that Louis Armstrong cracked open the first door to his future—a future that stood far from the poverty and ignorance that he knew all too well. As a stubborn and hot-tempered boy, he was sentenced to two years in a reform school for assault. Determined to salvage his life, which was spinning dangerously out of control, he taught himself, note by tedious note, to play the trumpet. For the next fifty years Louis Armstrong would teach others the world over the power of love and music, fashioning the title, "Goodwill Ambassador."

And it was by persistence that Shelton J. Lee—better known as Spike Lee—made bold statements about controversial, unpopular topics that major filmmakers were reluctant to bring to the big screen. In the rocky world of movie production, Lee persevered and patiently waited for his opportunity to come, by producing entertaining and provocative movies on shoestring budgets. As a young black producer with a succession of box office hits, Lee is on his way to becoming one of the giants of the film industry. "Persistence," he says, "is one of the keys to the kingdom."

These are just a few in the growing ranks of black achievers who have succeeded by application of this vital principle. *Now, will you persist in the face of your most formidable obstacle?* If you find you are weak in this critical area, you may want to reread the lessons on desire and faith before applying the instructions below.

Do You Persist?

Imagine for a moment that you are taking a personal inventory. Begin an accounting of the many blessings in your life. Here lies an opportunity for you to grasp one of your most prized possessions. Have you realized the vast treasure buried within persistence? Can you recall an occasion in your life where you persisted in the face of difficulty until you succeeded? Do you remember the joy of triumph, the sweet taste of victory? Of two men, one brilliant and with little patience, the other of average intelligence but great persistence, the second is far more likely to achieve grand results. *Sooner or later, the man or woman who persists will succeed!*

Do you persist? Here are a number of questions that will allow you to measure yourself against this all-important element. Answer these questions openly and honestly in order to uncover those areas of your life where you may lack persistence.

1. Reflecting on my life, can I cite specific cases where I have achieved something of note simply because I persisted?
2. Do I persist in my occupation or line of work?
3. Do I persist in the area of personal development?
4. Do I confront my obstacles or shrink from them?

If you have within you the ability to persist, you possess a priceless treasure. Consider for a moment these words written by Calvin Coolidge more than sixty years ago. They are just as penetrating today:

> Nothing in the world can take the place of persistence. Talent will not; nothing is more common than unsuccessful men with talent. Genius will not; unregarded genius is almost a proverb. Education will not; the world is full of educated derelicts. Persistence and determination alone are omnipotent.

You may wish to check the stories of A. G. Gaston, S. B. Fuller, Madame Walker, George Washington Carver, Mary McLeod Bethune, C. C. Spaulding, Ron Leflore, Alonzo Herndon, and Leontyne Price to recognize how each applied persistence in their lives, in addition to the other principles which contributed to their success. As you continue to read and analyze the case histories illustrated in *Think and Grow Rich: A Black Choice*, pay close attention to how the priceless quality of persistence kept the glowing flame of desire lit until it could be fanned into a searing laser.

Understanding Failure

We hear a fair degree of talk about genius, talent, and luck playing a large part in an individual's success. All are important factors. Yet the possession of any or all of these traits, unaccompanied by a definite aim or purpose, will not ensure success. Men and women drift into business. They drift into politics. They drift into religion. If the winds and tides are favorable, they continue to drift through life. That's a big *if*. But what if the winds and tides are *not* favorable? Whatever else may have been lacking in those whom we aspire to emulate, those men and women who have been conspicuously successful have all had one characteristic in common—doggedness and determination in the face of failure.

Failure's True Nature

To the common man the word "failure" has a negative connotation. For this reason alone failure has brought unnecessary grief and hardship to millions. But the refining fire of failure can also be the great educator of success. Most of us learn through episodes of trial and error, consequently transforming failure into a prerequisite for achievement.

The wise and ambitious always seek to learn something of value from each mistake. The loser, trapped within the hypnotic web of the fear of failure, gains nothing from the attempt and eventually comes up short. Look again at your failures. What you may label a failure may be only a temporary setback. Moreover, examine this minor stumbling block to see if it is really a defeat. It may be a blessing in disguise. Every adversity, every disappointment, every heartache, carries with it the seed of an equivalent benefit. As a great philosopher has said: "God never takes anything away from anyone without replacing it with something better."

Thomas Watson, the founder of IBM, was asked to offer his secret to success. In straightforward terms he barked, "Double your failure rate!" In other words, increase the number of risks you are willing to take—this is the most expedient way knowledge is generated. Neither temporary defeat nor adversity amounts to failure in the mind of the person who looks upon his setback as a teacher that will reveal a much-needed lesson. As a matter of fact, there's usually a good and lasting lesson in every reverse, and in every defeat—if we only search for it. And often enough, it is a lesson that could not have been learned in any other way.

"We've wasted so much time!" shouted a young assistant to Thomas Edison. "We've tried ten thousand tests, and we still haven't found a material that works."

"Ah!" responded the inventor. "But now we know ten thousand things that won't work!"

"Failure is, in a sense," says John Keats, the nineteenth-century English poet, "the highway to success inasmuch as every discovery of what is FALSE leads us to seek earnestly after what is true, and every fresh experience points out some form of error which we shall afterward carefully avoid."

The Lessons of Failure

My conversations with some of America's leading achievers have confirmed this hard truth: *If it is success you desire, failure is unavoidable.* There are no substitutes for the lessons learned in the "school of hard knocks." You should seize every opportunity to learn from your mistakes.

Theorists and psychologists have long agreed on the benefits of failing. Dr. Irene Kassorla writes in *Go for It*: "Winners make friends with failure and acknowledge the valuable lessons that it teaches. Failures offer valuable information and are helpful guides, not signals to give up." Dr. Kassorla explains that failure is a part of the success pattern.

"No one achieves their goals in one straight climb," she continues. "It's more like a jagged, uneven ascent with curves and plateaus."

In his best-selling book *Creating Wealth*, real estate expert Robert Allen quotes super-salesman Herb True: "Successful people often experience more failures than failures do. But they manage to press on." Allen, who built a multimillion-dollar real estate empire himself, says, "One good failure can teach you more about success than four years at the best university. Failing just might be the best thing that ever happens to you."

Arguably, one of the leading works in this field is *The Magic of Thinking Big*, by psychologist and college professor Dr. David Schwartz. Schwartz tells what he discovered about failure from interviewing social workers and public officials who had frequent contacts with the indigent. "We have all seen poverty and those struck by it," Schwartz explains. "These are the maligned, defeated, and bottomed-out people of the world. Men and women, young and old, some highly educated, some not—but all staggered by one of life's many blows." Schwartz learned that their personal tragedies are not significantly different from those who have experienced success.

Many times during his research he heard:

"I lost my job and my wife."

"I lost everything in a bad business deal with my best friend."

"My husband became ill, and we were wiped out."

These themes of hardship also turned up in the lives of achievers, who learned by failing, and went on to gain valuable experience and clearer insight.

Blessed Failures

The fine line between winning and losing is often drawn by our perception of failure. To the downtrodden who sleep in public rest rooms and on park benches, failure represents the end of the road. They interpret one of life's catastrophes as a kind of personal annihilation and allow it to totally destroy their sense of self, of purpose, and of relationships.

The man with a purpose, on the other hand, is able to accept failure as a temporary setback or distraction and use that experience to improve his performance. Failing can present life's most valuable lessons. Over and over I've heard declarations like "Getting fired was the best thing that ever happened to me," or, "The divorce, although a terrible blow, forced me to grow up, and now I'm a better person."

No one sets out to fail. It's something we dread and make every effort to avoid. But if we are to succeed, we must take risks and seize new opportunities, which can inevitably bring challenges and adversity. Schwartz argues again, ''It isn't possible to win high-level success without meeting opposition, hardship, and setback. But it is possible to use setback to propel you forward.''

Notice how some prominent ''failures'' have confidently drawn upon their defeats as learning experiences, while sticking steadfast and true to their ultimate goal.

The Miracle Worker

The television cameras had gone, and Benjamin Carson, M.D., was off the world's front pages, at least temporarily. The media had apparently decided that this understated, compassionate young man was a miracle worker. First, he performed a rare brain operation that had saved the life of a hydrocephalic baby still in the womb. Then, in 1987, he was part of a medical team that separated Siamese twins, born joined at the skull and sharing major blood systems in the brain. The operation left each twin alive and intact.

Today, Dr. Benjamin Carson is director of pediatric neurosurgery at the Johns Hopkins Children's Center in Baltimore, Maryland. A Yale University graduate who has won two of the most prestigious awards in surgery, he is a legend in his field. But just twenty years ago he was a poor black teenager in inner-city Detroit who nearly threw his life away.

''I had an explosive temper,'' Dr. Carson recalled. ''It was out of control. When I suspected someone of infringing upon my rights, I went to great lengths to ensure that they suffered as a result. I'd use whatever was available—rock, hammer, or bottle. One day I stabbed another teenager with a camping knife. Fortunately for me, his belt buckle stopped the knife from penetrating. Trembling and in tears after I realized what I had done, it finally struck me that had it not been for his belt, I would probably be either in prison or dead. This was the turning point of my life."

Ben Carson was the second son of divorced parents. His mother worked two and sometimes three jobs to keep the family together. More important, she worked hard to convince her boys that they could make something of their lives—even if their environment was telling them they couldn't.

"We got loads of negative input," Dr. Carson remembers. "But thankfully, our mother offset these negative images with positive words of encouragement. You might say she brainwashed us into believing that we could do anything."

As a part of a specialized educational program in a predominately white suburban junior high school, Ben did so well in the eighth grade that he won an award as top student in his class, proving what his mother already knew. But his success was short-lived when the program ended. After transferring back to the troubled, inner-city public school, he assumed the dead-end ways of his peers.

"My friends were experimenting with all types of drugs, and used crime to support their habits. As ridiculous as it seems, their influence began to rub off. I started to emulate them—I wanted to be part of the crowd." Soon, his grades and attitude plummeted, and what looked like a bright future began to dim.

His mother worked on him constantly, and convinced her son that he was headed nowhere fast. After a year, he agreed. He soon shifted his focus and began to apply himself. In storybook fashion, after three years of hard work, he graduated with honors and won a scholarship to Yale.

But the Ben Carson story doesn't end there. Pitted against many of the brightest students in the nation while adjusting to a new environment and tough curriculum, Carson had trouble at Yale. As a premed major, he came alarmingly close to flunking out his first year. "I realized

I had to manage my time and redouble my efforts. I had climbed so many mountains, overcome so many obstacles. I wasn't going to quit now."

This was the attitude that propelled Ben Carson through medical school, internship, and into a series of prestigious posts.

Dr. Carson looks back over his career and offers the following advice to anyone confronting failure: "The big difference between people who succeed and those who don't is not that the successful don't encounter setbacks. Everybody has roadblocks. If you look at obstacles as boundaries that prohibit your progress, then you're going to be a failure. But if you look at them as hurdles that strengthen you each time you clear one, then you're going to be a success."

Dr. Carson cleared his hurdles with a combination of persistence, courage, and compassion. He is something of a marvel in the medical profession. He has always resisted the opportunity to earn many times his income in private practice. Instead, he stays in academic medicine, searching for new challenges. In 1987, just out of curiosity, he read an account of 21 sets of Siamese twins joined at the head whom surgeons had tried to separate. In the majority of these cases, one child survived but the other either died or was mentally destroyed. The problem, he saw, was the mammoth loss of blood the operation entailed. If he was ever involved in such a case, he would stop the babies' circulation beforehand, lower their body temperatures, and then operate. But the chances of his ever seeing such a case, he thought, were minute.

Three weeks later a West German doctor arrived at Johns Hopkins with the records of a pair of Siamese newborns from his native country. Their mother was unwilling to sacrifice either child to save the other, but no surgeon in Europe knew any other method to separate them. Dr. Benjamin Carson was called in to consult.

"I looked at the charts and X rays, and said, 'Yeah, I can do this.' "

The operation took twenty-two tension-filled hours, and for fourteen of them Carson worked as a leading member of a seventy-person team—some of whom were doctors senior to him. What gave him the courage to step forward and tackle an operation so difficult and brimming with the possibility of failure? The same quality he discovered earlier in his career: "I guess I would have been afraid if I didn't have so much faith in God and my ability to overcome failure."

In like manner you may control your destiny to an astounding degree—simply by exercising your privilege of overcoming setbacks and failure. To the same degree that Dr. Carson transformed his life, you too can make life pay off in your terms, engaging in the sort of work best suited for you. How? *By taking a critical view of your failures and defeats.*

Hitting the Mark by Failing

How did Grambling University football coach Eddie Robinson hit his mark? By applying the same philosophy. College football's 300-win club consists of only four members: Glen "Pop" Warner, Amos Alonzo Stagg, Paul "Bear" Bryant, and Eddie Robinson. Robinson's record is the cornerstone of a legacy that he built with hard work, sacrifice, and persistence.

"I have no secret save persistence," says Grambling University's head football coach. "People look at my record and are awestruck by the three hundred wins. *They never realize that I lost more than a hundred games!*

"When I began coaching forty years ago, I did everything to keep the football program going—I mowed and landscaped the grass at our stadium; I repaired equipment, and even taped my player's ankles. I did whatever needed doing. Persisting through many tough times was a big part of my job." With more than 350 wins to his credit and currently the all-time leader in college victories, Eddie Robinson knows a good deal about the subject of failure and success.

There can be no such thing as permanent defeat for the man or woman who accepts adversity as a steppingstone to success. Life seems to have been designed so that every man who achieves great success must first undergo a testing period—sometimes many of them—through which he is tested for courage, faith, endurance, and the capacity to overcome.

"The persistent man never stops to consider whether he is succeeding or not," says "Mr. T." "Everything must be sacrificed for the attainment of the goal."

Born Lawrence Tureaud on Chicago's South Side, he was no stranger to life's recesses. The tenth of twelve children, deserted by their father, he was raised by a loving mother. For the better part of a decade his family hung on grimly, barely surviving on his mother's sporadic earnings and a monthly welfare stipend. Home was a three-room apartment in a public housing project. But like many fatherless boys of the Chicago slums, Lawrence was a fighter. He refused to succumb to life's difficulties and wasted no time with self-pity.

Thanks to his determination, persistence, and belief in the Almighty, "Mr. T," as he is now known, earns a handsome income in the world of entertainment and is seen by millions. Adversity was the yardstick by which he assessed his weaknesses. It also provided him an opportunity to balance his shortcomings. "Poverty is not a curse, it's a motivator!" In this sense adversity and defeat proved to be a blessing.

Adversity and Achievement

"There are three types of people in the world," said the inspirational writer Orison Swett Marden. "There's the *wills,* the *won'ts,* and the *can'ts.* The first accomplish everything; the second oppose everything; the third fail in everything." Dare to make a start. All the best-laid plans in the world will not help you as much as conquering the smallest obstacle in your path. And this book will not have served its purpose unless it demonstrates your ability to do so.

On every hand we see those who have turned back, people who had desire and enthusiasm enough to begin, but who were unable to overcome their adversities. Your ability to press on—to persist, to continue long after everyone else has turned back—is a good measure of your possible success. Don't be led astray by the so-called odds against you, or the obstacles blocking your path. These are old clichés. The doers of the world don't let such considerations deter them. If they had, they would have never become such noble examples.

You, too, have it within yourself to succeed. Monitor your thoughts and attitudes; take stock of yourself and your resources.

If you are reading *Think and Grow Rich: A Black Choice* with the intention of applying the principles it conveys, you will discover that *lack of persistence is one of the major causes of failure*. While the starting point of all achievement is desire, your desires may either be increased or diminished by the amount of persistence you apply to your goal. As history demonstrates, the lack of persistence is a common weakness in many men and women. Never forget the inspiring words of philosopher and writer Edmund Burke: "He that wrestles with us, strengthens us. Our antagonist is our helper."

If you are in need of persistence, build a stronger fire under your goal and stoutly assert your divine right to attain it. Believe you were made for the place you occupy, hold your head up, and put forth your entire energies.

Conquer or Be Conquered

Have you ever seen a man who had no quit in him, who would never let go his grip no matter what happened;

who, every time he encountered defeat, would come up
smiling and with increased determination to forge ahead?
Have you ever seen a man who did not know the meaning
of the word "failure," who never knew when he was
beaten, who had erased the words "can't" and "impossible" from his vocabulary; the man who no obstacles
could stop, who was not disheartened by misfortune? *If
you have—you've seen a conqueror!*

It is always of interest to watch a youth's first taste of
failure. It is the index to his life, the measure of his
success power. "A man's real courage," said Napoleon
Hill, "shows to best advantage in his hour of adversity."
The mere idea of his failure is not as important as *how*
he takes defeat. What does he do next? Was he discouraged? Does he conclude that he made a mistake in his
present undertaking and rush to attempt something else—
or does he stand firm?

No one is immune to failure, and everyone meets with
it eventually during a lifetime. Nonetheless, each of us
has the means by which we can overcome our failures.
Remember, you have control of the greatest tool ever
known—*your mind*—and you alone control its processes.

Failure usually affects people in one of two ways: It
serves as a challenge to greater effort, or it subdues and
discourages you from trying again. The majority of people give up hope and quit at the first sign of adversity,
even before it overtakes them. For instance, a significant
number of black Americans are born into poverty. Living
in a world of abundance, many accept their lot as ines-
capable and go through life wearing deprivation as an
albatross. However, it may very well be that poverty is
one of life's testing devices; whether it becomes either a
blessing or a curse depends upon the manner in which it
is received.

It has also been said that failure is part of nature's
plan, through which it prepares men and women of destiny to do its work. I have found much evidence to support this theory. One of the first lessons of life is to learn

how to snatch victory from defeat. It takes courage and stamina, when unsure and embarrassed by humiliating disaster, to seek in the ruins the elements of success. Yet this is the true mark of achievement. This measures the difference between those who succeed and those who don't. You cannot measure a man by his failures—instead you must know what he makes of them. With this in mind, it was Confucius who proclaimed, "A man is great not because he hasn't failed; a man is great because failure hasn't stopped him."

The leader is never subdued by failure, but is always inspired to a greater effort. By contemplating your failures, you will discover whether you have the potential for leadership. Your reaction will render a dependable clue. Nature often pummels aspiring men and women with adversity in order to find who among us will get up and make another go of it. Those who make the grade are people of destiny, programmed to serve as leaders of importance in today's world.

The next time you encounter failure, remember that every failure and adversity carries within it the seed of an equivalent benefit. Begin to recognize that seed, and plant it through action. You may discover that *there is no such reality as failure until you accept it as such!*

You may explore the secret of persistence by uncovering the ten most prevalent causes of failure:

1. Lack of a definite purpose, goal, or chief aim.
2. Lack of ambition to move past mediocrity.
3. A negative mental attitude.
4. Lack of self-discipline.
5. Lack of vision and imagination sufficient to recognize favorable opportunities.
6. The use of race, sex, or circumstances as a reason for inactivity.
7. Lack of belief in the existence of infinite intelligence.
8. Ill health.

9. Lack of persistence in carrying through to finish that which you start; unwillingness to go the extra mile or render a service; the habit of running away from unpleasant circumstances instead of mastering them.

10. The desire to get something for nothing.

You Can Make the Grade

Napoleon Hill had a clear vision of the potential power in persistence when he said:

> Those who have cultivated the habit of persistence seem to enjoy insurance against failure. No matter how many times they are defeated, they manage to move toward the top of the ladder. Sometimes it appears that there is a "Hidden Guide" whose duty is to test men through all sorts of discouraging experiences. Those who pick themselves up after defeat and keep on trying, arrive. The Hidden Guide lets no one enjoy great achievement without passing the persistence test. Those who can't take it simply do not make the grade.

From birth to death life poses a constant challenge to those who master failure with persistence, and it rewards with riches the men and women who successfully meet those challenges. If you accept defeat as an inspiration to try again with renewed confidence and determination, the attainment of your success will be only a matter of time. If you accept defeat as a final blow and allow it to destroy your confidence, you might as well abandon any hope of success.

Remember the words of the nineteenth-century American social reformer and writer Jacob Riis, who wrote, "When nothing seems to help, I go and look at a stonecutter hammering away at his rock perhaps a hundred times without as much as a crack showing in it. Yet, at the hundred and first blow it will split in two, and I know it was not that blow that did it—but all that had gone before.''

6

What Are You Worth?

"No one can make you feel inferior without your own consent."

—ELEANOR ROOSEVELT

"If I were you, I would stand for something—I would count!"

—BENJAMIN E. MAYS

"Self-hate is a form of mental slavery that results in poverty, ignorance, and crime."

—SUSAN L. TAYLOR

Every day the poor African farmer used to pray that he might have a good opinion of himself. "And why not?" he thought. "Can I ask another to think well of me when I do not think well of myself?" There's a piercing African proverb: "It never pays to respect a man who does not respect himself." In other words, it is senseless for you to claim to be worthy of the good opinion of others when you have a less than favorable opinion of yourself. If the world sees that you do not honor yourself, it will take you at your own value.

The world will look to you for your own rating. It will stamp its value of you based on the value you give yourself, and you cannot expect to pass for more.

There are two great objectives for which mankind seems to be striving. *One is to attain happiness; the other is to accumulate material wealth—prosperity.* You will see the role that a strong, positive self-image plays when you realize that neither of these objectives can be achieved without full application of this amazing principle. You cannot be happy unless you believe in yourself; you cannot accumulate riches—either material or spiritual—unless your self-image is worthy of the riches you seek. *Though it may be important to believe in others, it is equally as important to believe in yourself.* This can be accomplished only through a positive self-image.

When you bury this truth into the depths of your mind, a new, vibrant, renewed feeling of inspiration will embrace you. You will become conscious of a tremendous vitality and strength which you never knew existed. By uncovering the power of a positive self-image, you will take straight and true steps toward achievement.

What Are You Worth?

Before the atomic age, scientists estimated that a person's worth, from a strictly chemical and material standpoint, was approximately thirty-two dollars. In recent years this estimation has undergone startling changes. Researchers now calculate that if the electronic energy of the hydrogen atoms in the human body could be utilized, a single person could supply the electrical needs of a large, highly industrialized country for nearly a week. One noted theorist claimed that the atoms in our bodies contain a potential energy charge of more than eleven million kilowatt hours per pound; in effect, the average person, by this estimate, is worth nearly $85 billion. Moreover, these electrons and atoms are not just particles of matter, but waves of living energy. And as these waves ripple out, they spread themselves in patterns, reflecting and moving while remaining totally undetectable to the human eye. Furthermore, trying to mechanically reproduce the human brain would cost billions of dollars.

The point that I am trying to make is that you are much more than meets the eye. You are an *immensely valuable creature*. Not only are you immensely valuable as a human being, but you are unlike any human being who ever lived, or ever will live. *Despite your present conditions and circumstances, you are one of a kind.*

Now, why do I share this information with you? *Because you are priceless!* Though the wages you receive may not reflect this inherent treasure, you are capable of much more than you might attempt or accomplish. The purpose of this lesson is to help you discover your true net worth.

You Are Somebody!

The exhortations begin. "I am somebody! I *am* somebody!

"I may be black, but I am somebody!

"I may be poor, but I am somebody!

"*I am somebody!* I'm God's child." And with this liturgy completed, another session of Jesse Jackson's Operation PUSH is officially adjourned.

Jesse Jackson is correct. I am somebody. You are somebody. Each of us is somebody. But what we truly are is our perception of reality. And though you are somebody, how you feel about yourself will depend on the all-important variable that is known as your self-image. "How few young men realize," wrote the black historian Charles Wesley, "that their success in life depends more upon what they are than upon what they know. It is self-esteem that has brought the race this far."

Each of us, from childhood, weaves his own intricate web of self-images. These stem from the beliefs born in response to every thought and experience, every humiliation and triumph, every defeat and victory. Individuals behave, not in accordance with reality, but in accordance to what they perceive as reality.

How we feel about ourselves affects virtually every aspect of our lives: from the way we function on our jobs, to the jobs we take—or even seek—to the way we operate in society, and to the goals and aspirations we set before ourselves. Our responses to events are shaped by who and what we think we are. As the nineteenth-century inspirational writer Elbert Hubbard once wrote, "Man is not what he thinks he is—but what *he thinks*, he is." The dramas of our lives are the reflections of our innermost private visions of ourselves. Thus, self-image is the all-embracing secret to success or failure.

Whether we realize it or not, each of us carries within us a mental blueprint or picture of ourselves. It may be vague and ill-defined to the casual observer; in fact, it may not be consciously visible at all. But it is there, complete down to the last detail. This self-image is our concept of the *kind of person we are*. It has been erected from *beliefs* about ourselves. However, most of the beliefs about ourselves have unconsciously been formed from past experiences, our successes and failures, our humiliations and triumphs, and the way others have reacted toward us, especially during our childhood. From these experiences we mentally constructed a "self," or a concept of self. Once an idea or belief about ourselves is reflected in this picture, it becomes true, as far as we are personally concerned. We do not question its validity, but we act upon it as if it were true.

Your self-image becomes a golden key to living a better life because of two important discoveries:

First, all of your actions, feelings, behavior—even your abilities—are consistent with this self-image. In short, you act like the sort of person you perceive yourself to be. You cannot act otherwise, in spite of your conscious efforts. The man who perceives himself to be a failure will find some way to fail, in spite of all the good intentions, even if opportunity is virtually dumped in his lap. The person who views himself to be a victim of society will invariably find circumstances to verify his opinions.

The self-image is a premise, a base or foundation upon which your entire personality and behavior is built. Because of this, your experiences seem to verify, and thereby strengthen, your self-image, creating a positive or negative impact.

For example, the schoolboy who sees himself as an F student, or one who is "not very good in mathematics," will surely find that his report card bears him out. In the same manner, a young woman who is always "unable to land that certain position" or "to earn a lucrative income" will also find that her experiences tend to prove her self-image correct.

Because of this overly subjective "proof," it seldom occurs to people that their troubles lie in their self-image or their own evaluation of themselves.

Second, the self-image can be changed. It's been proved that one is never too young, too old, or the wrong sex or race to change one's self-image and thereby begin to experience a new life.

I used to think it was only I who was filled with doubts and fears—that I alone lacked confidence. In fact, while trying to overcome those very feelings of insecurity, I have searched deeper within myself, to discover higher ground. You are much more than what meets the eye; capable and equipped to make major triumphs in your life. Yet many of us live and die without ever experiencing our true greatness. It's time to develop a new and truer vision of ourselves; time to discover our individual uniqueness, our inexhaustible supply of divine wisdom and strength.

Most of us never experience what is best in us because we, too, readily accept the thinking and dictates of others. We live our lives trying to be what we feel is acceptable to the masses. Once again, that old bugaboo, conformity, rears its ugly head. Often we allow the people we care about the most to convince us we should move to their rhythm. We believe their thinking is more enlightened than our own—and then we resent them for not believing in us, for pulling our strings. But, more than anything, when we don't follow the stirring in our hearts, we feel a deep sense of frustration and personal failure. That essential part of our being—the *self* that is *you* and me—needs expression. It needs to grow wings, test itself in flight, in order to be.

To grow in self-esteem is to grow in the conviction that you are somebody, competent as well as worthy of success. As a result, you'll face life with increased confidence and optimism. This, in turn, helps you to reach your goals while experiencing fulfillment. To grow in self-esteem is to expand your mental capacity for success, to take on bigger challenges, opportunities, and responsibilities. If you master this concept, you will appreciate the idea that each of us has a substantial stake in cultivating his or her own self-image.

Protect Your Mind

This essential rule is crucial to the psyche of Black America. It is well documented that low self-esteem is the cause of most social problems. Often we allow myths, flimsy tradition, or negative half-truths to become chains that shackle our lives. We unnecessarily fall prey to the opinions of others, which eventually clouds our sensory data and does little to enhance the manner in which we view ourselves. *Ultimately, what shapes our self-image is not so much what happens to us as what happens in us.*

"Garbage in—garbage out" is a cliché of our times. During every moment of your life, you process and respond to millions of pieces of information fed into your mind. You will, in turn, tackle the rudiments of life with either a positive or a negative outlook, depending on this data. A vital step in developing a confident, positive personality lies within your ability to transcribe this information correctly.

Assume for a moment that you have in your possession a million dollars in gold. *Would you protect it? Would you safeguard this treasure? Would you respect its value?* Of course you would. You might even hire bodyguards or install security devices to ensure its safety.

In comparison, your mind and self-image are worth far more than one million dollars. *They're priceless!* Your mind is the exclusive source of all you will create spiritually, financially, or materially in your life. Your level of joy, happiness, and peace of mind originates from one place—your mind. *Now ask yourself, do you protect your mind as carefully as you protect your physical assets?*

In all honesty, the answer is probably no. Many of us permit all types of image-destroying garbage to seep into the archives of our minds and penetrate our thought processes. More than we would like to admit, many of us have allowed negative attitudes and counterproductive thinking to enter and program our mental computers. And the results are all too obvious—broken families, drug abuse and alcoholism, teen pregnancies, soaring crime rates, and a waning of educational achievement.

Learn to protect your mind! Your environment and well-meaning family and friends combine with the events of your day to strongly influence the manner in which you view yourself. Whether you realize it or not, each of us maintains within the spectrum of the mind a personal recorder. You must become extremely particular concerning the type of data that is fed into your mind and permitted to take root, for the sole function of the self-image is to follow the instructions given to it implicitly by the mind—like an obedient personal computer reading its program and responding automatically.

Your mental image of yourself forms the very core of your personality; to have a positive self-image is to feel confidently appropriate to life, that is, competent and worthy. To possess an average self-image is to fluctuate between feeling appropriate and inappropriate, right and wrong as a person, and to manifest these inconsistencies in your behavior. To possess a low self-image is to feel inadequate and ineffective in life.

The more positive the self-image, the better equipped you are to cope with life's adversities; the more resilient you become, the more you are able to withstand outside forces. The more positive the self-image, the more creative you become in your daily approach toward life. The greater the self-image, the more ambitious you will be—not necessarily in a financial sense, although this does often happen, but in terms of what you hope to experience in life. The greater the self-image, the more inclined you will be to treat others with respect, kindness, and sincerity, since those you face will not be perceived as threats, inferior or superior. Succinctly put, self-image is what *you think* and *feel* about you. *There is no greater force at your service than your own mind coupled with a strong, positive self-image.*

See Yourself as You Will One Day Become

In *Pygmalion,* George Bernard Shaw's whimsical masterpiece, Henry Higgins, the proud phonetician, admonishes Eliza Doolittle, the unassuming flower girl, that she should *see herself as she will one day become.* "Think like a duchess, act like a duchess, talk like a duchess, and one day you will be a duchess!" he advises.

Dr. Maxwell Maltz, author of *Psychocybernetics,* developed a process for unlocking self-direction. He wrote: "The lucky or successful person has learned a simple secret. Call up, capture, evoke the feeling of success. When you feel successful and self-confident, you will act successfully. Define your goal or end result. Picture it to yourself clearly and vividly. Then simply capture the feeling you would experience if the desirable goal were already accomplished."

What do you think and feel about yourself? Do you like who you are? When you look in the mirror, do you see the person that you will one day become? Perhaps the following story will help you answer these questions.

There was once an African prince who was born a hunchback. On his twelfth birthday, his father, the king, asked him what would he like to receive as a birthday gift. Bent over and looking up, the boy replied, "I would like a statue of myself."

Upon hearing of his child's desires, the father was confused. He wished he had never brought up the subject. The last thing in the world he wanted for his young son was for him to be mocked. In an effort to change the boy's mind, the king asked, "Certainly there must be something else that you want?"

But the prince replied, "No, I want a statue of myself. But don't misunderstand me, Father. I do not want a statue of myself as I appear now. Rather, I would like a statue of how I would look *if I stood straight!*"

Well, the poor king was distraught. He thought his son's reasoning was even worse.

"Furthermore," said the prince, "I'd like the figure to be placed outside my window in the garden, where I could see it every day."

Reluctantly, his father finally agreed to his son's wishes, and the statue was erected. Every day, in a routine, methodical fashion, the boy would stand before his statue. Day in and day out he would stretch and reach and extend and strain to mimic the six-foot replica. He did this without fail several times a day, each day, *for eight years!*

On his twenty-first birthday something happened! The prince stood with his shoulders erect, head straight, staring eyeball to eyeball with his likeness. For this once humped-back, four-foot-tall youth was now the epitome of strength and power, with a statuesque body and an equally impressive self-image. *What was the young prince's secret?* Well, as the poet says, "What thou seest, that thou beest!"

How do you visualize yourself? What are the words, pictures, and images that cross your mind when you think of yourself? Get centered by seeing yourself as you really are—as you will one day become. Words, pictures, and images have incredible power. You must recognize this power and use it as if your life depended on it—because it does. This is the first step toward bringing about the physical equivalent of your thoughts.

Loving Your Neighbor as Yourself

The Bible speaks of the necessity of a positive self-image in the second commandment: "Love your neighbor as yourself." It is important that we love our neighbor, but the first and last words of this directive indicate a vital key to riches—*love yourself*. By following the intent of this commandment, you will do the things that will ultimately allow you to perform on a level of personal excellence, providing an added measure of self-confidence.

Love yourself, not in a narcissistic sense, but from a vantage point that respects and believes in your own abilities. This builds ego strength. Any man or woman who truly wants to change the circumstances of his life must first change from the inside out—he must change the innermost picture he holds of himself.

You Are Worthy of Success

He was a young black man who had grown up an orphan in Louisiana. He had lived in fourteen different foster homes before he drifted to southern California. There he resumed his education in a small public school near Los Angeles. It was obvious the boy had a deep-seated inferiority complex, which his teacher tried to change through counseling him.

One day in class he blurted out: "You have to remember that I'm black and that we're inferior. We're the products of slaves."

"That's not true," his teacher countered. "You are not inferior."

"What do you mean?" he asked.

"You and every black American can trace his or her genealogy to Africa," she explained. "You can take pride in your genetic roots. Why? Because you are the offspring of survivors. The weakest slaves, unfortunately, did not clear the middle passage. Some died aboard ship. Some threw themselves overboard and were drowned. Others died as soon as they reached these foreign shores. But those Africans who survived the tumultuous ordeal— *your forefathers*—had the courage, fortitude, and state of mind that would not let them die. They were emotionally superior—*they would not give up hope in spite of the obstacles!* Every black American is a genetic descendant of the toughest and best bloodlines. And that's the kind of blood that you have, Bert.''

The caring teacher made her point. The boy left school that day and thought about all he had learned. Today that young black child—Bert Duncan—is a practicing physician in Los Angeles. He successfully achieved his potential, but first he had to change his self-image.

Most of our battles are not fought with physical weaponry, but in the scope of mental images. If we believe subjective statements about ourselves—"I'm fat, I'm ugly, I'm poor," for example—these images, if unchecked, will eventually take root in our lives. *No one is superior or inferior to another.* It is up to each of us, individually, to nurture our own sense of self-worth.

For those with poorly developed self-images marked by a lack of self-confidence and diminished self-worth, I point to the virtue of establishing a success consciousness.

Overcoming Mental Slavery

To fully understand the meaning of being black in America, you must assess the impact that generations of racism, oppression, and bias have left on the collective psyches of a race of people. For more than 300 years Black America has been chained by slavery, segregated by discrimination, and systematically excluded from equal participation in the life and culture of a society at large. The most conspicuous consequence of this pattern of discrimination and exclusion, and arguably the most horrendous transgression any human being could confer on another, is an obtrusive self-hatred.

Fortunately, these problems are of our own making, and without exception the solution to these barriers lies within our power to find. Those who base their beliefs on a loving God—infinite intelligence—who acts in their behalf, and who believe that they are created in His image, tend not to think less of themselves or others. Physical or emotional differences are not breeding grounds for personal shame or humiliation. Problems must be seen as opportunities for growth. There is a God-shaped vacuum within us all, and those who base their foundations on this revelation find joy, hope, and peace of mind.

As you discovered in the introduction of this chapter, you are immensely valuable—as perfect a creature as is capable of being created on this planet—no more, no less. You are the result of millions of years of evolution. The handiwork of the Creator provided the most solid foundation for building a healthy, positive self-image. Those possessing a strong self-image are able to place their own personality in complete harmony with those around them; enjoying every moment of their lives, treating people like people, regardless of race, creed, or color.

Can you overcome years of mental slavery? Will you struggle to uncover and express your self-worth?

Again, Protect Your Mind!

To protect yourself against negative influences, whether of your own making or as the result of the input of negative-thinking people, realize that you have willpower, and you can use this power to create walls of immunity against negative influences in your own mind. Successful men and women always protect their most valuable assets—their minds. The poverty-stricken never do—leaving their most cherished gift exposed to be either stolen, abused, or overtaken by destructive thoughts.

Those who succeed in any calling must prepare their minds to resist the ignorance of the world. If you are reading *Think and Grow Rich: A Black Choice* to gain insight to the secrets of success, you should examine yourself first to safeguard against any negative influences. If you overlook this most basic duty, then any goal or desire you henceforth aspire to could be in jeopardy. The most common weakness of all human beings is the habit of leaving their minds open to the negative influences of others.

You may control your mind by feeding it whatever thought impulses you choose. You are the master of your own earthly destiny just as surely as you have the power to control your own thoughts. You may influence, direct, and eventually control your own circumstances, making your life what you want it to be—or you may neglect to exercise this privilege and pay the price for failure.

Right now you are somewhere on a scale between positive and negative self-esteem. Ask yourself whether it might be profitable or desirable to move up that scale—to move in the direction of a more accurate, valid, or honest appraisal of your real worth and significance as a person. If you can accept the possibility that you may genuinely be a worthy human being, then take deliberate action to march in the direction of an even greater self-acceptance.

This is a critical time for Black America. *Black America needs strong men and women with equally strong self-images who are fit, focused, and armed with a plan of action for personal and collective empowerment.* Now, more than ever, we need a renewed positive vision of ourselves and each other. Once we discover the best in us, we can move on to our larger purpose of uplifting the race. *But first we must focus on self, accept self, and believe in self.*

Dr. Carter G. Woodson, the eminent black historian,

expressed his respect for the power of the self-image when he wrote:

> When you determine what a man shall think, you do not have to concern yourself about what he will do. If you make a man feel inferior, you do not have to compel him to accept an inferior status, for he will seek it himself. If you make a man think that he is justly an outcast, you do not have to order him to the back door; he will go without being told; and if there is no back door, his very nature will demand one.

Remove from your mind all forms of unrealistic limitations, fears, and subjective ideas that may have led to the disintegration of your self-image. Through deliberate affirmations and conscious effort, you can strengthen your self-esteem, thereby drawing a better, more truthful image of yourself. To prove the accuracy of this statement, read and utilize the following points which will help you rebuild or strengthen your self-image.

1. Make a list of at least ten positive attributes you possess. Be generous but honest when listing those qualities that you like about yourself. When your list is complete, write a brief expression of gratitude for all who have helped—family, friends, the Almighty.
2. Conversely, make a list of all the things you wish to change. Don't be ashamed, change is normal. Place a check mark beside those traits you feel you can change. Write a personal statement of acceptance acknowledging the things that you don't like but can't change and a pledge to change all the things you can.
3. Write a short personality profile describing the person you have identified yourself to be. Give full attention to both strengths and weaknesses.
4. Know that in order for you to succeed, you need only believe in yourself.
5. Understand that life is thought. Therefore, concen-

trate on becoming the person you intend to be. Draw a mental picture of this person so as to transform this image into its physical expression.

6. Master the principles set forth in this book. Through constant study you will become increasingly aware of your God-given powers.

7. Become self-reliant. Learn to stand on your own feet, and express yourself in a manner that will carry conviction. Cause others to become interested in you because you will first become interested in others. Eliminate selfishness and develop a spirit of service in its place.

8. Never downgrade yourself or your importance in life, nor allow others to berate you. If you are forced to listen to such nonsense, dismiss it immediately. Remember, the quality of your thoughts, your feelings, and attitude produces results.

9. Repeat positive affirmations to yourself with conviction—*"To be enthusiastic, act enthusiastic!"* or *"Do it now!"*

Think of this list as a blueprint or detailed description of the person you want to be. By utilizing the list in this manner, you should not doubt for one moment the plan for your new self-image that you'll one day resemble. Review this list as much as possible, and remember, your thoughts produce corresponding results within your life.

7

Self-Reliance

"All work and no play makes Jack a dull boy; but all play and no work makes him something greatly worse."

—SAMUEL SMILES

"God bless the child who's got his own."

—BILLIE HOLIDAY

"What we, the colored people want, is character. And this nobody can give us. It is something we must earn for ourselves."

—FREDERICK DOUGLASS

"Heaven helps those who help themselves" is a well-tried maxim embodying in a small compass the results of vast human experiences. Biographies of black men and women of achievement are the most instructive and useful incentives to others. Some of the best are almost equivalent to gospels—teaching high ambition, right thinking, and energetic action to further their aims. These valuable examples exemplify the power of integrity, self-help, individual initiative, and patient purpose.

Great men and women of science, literature, and the arts have belonged to no exclusive class or social rank. Some of the Master's greatest apostles came from the ranks. The impoverished have sometimes risen to the highest stations. And the most indigent proved insurmountable obstacles no great task.

Take for instance Frederick Douglass, the esteemed orator and ex-slave, who said, "Our destiny is largely in our own hands. If we find, we shall have to seek. If we

succeed in the race for life it must be by our own energies, and our own exertions. Others may clear the road,
but we must go forward or be left behind in the race for
life. If we remain poor and dependent, the wealth of
others will not avail us. If we are ignorant, the intelligence of others will do but little for us. If we are foolish,
the wisdom of others will not guide us. If we are wasteful
of our time and money, the economy of others will only
make our destitution the more disgraceful.''

Also from the humble ranks sprang Marcus Garvey,
the twentieth-century ''Black Moses,'' who suggested:

> There is no force like success, and that is why the
> individual makes all efforts to surround himself
> throughout life with the evidence of it. As of the in-
> dividual, so should it be of the race. The glittering
> success of Rockefeller makes him a power to the
> American nation; the success of Henry Ford suggests
> him as an object of universal respect. The black man
> must be up and doing if he will break down the prej-
> udice of the rest of the world. We must strike out for
> ourselves in the course of material achievement, and
> by our own effort and energy present to the world those
> forces by which the progress of man is judged.

In both these cases, strenuous individual application
was the price paid for distinction. This lesson will single
out those who will embark on this same great adventure
in the arena of self-reliance.

Who among you is not afraid to stand alone? Who is
bold, original, and resourceful? Who is ready to strike
out for his own independence? Who is one of the auda-
cious few who possesses the fortitude to venture where
others have never been, to do what others have never
done, in order to live life as others rarely will, by leaving
his mark on the times through the power of self-reliance?

Nine out of ten men past mid-life, if asked why they
are only barely earning a living, would tell you that they

never had a chance—that they were kept back, and that circumstances were against them. Chances are they would say that opportunities eluded their grasp or that they didn't have access to the proper schooling. Today, millions of young blacks who are searching for a start in life seem to think they have very little to do with good opportunities except to discover them. *But no matter where you go, no matter what your background or educational level, your best opportunity always lies within yourself.*

The grandest fortunes ever accumulated on earth were and remain the fruit of endeavor that had no capital to begin with, save energy, intellect, and will. From L. Douglas Wilder, governor of Virginia, to John Johnson of Johnson Publishing, the story is the same, not only in the securing of wealth, but also in the seizing of greatness—*those men and women who have won most, relied mostly upon themselves!*

The habit of depending on self, the determination to find one's resources within one's self, develops strength. Crutches were intended for the physically disabled—*not the able-bodied*. Whoever attempts to go through life on mental crutches will not go far, nor will he be successful.

President of Your Own Company

Within the pages of the previous lesson, you learned of the hidden capacity for achievement lodged within yourself. It is mandatory that you discover your personal worth, not just from a physical point of view, but as a person, right now, on the market in today's society. Having ascertained your present worth, ask yourself, what do you intend to be worth next year, three years from now, or even five years from now?

In the final analysis every person is in business for himself; that is, he is building his own life regardless of who signs his paycheck. Within a free and open society, all of us are entrepreneurs. Each of us, individually, is the president of his or her own corporation. As you as-

sume this office, you, and you alone, are solely responsible for your firm's success or failure. You and the members of your family are stockholders in your corporation,
and it is your responsibility to see that the value of your
stock *increases* in the years ahead. Your family has displayed faith in you, and it is your responsibility to prove
that their faith is justified.

While the operations of a corporation are multitudi-
nous and complex, they can be reduced to four basic
functions:

- FINANCE
- PRODUCTION
- SALES
- RESEARCH

Without proper financing, there would be no production; without production, your company would have
nothing to sell. Without sales, your corporation would
have to completely stop production. And without research, your firm could not hope to stay abreast or ahead
of our rapidly changing times. Slight any one of these
four vital functions and you have a crippled company—
much like our individual braced on mental crutches. And
if you slight one factor long enough, you'll commit corporate suicide.

For the purpose of conserving time, we will discuss
the subject of finance and money in a subsequent lesson.
For now, let's concentrate on research, production, and
sales—the head, hands, and legs of your company.

How many once-large companies and trade names can
you think of that were once giants and have since disappeared entirely from the corporate landscape? Names
that were once world leaders in their fields and are now
only memories? Think about this for a moment. Why did
they go out of business? Simple. They failed to keep in
balance these four crucial functions. When I mention
crucial functions, I speak of the intangible and nonfinan-

cial assets your company has to have in order to become profitable and successful.

What about research for your personal corporation? Research can be said to exist in two areas—present and future. That is, the research of your company should be devoted to the ways and means of improving its present products or services, present production and present sales. Future research is concerned with the ways and means of developing new products and services, new methods of production, and new methods of marketing.

Are you looking for new and improved ways to enhance *you*? Are you presently researching the many areas in which your personal development can be effectively increased? Many people dream of starting their own business without ever realizing they're in business for themselves right now!

Life Moves Forward

It was an interesting conversation. An eighteen-year-old girl was talking with a learned old man. He had inquired about the direction of her life, particularly what line of training or career she would pursue. She said, "Well, you know, sir, I would like to become a psychologist, but it requires so much training that I'm afraid I would be too old when I finish."

The wise man sat in silence for a few moments, smiled, and then asked, "Young lady, how long would it take you to become a psychologist?"

"About seven years," she replied.

"How old would you be then?" was the next question.

"I will be twenty-five."

Then the man asked, "How old will you be in seven years if you don't become a psychologist?" Of course, her answer was the same. "Well, I guess I would be about twenty-five."

Time waits for no one. How many people have cheated themselves—thereby selling their company short—because they relinquished their desires or forfeited their dreams? Remember, your future is exactly what you make it. Five years from today you will be five years older. The question to ask is, Will you be five years wiser?

Abraham Lincoln said, "I am a slow walker, but I never look backwards." I suggest that you never look backward. Life is a forward impulse and the past is gone. You can live only in the here and now. But there are compulsive people who insist on looking backward. Rigid, attempting to stay in boundaries as though wearing blinders, they look to a past that cannot be relived or experienced again. They fail to understand that, at best, all they can do is react emotionally to the past. The past can never be resurrected—yesterday is gone. *Never look back!*

When Orpheus looked back, he lost his beloved Eurydice and eventually his life. Lot's wife looked back and turned into a pillar of salt. The point of these tales is that life is growth. *Life always moves on!* If you are living in the past, life will *still* move on—but it will move on *without you!* Living in the past means clinging to nonproductive attitudes and remaining in situations that hinder your personal growth and development.

St. Ignatius wrote in the first century, "He who is not getting better is getting worse." Like most words of wisdom, these words are just as applicable now as they were when they were first stated. The world is large, with much to learn and a lot to experience. If you are living in the past, you are preventing yourself—your company—from participating actively and fully in life.

Select an Area of Interest

One sure way to enhance the chances of your company's success, and in turn your own success, is to become a specialist in a particular field of knowledge or skill. Every day new knowledge is made available to you. This means that the sheer volume of information will make it increasingly difficult for any one individual to possess all the facts in any one particular field. Therefore, one way to improve your company is to become more skilled, better trained, and better educated.

Choose an area of interest that is of extreme importance to you. Research it from every possible angle. Our public libraries are free and open for all who wish to use this immense resource. Study trade journals, read all available materials, meet with experts and recognized leaders in the field, and in general make yourself a valuable storehouse of information. Make others aware of your activities and what you can offer. What you are really doing when you undertake such a project is making your organization—yourself—more effective.

Your corporation has two factors to consider—the present and the future. How successful you are in meeting these challenges will determine your present profits (what you earn) and future growth (what you will earn in the years to come).

Change Is Normal

The one constant thing in life is change. Change is everywhere—in your environment, in your emotions, in your beliefs, and in the way you think. How you generate change, what you do with change, and how you react to it determine whether you grow or stagnate. In spite of the concept that change is constant, there is nevertheless a strong tendency to resist it. Why? Because it presents an unknown factor in our lives. Though each of us may have problems, we are often tempted to maintain the status quo rather than venture into the unknown. By sailing in supposedly "safer" waters, we isolate ourselves as much as possible from the impact of change, trying to live with problems rather than solving them. Consequently, we become experts in negative, limited thinking, almost immunizing ourselves from any possible success.

To participate in change is to grow. Nothing grows that does not change. The tiny seed becomes a tall blade of grass; the bud becomes a flower; the egg hatches into a bird; and the child becomes an adult. The very act of life is to experience change and growth. *To earn more, you must first learn more.* Those who accept and adjust to change keep growing and learning. Those who cannot accommodate change do not grow. They stagnate by the wayside—a mental, physical, or spiritual death.

Why are all companies concerned with growth—even in a period of prosperity? It's because of the law that operates with companies as well as human beings. The law simply states: *Nothing in the world stands still! Nothing in the universe stands still!* A law of physics confirms that a body in motion tends to remain in motion until acted upon by an outside force. A company that is growing has a tendency to continue to grow. In other words, it is doing things right. Conversely, a company that is shrinking has a tendency to shrink until acted upon by an outside force. That is, it will shrink until it (or the individual) takes in additional information (personal development), or improves production and increases sales. All responsible company officials know that unless a company is growing, it is developing the first signs of stagnation or going out of business. As the head of your personal corporation, you should realize this law applies to you as well.

We are living in an age of discovery. A day rarely goes by when the media do not report the discovery of some new technological innovation or advance. The pace of scientific discovery seems almost unbelievable. The automation of production, computerization of information, supersonic transportation, communication by satellite, exploration of space, new uses for nuclear energy—all developments of the last twenty-five years—are only the beginning.

It has been estimated by scientists and scholars alike that man's total body of knowledge doubled between 1775 and 1900. A period of 125 years. It doubled again between 1900 and 1950, a period of only 50 years; and again between 1950 and 1958; *and it is now thought to be doubling every five years.* This is a tribute to man's curiosity and relentless movement forward. Now each of us, as president of our own corporation, can decide what to do with our lives. We can either grow and move forward, or go backward. We cannot stand still, even if that was desirable.

These ideas will give you an opportunity to stand back and view yourself and your future objectively, just as an intelligent bystander might. Ask yourself, how much am I worth right now, as a corporation? If you were an outside investor, would you invest in *you* as a corporation?

> THE MARKET DOESN'T PAY FOR EFFORTS—
> IT PAYS FOR RESULTS.
> YOU MUST PRODUCE!

What about productivity? A company growing at the rate of 10 percent a year will double in size in about eight years. What attention are you giving to the production of your personal corporation? Can you grow and improve as a person at least 10 percent per year? Of course you can.

Think and Grow Rich: A Black Choice is filled with countless stories of men and women who have exceeded their previous performance to an almost unbelievable degree. Achievers in all walks of life have multiplied their personal effectiveness (increased productivity) many times over.

We are constantly reminded of the energy being wasted, both by corporations in general and ourselves in particular. Giving an all-out effort doesn't seem to be as popular today as it was in the past. This might explain why so few individuals rise above the ranks, and why this author believes it is so much easier to succeed today. No matter what the field, most people find it easier to stay within the warmth of the huddled masses rather than risk failure. They submerge themselves in mediocrity, ultimately suffocating at the hands of conformity. As corporate presidents, some with brilliant minds and all capable of fulfilling a specific purpose in life, they refuse to go all out, forcing their companies to teeter on the verge of liquidation.

But this habit can easily be overcome. *Give and it shall be given to you.* This simple statement grants you the ability to advance *you*—your biggest asset. By giving to others—of your positive attitude, your loyalty, your commitment, your faith, your winning example, and the will to win—by giving your talents and energies to others, you will enhance this product called *you*. This is probably the greatest deed you could ever perform. If it is true that life will defeat the person who lives only for himself and his own personal satisfaction, then it is equally true that the same individual will receive strength, love, happiness, and success by giving of himself or herself. As Andrew Carnegie said to a young and highly inquisitive Napoleon Hill when pressed for the single key to achievement, ''The greatest service that one can render to God is by helping others.''

Nature employs this law in behalf of the tillers of the soil. The farmer carefully prepares the ground, then sows the seed and waits while the ''Law of Increasing Returns'' brings back the seed he has sown, plus a manyfold increase.

I am stressing the importance of this function of production as a means of enabling you as a corporation to promote yourself to an even higher station in life. Compliance with this feature will render a twofold reward. First, it will offer a greater material gain than that currently enjoyed by those who do not observe it. Second, it will produce the rewards of happiness and satisfaction, which come only to those who render such service. You will be trusted with even greater responsibilities as your level of production and service increase. This is the rule.

So, how's your production? Is there a way in which it can be improved? Are there ways to enhance output? These are all questions that must be answered by you, the president of your corporation.

Don't Forget Sales

And finally, what about sales? How can they be improved? Sales encompass more than just selling a product or service. This is the manner in which you sell yourself to everyone with whom you come in contact. It is the way you get along with your spouse, your children, your neighbors.

We are living in an age of cooperative effort. For centuries the pyramid structure was the way we organized and managed ourselves. Information, communications, and power, simulating the second law of thermodynamics, moved one way—from the top of the pyramid down to the bottom. However, over the years this, too, has changed. Nearly all successful companies are becoming more self-reliant. The pyramid has given way to *networking*—people talking to each other, at all different levels and in different directions, sharing ideas, information, and resources.

Networking exists to foster self-help, to exchange information, to change society, to improve productivity and work life, and to share resources. The important component is not the network, the finished product, but the process of getting there—*making contacts*. Within our personal universe, demographers have estimated that each of us knows nearly 270 other individuals—some more personally than others. This indeed may be the pathway to lead to even greater self-reliance and to the attainment of your goals.

The Most Important Sale

How's your level of salesmanship? How are you marketing your most important product—*you*? Regardless of who you are or what your chief aim is, your success will depend on your ability to sell yourself to others.

Selling is nothing more than the personal persuasion of ideas and thoughts. You need not go back into history to realize how fundamentally necessary salesmanship is for any successful venture. People will be persuaded more by the depth of your conviction than by the height of your logic; more by your enthusiasm and your belief than by any proof. Or as the master salesman Percy Whiting wrote, "Selling, to be a great art, must involve a genuine interest in the other person's needs. Otherwise it is only a subtle, civilized way of pointing a gun and forcing one into a temporary surrender."

Self-Reliance Through Selling

In the modern world of business and commerce, the ability to generate sales is the indispensable prerequisite for success of all competitive enterprises. It is the effectiveness of the salesperson that determines whether companies, industries, and even countries decline or prosper. Regardless of your occupation or profession, you must be a master salesman. Salesmanship is the key to the attainment of whatever you desire from life as long as your goals do not violate God or the rights of your fellowman. This applies not only to those who sell professionally, but to housewives, students, and anyone who may desire to reap his share of life's blessings.

The major advances in all fields—science, education, industry, technology, religion—have been made, for the most part, by men and women who possessed and utilized the power of persuasion. Numerous variables enter into the development program of the successful salesman. Most of these are personal in nature, having a greater bearing on the salesman himself than on the product or service he offers, or the organization he represents.

By reading the preceding pages and carefully applying their contents, you have already taken the first step toward becoming a master salesman. In addition to the valuable information in the foregoing chapters, there are essential qualities that you must possess if you seriously intend to become a successful person. The qualities are: *persistence, planning, common sense,* and *showmanship.*

Pay close attention to the examples that follow, and observe how these particular traits were used. If you are ready to take the first step to a more productive life, perhaps you will profit from the sales strategies of America's top black salesmen.

Persistence

The word "salesmanship" goes a long way toward explaining Earl Graves. In high school in Brooklyn's Bedford-Stuyvesant section, Graves sold his relentless energy by working three jobs at once. At Morgan State he paid his way through college by working as a swim instructor and dorm counselor. He even ran track for his meal ticket.

Graves majored in economics, and by his junior year launched a business from his dorm room—landscaping. He had a friend type a flyer that promised experienced lawn service at reasonable rates, and he stuffed every mailbox in sight. Anticipating only a modest response, he was totally unprepared for what followed. *More than forty homeowners signed up the first week!*

Graves graduated from college and entered the Army in 1958. Here, he developed and sharpened his sales skills. Though he made first lieutenant ahead of schedule, the military was clearly not a career; Graves had other things on his mind. When he completed his tour, he went back to New York and tried his hand in real estate.

In his first three months he sold nine houses—enough to pay for a wedding and furnish a modest apartment. In 1965, Graves went to work for the Justice Department, a job that was to eventually lead to his working for Robert Kennedy, then a New York senator. Working for Kennedy introduced Graves to a world he had never seen: a world where power was a natural heritage; where the word *can't* did not exist, *and where everybody practiced salesmanship.*

"Working for the senator played an enormous part in, my personal development," said Graves. "Robert Kennedy was a man who was totally unfamiliar with failure."

Graves recalled an incident where he was asked by the senator to contact then Secretary of the Interior Morris Udall. At the time, Udall was vacationing in Colorado, rafting down one of its more popular rivers. After several unsuccessful attempts to contact the secretary, Graves informed Kennedy that he was unable to reach Udall. To this the senator crisply responded, "Graves, that raft is not going down that river all day. It's going to stop somewhere, *and when it does I want Udall standing there with a phone in his hand!*" Those words still penetrate Graves's psyche today.

"That story is a part of my personal philosophy. You would be surprised how many people quit when faced with obstacles. As every good salesman knows, everything may not be possible today—but sooner or later, it is possible."

For nearly twenty years Earl Graves would apply this maxim as he and a cadre of loyal employees strove to keep *Black Enterprise* magazine at the forefront of the business-monthly circulation charts.

Planning

When the annals of black business history are written, Henry Parks and the Parks Sausage Company will be listed as major contributors. Starting with every nickel he could scrape together, and with his most important asset—a knack for planning—Parks was one of the first black businessmen to sell his product to the general market and convince the white banking establishment to invest in minority enterprises.

In 1951, he did just that, and achieved what few black entrepreneurs managed to do: expand his company beyond the confines of the black consumer dollar and carve a niche within the general market. Since the Baltimore-based manufacturing company began grinding out sausage in a small converted dairy, 1990 sales have grown to nearly $30 million.

Parks had begun his career with a blast of confidence, graduating with honors from Ohio State University. He was hired as a salesman by the Pabst Brewing Company after showing the firm a plan to market more beer among blacks. Parks's sales strategy was to reach the general market through ethnic consumers—a tactic that is practiced by Fortune 500 companies today. He succeeded beyond their wildest expectations.

By placing salesmen in supermarket parking lots and pitching Pabst to every black cook, chauffeur, and domestic who came to shop for their white employers, Parks infiltrated both black and white markets. To dislodge Budweiser as the exclusive supplier to America's railroads, he befriended dining-car waiters and Pullman porters, convincing them to stock Pabst on trains, in nightclubs, hotels, and union halls.

In 1951, Parks threw his sales skills into high gear and launched Parks Sausage—but soon ran out of money. He saw that his survival in food retailing would depend on his going beyond the minority market, so he bore straight ahead into promotion. He staged cooking demonstrations and taste tests in supermarkets—the first of their type.

Though cash was tight, Parks kept quality high and poured thousands of dollars into advertising—with ads like, "More Parks Sausages, Mom!" In a few short months trucks were seen rolling into some of the largest grocery chains on the East Coast, stocking the shelves in white-owned food stores.

"Every market has a key," Parks claimed. "And if you turn that key, you'll undoubtedly capture that market. I've proved that with proper planning, you can sell to anybody."

Common Sense

It would seem that a man who has amassed enough wealth to be ranked among the richest men in America—a personal net worth of more than $150 million—would know a bit about selling. How did he do it? "By using common sense to pry open markets."

In 1942, John H. Johnson borrowed $500 from a small loan company on the security of his mother's furniture, and used it to start *Negro Digest,* a black version of *Reader's Digest.* The magazine started slowly due to the reluctance of local distributors who refused to stock his journal. To solve this problem, Johnson called on friends and relatives, who canvassed Chicago buying up the entire press run of the magazine. Ecstatic distributors who were unaware of Johnson's tactics clamored for more copies. In one issue, circulation jumped from 50,000 to 150,000 copies, and *Negro Digest* soared. Three years later Johnson got more ambitious and launched *Ebony,* a clone of *Life* magazine for blacks.

In 1973, Johnson used the same strategy to win support for his cosmetic line. For three decades Johnson has sponsored the Ebony Fashion Fair—the world's largest touring fashion show. When he had trouble finding cosmetic shades dark enough for black models, he tried unsuccessfully to convince Estée Lauder and Revlon to develop a product. When they said no, he created his own products. But it wasn't that easy. His line was new, untested, and black. *How could he break in?*

After numerous proposals to department store executives, Johnson couldn't find any takers. Finally, he convinced the president of Chicago-based Marshall Field's that his cosmetics, Fashion Fair, were worth stocking. The executive purchased a small order but warned the black tycoon that his line would be yanked if it didn't sell. Johnson had to produce. Once again common sense prevailed. Using the plan that had worked before, Johnson had female employees purchase various amounts of Fashion Fair products for several months. Store buyers who monitored sales were excited and quick to reorder.

Johnson was equally quick to repeat the maneuver as he stocked the shelves of some of America's most exclusive and acclaimed department stores.

"I love to sell," Johnson states emphatically. "I sell even when there is no monetary advantage to be gained. The only advantage I have is a lifetime of experience." John Johnson possesses a quality shared by few in his time. Common sense has its rewards, and Johnson has reaped them.

Showmanship

Some call him a promoter, others say he is a public relations wizard—but neither title adequately describes what he does best. Wally Amos is a salesman who uses flair, hype, and showmanship to convey his message. With the help of an aunt, he began baking as a hobby that he would maintain throughout his promotional career. As a teenager Amos attended a New York City trade school, with an apprenticeship at a local hotel as a cook. Disenchanted, he quit six months prior to graduation and joined the Air Force. After a four-year stint he returned to New York and joined the William Morris Agency, where he started in the mail room before becoming a top agent, handling such acts as Simon and Garfunkel, the Temptations, and the Supremes. Amos perfected his self-promotional skills well while passing out his chocolate chip cookies at concerts, auditions, and meetings.

Friends and clients urged him to sell the treats, but he never gave the idea much thought.

But in 1974, fate intervened. Amos's personal management business was on the rocks. In a period of depression, he turned to his first love and started baking cookies full-time. After opening his first store on a shoestring, his funds waned and his cookie business went reeling. Amos recalls his toughest moment:

"As I look back, I realize that I was grossly undercapitalized. But I was too naive to consider failure. With no money, I had to stir up my creative juices and promote my cookies the same way I promoted my clients."

Amos wrote a business plan, raised some start-up capital from his show business contacts, and took a leap of faith. A few months later, amid flowing champagne, a strolling band, valet parking, and 1500 people, Wally Amos set his chocolate chips above all others—he called them "Famous Amos chocolate chip cookies."

Starved for cash, he once traded a day's worth of cookies ($750) for advertising time on local radio. He had professional models distribute cookies to passersby in neighboring Beverly Hills and Hollywood. "I knew I had the best product. All I needed to do was to convince the public of something I already knew. In 1975, a star was born and I was its showman."

Carefully consider these four qualities. Question yourself about the characteristics you honestly possess and those in which you are deficient. *Work at improving your persistence, planning, common sense, and showmanship.* Master salesmanship is an art and a valuable tool for the development of self-reliance.

Successful commercial and financial enterprises are managed by leaders who either knowingly or unconsciously apply the ideas described in this chapter. You too can become a recognized leader in the field of your choice by utilizing these principles—finance, production, research, and sales—in your life.

Self-Help

There are no open doors to the temple of success. Everyone who enters must forge his own way. Grand success waits patiently for anyone who has the fortitude and determination to seize his share of the American dream. But you must remember that it is *you who creates your own opportunities—not fate, luck, or chance*.

Lack of opportunity is ever the excuse of the poorly directed. Every life is full of opportunity. George Bernard Shaw once said: "God has given us a world that nothing but our own folly keeps from being a paradise." In other words, we live in a world that always has the potential for affluence.

Life is a lesson, and every lesson, regardless of where or when it occurs, is opportunity. Every business transaction is opportunity. Where there are people, there is opportunity. Existence is the privilege of effort, and when that privilege is met, opportunities to succeed along the lines of your aptitude will come faster than you can handle them.

If a slave like Frederick Douglass can elevate himself into an orator, editor, statesman, and successful businessman, then what ought the poorest black child born today, who is RICH in opportunities, accomplish with his life? Just think for a moment. If the average slave who suddenly found himself free, with no food, no shelter nor clothing, could lift his life from the "*gutter-most*" to the "*uttermost*," then what should the black American of today accomplish? A lowly beginning or humble origins are no barriers to opportunity.

The ranks are full of those who miss the boat called self-help. Generally, there are two alibis for missing the mark. "I'm not a genius" is one; the other, "Opportunities do not exist today as they did in the past." Neither excuse holds. The first is beside the point; the second is altogether wrong. It's the old failure "woe is me" syndrome expressed by "Someday my ship will come in."

In truth, opportunity first takes shape in your mind. It is an expression of how you perceive yourself as well as how you perceive your environment. The achievers, the innovators, and the movers and shakers are those with the courage and the insight to say, "Yes, I can! There is a way—and I'll find it!"

They are those rare individuals who accept life with its challenges and who work to turn those challenges into successes.

Opportunities abound! YOU ARE OPPORTUNITY, and you must knock on the door leading to your destiny. *You create* opportunity as you turn your crises and defeats into success. You must stop complaining about your unfortunate past or bad luck and realize the opportunities that exist around you.

Self-help is the offspring of adversity, the progeny of defeat. The spirit of self-help is the root of all genuine growth in the individual. If you rely on others for help, you lose the stimulus to improve yourself, which in effect renders you comparatively helpless. Put forth the effort, and practically anything you desire is yours. When opportunity is seized, self-help is simultaneously activated. The path to greatness and success is paved with self-reliance.

Don't Wait for Opportunity!

Don't wait for opportunity—make it! Make it as Thomas Burrell made his when he first conceived and created Burrell Advertising.

Born in Chicago in 1939, Tom Burrell was raised by his mother in a tough section on Chicago's South Side. Though he barely managed to stay out of trouble, he scored well on a scholastic aptitude test that would eventually give his life new meaning. With a newfound direction, his aim, attitude, and academic performance improved, leading him to college, where he majored in English and advertising.

Prior to graduation Burrell landed a job with a Chicago ad agency, working in the mail room for less than fifty dollars a week. *It was here that Burrell made his opportunity!* Within three months he advanced to copywriter, then on to various television and print campaigns. Burrell mastered his trade well, sharpening his skills with every new assignment. But when he launched his own agency, he wondered if he had made a serious mistake. It took six nervous months before his shaky firm secured its first account. As time wore on, Burrell pushed his fear aside and performed admirably.

Today, with more than $50 million in annual billings, and clients such as Coca-Cola, Sears, Procter & Gamble, and McDonald's, Burrell Advertising is the fastest growing black-owned advertising agency in the U.S.

Make your opportunity as Percy Sutton made his, by utilizing his many talents. It was in 1964, during the Harlem riots, that Sutton quelled a hostile crowd by using a local radio talk show as a forum for peace. Impressed by his performance, the station owner offered Sutton the chance to purchase one of his New York stations. But Sutton was nearly broke. Eight years later he organized a consortium of 33 investors, some of whom used their homes as collateral to obtain bank loans to purchase the $2.1 million radio station. Since then Sutton's company, Inner City Broadcasting, has diversified into a variety of fields. The parent company, which now has more than sixty stockholders, operates a cable station, New York's Apollo Theater, and a number of profitable radio stations nationwide.

Make your opportunity as Alice Walker made hers. As the youngest of eight children, Alice experienced a childhood in rural Georgia punctuated by poverty. Her parents' annual income—her father was a sharecropper, her mother a maid—never exceeded $5000. Nevertheless, she still unearthed the secret to success by clinching a rare place in literary history. In 1983, she became the first black female novelist to win the coveted Pulitzer Prize for fiction for her masterpiece *The Color Purple*.

Make your opportunity as Carl Rowan made his. Carl Rowan and his family knew the kind of poverty that is thankfully rare today. He was raised in a rat-infested house in rural Tennessee that had neither a clock, electricity, running water, telephone, or radio. His family survived on black-eyed peas and navy beans. But out of this milieu emerged a black child who would go on to become a naval officer, a member of the Foreign Service during the Kennedy administration, and, arguably, *Black America's most successful syndicated columnist*. At every step along the way he challenged mediocrity and complacency. Though racism and poverty tried desperately to put him on his knees, neither succeeded.

And make your opportunity as Ron Brown, chairman of the Democratic National Committee, made his. Brown discovered the genius that slept dormant within. As a freshman at Middlebury College, he confronted the racial restrictions of an all-white fraternity. Poised, talented, and competent, he refused to offer the organization any reason to deny his acceptance except skin color—something the fraternity was unwilling to do. Thirty years later he placed the Democratic party leadership in the same position.

The achievement of Ron Brown, as well as those mentioned above, is due, in large measure, to their ability to digest and apply the central rule of success: *Don't wait for opportunity—make it!*

The call of the twentieth century is for those who will climb into the rare air described by all who have ascended to a greater self-reliance. There is no corner of the market that is not seeking young men and women of ability, who will help themselves by relying on their own splendid talents.

There is some one thing that you can do better than anyone else. What is it? Search until you find *your area of excellence,* and then organize all of your forces and attack it with the belief that you are going to excel. Keep in mind, the man who complains he never had a chance probably hasn't the courage to take a chance. And the man who says it can't be done is busy getting out of the way of the man doing it. He who attempts the impossible has little competition. Make your opportunity as all who've embraced riches have done—*by seizing it!*

Self-Reliance Is Your Responsibility

So many times we witness the birth of another child born into the clutches of poverty within the black community. Born into a world of few resources and even less motivation, the child finds himself discriminated against at every turn. More often than I care to remember, I have personally observed this child mature into adulthood and consume the blight and decay that surround him, proclaiming to all, "What's the use? My obstacles are insurmountable!" He mistakenly concludes that he has every right to quit, to fail, blaming his conditions on the circumstances of his birth. Too many in similar conditions have succumbed to this seductive spirit of blaming others for their troubles. They would serve their purposes much better to examine their inherited advantages revealed within this text. What they would discover is a basic keynote to success: *You are accountable for what you do with your life!*

Are you disenchanted with the hand that life has dealt you? Then change those circumstances to some more favorable. Never give up hope. Without hope there is only emptiness between the cry of the newborn infant and the sound of the closing casket. Understand, you will get exactly out of life what you put into it. You will reap tomorrow what you've sown today.

No one knows this better than Darryl Stingley, a former star football player who was paralyzed from the waist down as a result of a ferocious hit during a football game. Though flat on his back, Stingley is conscious of the above axiom and refuses to give in to his circumstances. Here's what he says about the agony of his daily physical therapy: "Naturally, the pain means there's feeling there. I've developed a philosophy about pain: I like it because it makes a man think, and thinking makes a man wise, and knowledge and wisdom are the keys to a peaceful life. Life is what you make it!"

Responsibility and choice are opposite sides of the same coin. Freedom of choice and responsibility for one's own actions are precious gifts. Physical drudgery is not the intention of the Creator. It is the responsibility of each of us to carve out a meaningful life in our existence as we see fit. You have the power to either subdue the earth or starve.

Self-reliance is not a question of what someone can do on your behalf, *but what you can do for yourself.* And you can do whatever *you* decide to do. You don't have to work, pay taxes, have children, or even get out of bed in the morning—millions don't. You decide to do whatever you wish because it is profitable to you, and whatever you choose to do is the best *choice* among the alternatives available to aid you in reaching your goals. You have the choice to succeed on the scale of those highlighted in this book, or to exist in poverty and lack—if *you* so choose. And having made this choice, it is not the responsibility of your fellowman to serve as a never-ending caretaker. Though choice includes the right to do or not to do, it is equipped with the added requirement of responsibility. *Tough words?* I agree, but totally necessary if you are to experience the true riches of life.

There are two keys to this principle of responsibility that you would do well to remember:

1. The greater your lot, the greater your responsibility. The man in the biblical story who was given five talents to invest was answerable for the full responsibility of those five talents. If you acknowledge the talents given to you by the Creator—*imagination*, *creativity*,

the ability to control your thoughts, and *choice*—then you must know that you are eventually answerable for these talents also. This statement takes into account the different levels at which people start their lives, while holding each of us accountable at the level at which we find ourselves. Notice, I did not say that it removes this requirement of responsibility—for this is one of the greatest stumbling blocks of largesse.

2. Each day ask yourself, "What can this day mean to me as a person?" Upon deciding what it is that you desire, you then must become aware of how each experience fits into the meaning you seek. You are given twenty-four hours a day, seven days a week, in which you are held accountable. You are free to work at your leisure or extremely hard, if *you so desire. But you are accountable to life—life is not accountable to you.*

As you continue your journey through the pages of this text, take with you the following pledge of responsibility. Many of America's most eminent leaders have silently taken this oath. Grab the full message of Marcus Garvey, who reminded the masses of their task in the midst of poverty and rampant oppression: "Black men, you were once great; you shall be great again. Lose not courage or faith, go forward."

I, too, encourage you to be bold enough to step out on your own through individual initiative, independence, and greater self-reliance. *Your destiny is in your hands.* Do you wish to be self-reliant? Then let me see it in your actions. If I see that all-consuming, all-absorbing fight to succeed, braced by a dominant desire to be self-reliant, I will know that you have subscribed to the guidelines of success proposed by inspirational writer Danny Cox, who stated his Declaration of Personal Responsibility:

I currently possess everything I've truly wanted and deserved. This is based on what I have given to society to date. My possessions, my savings, and my lifestyle

are an exact mirror of me—my efforts and my contribution to society. What I have given, I have received.
If I am unhappy with what I have received, it is because, as of this date, I have not paid the required
price.

I have lingered too long in the quibbling stage. I
fully understand that time becomes a burden to me
only when it is empty. The past is mine, and at this
very moment, I am purchasing another twenty-four
hours of it. The future changes quickly into the past,
at a control point called the present moment. I not
only truly live at this point, but have full RESPON-
SIBILITY for the highest and best use of the irreplaceable
now.

I accept full RESPONSIBILITY for both the successes and failures in my life. If I am not what I desire
to be at this point, what I am is my compromise. I
choose no longer to compromise with my undeveloped
potential. I am the sum total of the choices I have
made, and I continue to choose daily. What I now put
under close scrutiny is the value of each upcoming
choice. Therein lies the quality of my future lifestyle.
Will my future belong to the "old me" or the "new
me"? That answer depends on my attitude toward personal growth at this very moment. What time is left is
all that counts, and this remaining time is my RE-
SPONSIBILITY. With a new-found maturity, I accept
full RESPONSIBILITY for how great I can become at
that which is most important to me. I AM SELF-
RELIANT!

8

A Pleasing Personality

"A man without a smiling face must not open a shop."
—ANCIENT CHINESE PROVERB

"Perseverance and tact are the two most important
qualities for the individual who wants to move
ahead."

—BENJAMIN DISRAELI

Having found the patterns that define the image of our
self, and having believed through faith that who we are
and what we are is a valuable asset to be cultivated, stimulated, and enjoyed, we then begin to think about how
we affect those individuals around us. Tact and skill
in handling people are required, more than ever, in our
fast-changing, highly technical world. Yet, this simple
principle does not require the use of special tools or techniques.

It has been said, and perhaps correctly, that "courtesy" represents the most valuable characteristic known
to the human race. Common courtesy costs nothing, yet
it returns dividends nearly a thousandfold if it is practiced as a matter of habit, in a spirit of sincerity. Today,
there remains a crying demand for those individuals who
understand that success depends on a number of factors,
among which is the *support of other people.* Basically,
the only hurdle between you and what you desire is the
support of others.

Furthermore, let's unmask the illusion that success is

altogether a matter of complicated knowledge. Or that all
we ever need to know are the intricacies of our jobs,
professions, or livelihoods. We are told by some of the
world's most able men and women that all of the technical knowledge that we can stuff into our minds, while
indeed important, still does not exceed in value the ability to achieve harmonious relationships with those around
us. Now, don't misunderstand—I certainly do not wish
to belittle the need for technical knowledge. But you must
realize that we commit few technical errors because we
are such experts at our jobs or occupations. *However, it
is shocking to observe how often we all bungle the job of
handling people.* If you develop the skill that caters to
the feelings, pride, and emotions of those around you,
not only will you unlock one of the doors to success, but
once inside you will be able to carry away all of the
riches that your pockets will allow. If you develop the
ability to skillfully handle people, you may not need any
other skill. However, on the other hand, if you do not
refine this characteristic, it will not matter what additional skills you may possess.

Too many of us are trying to substitute rules, logic,
and knowledge for appreciation, praise, and a better understanding of human feelings and emotions. You must
remember the immutable fact that the minds of people
are set into motion almost entirely by *the way they feel
toward others*—not by logic or reason.

The Lamplighter

In his classic tale *Don Quixote*, Miguel de Cervantes, the
sixteenth-century Spanish writer, tells of an old lamplighter who lived in a small village. It was the daily duty
of the lamplighter to care for and light the lamps on the
streets of Madrid. Each evening before dusk, he ventured
into the city with his sturdy ladder and supplies. He always started with the first lamp at the lower end of town.
With increasing precision he would meticulously ap-

proach each lamp post, position his ladder, and climb up to reach the wick. Almost methodically, he would then clean the glass windows and light the lamp. Down the ladder and on to the next lamp post he would go.

His daily routine would continue for many hours, lighting one lamp and then the next. He could be seen by the villagers as he disappeared up the hill, out of sight. The townspeople often commented that they could always tell where he had been by the lamps he had lit.

Each of us has the opportunity every day to light a lamp of kindness for someone else. Or, if we so choose, we can blow out the flame, causing darkness where light once shone. If we really desire, we can develop the skills that will enable us to get along graciously with others. Surely, each of us wants to live our lives so that people will say that they know *where we've been by the lamps we have lighted in the hearts and lives of others*. This is done through a pleasing personality.

What Is Personality?

What is personality? Personality is the sum total of an individual's mental, spiritual, and physical traits and habits that distinguish him from all others. It is the factor that more than anything else determines whether one is liked or disliked by his fellowman.

Your personality is like an enormous iceberg, since much lies beneath the surface. The "real you" is expressed by the simplest smile or friendliest gesture. The real you is not only the outwardly verbal, but also the deepest of personal feelings, which are nonverbal. Your personality consists of clearly visible expressions as well as the "invisible you" lying at the deepest level of your human experience. Personality transmutes into "persona"—the way you make others feel upon immediate contact. It is the manner in which you greet strangers; it is the way you walk and talk, as well as the things you do that provoke emotions in those around you.

Your personality is often revealed in the expression of your eyes and the words you use. Your personality portrait is painted for all the world to see, by the way you dress, the habits you cultivate, and how you treat others.

The degree to which we exhibit positive personality traits may vary greatly from person to person, but we all have them, or at least have the potential to develop them. If we encourage rather than suppress them, we become more proficient at summoning up the personality traits—on demand—that will help ensure success in any situation.

Do you smile while speaking, use tact in your conversation, and express sincerity, fairness, thoughtfulness, tolerance, and patience? Hopefully, you do. All are expressions of your personality. In simple terms, the impact your personality makes on those around you determines the way other people will view and react to you as a person. Never underestimate the power of a smile, a firm handshake, or a warm greeting. These are the tools that fashion long-lasting, positive relationships.

A Pleasing Personality

To reach your definite purpose, you must have a personality that meets certain standards. Few of us are born with sparkling personalities, and we may have allowed negative thinking and unattractive habits to spoil the impression that our personality may have transmitted in the past. Nonetheless, we can brighten our outward demeanor and raise the spirits of those with whom we come in contact, if we truly wish to do so.

What constitutes a pleasing personality? The Bible offers a well-known guideline: "And as ye would that men should do to you, do ye also to them likewise." This statement appears in various forms in many religions and philosophies. It is appropriately called the "Golden Rule." You and I are forced to coexist in a world inhabited by others. How we approach and treat all members of society—and how society reacts toward us—is partly determined by how well we adhere to this mandate.

Life Is a Mirror

Like attracts like. The way we hope others will respond to us is the manner in which we must express ourselves.

Perhaps you have heard it said that a child's behavior reflects the manner in which he or she is treated. If he is treated with love, he becomes loving; if he is treated spitefully and ridiculed, he becomes cruel and spiteful. To some extent the same is true in our lives. *We get from others what we give.* This is a basic function of our personality.

Life is a mirror that reflects your expressions. If you smile, it reflects a cheery disposition. If you are irritable, it shows a true picture of your contemptible self. In essence, what you say of others is said of you. You will find nothing in the world that you will not find in yourself first. Nature takes on your moods. If you rejoice, the world rejoices. If you trust, you are trusted. If you love, you are loved. If you hate, you are hated. You will cast your own reflection.

An Opera Star Uses the Golden Rule

Men and women have found the Golden Rule to contain all that was needed as they marched down the road to achievement. Leontyne Price, the celebrated opera singer, tells a fascinating story in which this principle changed her life.

In the late 1950s Leontyne Price was a schoolteacher fresh from the ranks of Central State University in Wilberforce, Ohio. Though she had graduated with honors at the top of her class, she remained unfazed by her accomplishments. Sadly, teaching offered little challenge to the talented young woman. She loved her students but was extremely bored. And why not? As a child she was able to read music before she could read books. Singing was her first love. An inner voice called to her, making her frustrated and depressed. She secretly longed for a career in the great concert halls. One day after school, as she watched the children playing outside, she began taking stock—the bitter with the sweet—and realized that she was at a crossroads. Beseeched by her fellow teachers to keep her job, she listened to the beating of her heart instead. The following day Leontyne resigned.

Leontyne was dead broke when she looked down the rainbow toward her dreams. She had all the qualities to become not only a good opera singer—but a great one! But would she get the chance?

In order to pursue her goal she would need additional training and substantial monetary support—maybe even a sponsor. Encouraged by her new sense of purpose, her parents supported her decision to sing. But as a product of limited means—Leontyne's father was a carpenter, and her mother a midwife—they could offer her everything *except money*. Without the added assistance for voice lessons, extensive travel, and other mounting expenses, a career leading to Carnegie Hall and Lincoln Center would be difficult, if not impossible. *But the harmony of the Golden Rule knows no boundaries or limits.*

Long before she ever dreamed of success, Leontyne spent many happy, carefree days in her hometown of Laurel, Mississippi. With her two closest friends, the Chisolm daughters, who lived nearby, life was fun-filled and full of new experiences. Though time and circumstances had split the playmates apart, their feelings and remembrances remained intact. During a periodic visit home to buoy her spirits, Leontyne sought out her ex-playmates, who had long since moved. Hoping to find her childhood friends, Leontyne was greeted by their mother.

Elizabeth Chisolm was a kind and gentle woman who had remembered her daughters' companion. During this brief visit, Leontyne shared with the woman her dreams and goals. As she peered forlornly through a neighbor's front-yard fence, Leontyne couldn't hide her pain. Almost apologetically, she told Mrs. Chisolm that she was prepared to resume her teaching career. Her dreams of entertaining millions as a singer would remain just that—dreams.

Before Leontyne had time to dry her eyes, the generous woman made a magnificent gesture. Mrs. Chisolm provided the skillful singer with much-needed funding, eventually helping her continue her studies at the prestigious Juilliard School of Music, studying under the renowned Florence Page Kimball, a former opera singer. But Mrs. Chisolm's support did not come unattached. Aware of the power of this principle, Elizabeth Chisolm stipulated that she would help the would-be opera star only if Leontyne would agree that if she ever occupied a position where she, Leontyne Price, could render a helping hand to any aspiring individual, she would do so, thereby passing on the torch of the Golden Rule. Price accepted the offer and has adhered to her agreement many times over, frequently coming to the aid of many young, struggling artists.

Since the Creator wound the hands of time, men and women have constantly preached the Golden Rule: "Do unto others as you would have them do unto you." Unfortunately, the world has all too often accepted the letter while completely missing the spirit of this divine guidance. Mankind has embraced this philosophy merely as a sound rule of ethical conduct, but has failed to comprehend the precept upon which it is based. Why? The answer lies within the various mental laws we discussed in the opening pages of this text.

There are mental laws through which all life operates. When you select the rule of conduct by which you'll guide yourself and your dealings with others, you will be fair and just if you realize that you are setting into motion a power that will in turn run its course back to you. It's your privilege to deal unfairly with those around you. But if you understand the law upon which the Golden Rule is based, you must know that your unjust attitudes will come home to roost.

If you wish to know what happens to a man who totally disregards the law upon which the Golden Rule is based, choose any individual in your community who lives for the single purpose of accumulating wealth, and who has no conscience as to how he accumulates that wealth. Study this man and you will observe there is no warmth, no kindness, no welcome to his words. He has become a slave to the desire of money; he is too selfish to help others enjoy it. It would be extremely foolish to equate success with this man. There can never be success without happiness, and no man can be happy without transmitting happiness to others.

The Secret of a Pleasing Personality

Though force can achieve many things, its use does not make for lasting relationships. When another person likes you, laughs with you, and harmonizes with you, then you can be sure this same individual will think with you, help you, and even share with you. A pleasing personality is one of your most important social tools.

What is the secret of a pleasing personality? We have all known them, people who just seem to attract others—friends, clients, or acquaintances. We say that people are drawn to such individuals, as if there were some physical force at work. This phrase is quite descriptive, for you cannot force someone to like another. But you can draw or attract people by satisfying the basic hungers prevalent in all human beings. The following story reveals one such need.

A very prominent black businessman arrived one morning in his downtown office, a couple of hours earlier than usual. He had some things he wanted to do before his employees reported to work. No one was there when he arrived except George, the custodian of the building.

George was a faithful employee with many years of service to the firm. When his boss walked into his office, there was George, as usual, emptying trash cans, dusting furniture, and cleaning the office.

When George's boss noticed him going about his routine, he said, "George, you know, as I look around the building, I can't help thinking what an asset you have been to our organization for all of these years. You have kept this place clean and tidy for our employees and customers to enjoy.

"George," he continued, "you are an important part of this organization, and I want you to know that I appreciate you and all that you have done."

George paused and then replied, "Thank you, sir," and walked out of the room with his dust cloth in hand.

A few minutes had passed while his boss settled down to work at his desk. Suddenly, the office door opened and in walked George. His eyes were moist, there was a tear on his cheek. His boss could not understand. He said, "What is wrong, George—did I say something to offend you?"

George forced a smile and then replied, "No sir, you did not offend me. But I have something I would like to share with you." A deep silence fell across the room. "You know, I have worked for this company for seventeen years—twelve of those years for you—and this morning is the first time anyone has ever told me that they appreciated anything I've ever done."

He continued, "I just want you to know, sir, that I appreciate what you said to me this morning more than I've ever appreciated my paycheck! I just wanted to let you know." He then turned and walked out of the room.

The deepest craving in human nature is the desire to be appreciated. Man will not give his best for money alone, but he will give everything possible for a bit of appreciation. When you resolve not to criticize or condemn, but instead look for every opportunity to drop a word of honest appreciation, you will find that others will desire your company. They will truly want to be around you. By making it a habit to give sincere and honest praise, you will have taken a giant step toward enhancing your own success and happiness.

Do you receive praise, approval, and appreciation at home or on your job? When is the last time you praised someone else or gave a sincere word of appreciation? The two go hand in hand.

Too many people today are frazzled. With circumstances as they are within many inner-city neighborhoods, emotions run high. When our emotions get out of control, which may be surprisingly often, we handle others with quickly chosen words, gestures, and decisions, emanating entirely from how *we feel*. However, it is much wiser to reverse the procedure. Set your feelings aside. Stop, listen, think, and reason with yourself. *Think how the other person feels, not how you feel.*

When you look into a mirror, you expect to see your reflection. Likewise, the other person is always looking for himself to be reflected *in your mirror—his ideas, his point of view*. Think of the pride, emotions, and feelings of others, not your own. You will be surprised how quickly people will acquiesce to *your* point of view. You can now see the opportunity and importance of treating people by the way *they* feel, and not the way *you* feel.

What a Pleasing Personality Can Do

Personality, to be successful, must be lastingly effective. The remarkable career of Daniel "Chappie" James points up the fact that a pleasing personality not only can open many doors, but can help you attain a high degree of efficiency.

Chappie James grew up in the darkest times of Jim Crow in Pensacola, Florida, when the city was a symbol of the South's racial wrongs. Years later he would overcome segregation in the armed forces to become the second black American promoted to the rank of general in the U.S. Air Force, and the fourth in the history of the military services. James's riches rested within his ability to effectively use the advice that his mother shared with him as a child.

"My mother taught me the basics," he reflected. "Love of God, love of country, and love of fellow man. And not to be so busy criticizing that you forget to look at the good which is in us all.

"With some people you may have to search a little bit harder to find that good, but everybody is worthy of praise and appreciation. Despite the injustices I've encountered, I knew the value of appreciation. If I could compliment a recruit or praise my support staff, I was more than happy to do it."

James carried this wisdom throughout his life. He had a knack of making those around him feel special by simply singling them out for tasks well-done. He sidestepped the myth that most people you meet feel superior to you in some way. He cut a path to the hearts of his subordinates by acknowledging their importance and contributions. He gave them what they desired most—*open and honest praise, and appreciation*.

I sincerely hope you don't overlook this simple but perhaps most meaningful gift that you can give to another person—*appreciation*.

A Simple Formula

If you still have lingering doubts that praise and gratitude have something akin to a miraculous power, study the next example. The story that follows may be old, but its message is still ahead of its time.

It was the custom of the old man to sit outside the wall of the ancient city where he lived, watching passersby come and go. He always sat in the shade, usually surrounded by children, retelling stories which they loved to hear. Through the course of the day, many travelers would stop to chat. One hot summer day a stranger stopped to visit for a few minutes with the old man, who was entertaining his young friends. The stranger approached the old man and asked, "I am thinking of moving to your fair city. Tell me, sir, what kind of people live here?"

Quickly the old man replied, "What kind of people live in the city where you're from?"

"The people in my town are unkind," said the stranger. "They cheat and steal and lie; they speak badly of each other. I am leaving that town because of the undesirable people who live there."

The old man gazed sadly at the stranger and said, "I'm sorry to inform you, but you will find the same type of people in this town." And without a word the stranger turned and walked away as the old man continued his tale to the children.

A short time later another stranger came down the road toward the gate. He, too, stopped to chat.

He said, "My good man, I need to move to a town such as yours. Tell me, sir, what type of people live here?"

The old man asked the same question, "What kind of people live in the town where you're from?"

The stranger replied, "The people in my town are good. They are friendly, courteous, and are always looking for an opportunity to do a good deed for someone. I truly hated to leave that town because of the warmth and kindness of its people, but my work requires that I move."

The old man clasped the hand of the traveler and said, "You'll find the same type of people here. *Welcome to our fine town.*" The stranger walked happily through the gate.

The children sat in silence. Finally, one of them approached the old man and asked, "Why, sir, didn't you tell those men the truth? You told one that our people were bad and the other that they were good."

The old man begged them to sit while he explained.

"I did tell the truth," he said. "You see, no matter where you go or what you do, you will find in other people just what you are looking for. *If you search for the good, you will find it; but if you look for the bad, that is what you will undoubtedly see.* Almost everyone has far more good qualities than bad. Always look for the best in others."

Appreciation and Praise

Robert Louis Stevenson once said, "I know what pleasure is, for I have done good work." The ego craves appreciation and receives pleasure from the approval from others. Approval, praise, and love are the great motivators in life. When we're patted on the back we feel happy and worthwhile. When we're criticized we feel inadequate and out of balance. Why do we feel good when we are praised? Because praise is an acknowledgment and confirmation of our worth. Praise tells us that we are respected, needed, and appreciated—*that we belong*.

So often we withhold praise. Sometimes because we don't want to appear patronizing or too personal. At other times we simply don't make the effort. We forget that everyone enjoys appreciation, a pat on the back, a word of praise. Praise is the confirmation of our own worth. Praise is welcome testimony that our self-esteem is justified. It tells us that we are needed.

So praise others, and don't forget to praise yourself when you deserve it. Praise life. It is so easy and so pleasurable to participate in someone's life by saying a few constructive words. Sincere praise takes little effort and less time. But the effect is enormous and immediate. The recipients of your praise will hold their heads higher and try a bit harder to confirm your opinion. You will feel a glow from the warmth you have spread.

Remember the key insight uncovered by Chappie James. Look for the good and learn to appreciate small things, as well as large. Small contributions and simple actions also deserve your support. Good is good wherever you find it.

Far too few of us recognize just how important it is to our world that credit be given where credit is due. People everywhere—in the home, school, and office—hunger for praise and appreciation. *Wouldn't it be a wonderful idea if mankind engaged in such a generous undertaking?*

"The measure of mental health is the disposition to find good everywhere," said Emerson. If you want to increase your own peace of mind and personal happiness, there is no more certain formula than to start looking for the good in others. The next time you find yourself confronted by someone who irritates you, try searching for areas in which to compliment him. Not only will his attitude change for the better, but so, too, will your opinion of him change.

There are subtle rules to remember when giving praise and appreciation. Use these keys as a daily guide.

- Praise must be sincere. Mere flattery is shallow. Praise a person for what he does, not what he is.
- Thank others by name. Personalize your appreciation by calling others by their names.
- Be generous with kind statements, and thank others when they least expect it.
- Take into consideration the other person's point of view.

Look around. As you do, think for a moment. Are the most successful people you know those with the highest intellect or superior skills? Are those who live life to the fullest and who receive the most fulfillment smarter than you? If you stop and think for a moment, chances are the most successful and happiest people are those who have mastered the principle of a pleasing personality. There are millions of people today who are self-conscious, shy, timid, ill at ease in social situations, and who have low self-esteem. They've never realized that their real problem is one of human relations. They have never discov-

ered that their failure as people is really a failure to learn
how to handle and treat those around them.

First Impressions

It has been said that God looks upon the heart. Though
this may be true, *He is the only one who does*. You get
only one chance to cast a first impression.

A musician can often listen to the very first note of a
piece of music and tell you in what key the composition
is written. The manner in which you approach those you
come in contact with—your first words, your actions and
conduct—sound the keynote for your entire relationship.
You are more responsible for how you are accepted than
anyone else. While many people worry about what others
think of them, few realize that the world forms its opinions of them largely from the opinion they have of themselves. If you aren't accepted as you would like, maybe
the blame lies within. Act as if you are a nobody, and
the world will treat you at your own value. But act as if
you are a somebody—sincere, honest, and praisewor-
thy—and the world has no choice but to treat you as such.

Emphasize those aspects of your personality that you
like in yourself and that others find attractive. Because
we are all complex individuals with a full range of positive and negative emotions, it would be totally unrealistic to expect everyone you meet to appreciate every
aspect of your personality. But by directing your thoughts,
you can control the kind of person you wish to become;
a positive thinker becomes a positive person, someone
others like to be around.

A gracious, genial presence, a pleasing personality, a
refined, fascinating manner are welcomed where beauty
is denied and where mere wealth is turned away. A pleasing personality will make a better impression than the
best education or the highest attainments. A sincere first
impression, even without great ability, often advances one

when talent and special training will not. Everywhere, a pleasing first impression wins its way.

How to Make a Favorable First Impression

How can you make a favorable first impression? You can begin by making a conscious effort to upgrade your personal appearance and habits. High achievers display a simple, radiating charm. They project a warm glow that emanates from the inside outward. Most importantly, their self-esteem is transmitted with a smile, which is the universal language that opens doors, melts defenses, and saves thousands of words. Their smile is the light in the window that tells all there is a caring, sharing person inside.

The successful recognize that first impressions are powerful and create fond memories. They understand that interpersonal and professional relationships can be won or lost in a matter of seconds during a conversation. They have learned through experience that—fairly or unfairly—people project and respond to an intuitive or gut feeling, which is nearly instantaneous.

Clifton R. Wharton knows the power that a favorable first impression can project. Few individuals of any race have surpassed his records of achievement. Throughout his distinguished career, Wharton has blazed new paths and has placed together an incredible string of "significant firsts," including his past position as president of Michigan State University. Today he is the chief executive officer of America's largest private pension fund. Though armed with little experience in pension fund management, his poise and disposition so impressed the corporate board of the Teachers Insurance and Annuity Association/College Retirement Equities Fund that during their search in 1987 for a CEO, Wharton was unanimously chosen for the prestigious position.

Don't misunderstand—this is not to say that Dr. Wharton did not possess the skills and attributes for the office he assumes, because he does. His professional and scholarly credentials are impeccable. Among his peers he is widely regarded as a genteel, diplomatic, and intelligent man. But in large part, Dr. Wharton's easygoing, personable, and statesmanlike manner landed him this position. The man with an attractive personality and disarming smile knows how to make a first and lasting impression.

"I always try to treat others with the same dignity and respect that I am afforded," Dr. Wharton says. "I look for the best in those around me and then search for ways to enhance their strengths."

Is it any small wonder as to why he is the chairman of one of the nation's largest private pension funds?

Scan the pages of history and you will find that the majority of leaders possess this unselfish spirit, this cordial, kind manner toward all.

How a Thirteen-Year-Old Girl Scout Sold 32,000 Boxes of Cookies!

The business world demands a magnetic personality. A favorable first impression becomes crucial. Read the story told by Markita Andrews, a thirteen-year-old Girl Scout who discovered the impact that a favorable first impression and a pleasing personality can have on others.

I was seven years old and in my second year of scouting when I learned a valuable lesson about sales in particular, and people in general.

My mother and I moved from California to New York when I was six. I was in the first grade and, unfortunately, didn't have many friends. My aunt, who lived in the same apartment building, suggested I join the Girl Scouts in order to meet other children. I took her advice and joined a local Brownie troop. Our first major project was to sell Girl Scout cookies.

Since there were few Scouts in my building, I decided this would be a good place to start. At first I was sort of shy and didn't have much confidence. I didn't know a thing about selling. My troop leader told me to do my best and to have fun, which is what I did. I managed to sell 648 boxes my first year using a few sales techniques.

Things began to happen fast. I sold 1148 boxes my second year and 1754 my third. *And I have been selling ever since!* People began to approach me about giving talks on my selling skills. I spoke at my first convention—a meeting of the American Bankers Insurance group. This led to other engagements: IBM, AT&T, Pacific Telephone, and other corporations. When I was nine, I made a movie with Walt Disney Productions called *The Cookie Kid*, which is still shown at various sales conventions.

Ironically, I haven't read many books on selling, though there are tons of them. To me, most of them are confusing and difficult to understand. But selling is *about people, not ideas*. My strategy isn't something to follow word by word. It stems from a simple approach that I have learned along the way. You may want to keep these thoughts in mind:

You have to think about how you come across to others. Being polite and having good manners are the most important keys. You would think that the first thing people notice about you is your appearance. But generally this is not the case. What others notice more than looks are the positive things that you possess—your smile, your self-confidence, your sincerity, and your attitude. All of these qualities have a bearing on how others perceive you.

When selling, I usually engage in a friendly conversation with my prospect. I try to find his interests and usually offer a kind word. My goal is to become his friend, not just to sell him cookies. I have found that a friendly smile, a firm handshake, and a sincere interest in the other person work wonders. I have discovered that this is what people notice first, and immediately base the relationship upon. People like doing business with people they like. *You have only one chance to make a first impression.* Make it count!

Here is a young girl who carefully took stock of her abilities and her circumstances as she saw them. Exhibiting faith, hard work, and a pleasing personality, she seized undreamed-of success. By effectively employing the guidelines of a pleasing personality, Chappie James, Clifton Wharton, and Markita Andrews have earned enviable records in their chosen fields.

A Program for Improvement Through Personality

Your personality is the medium by which you will negotiate your way through life. Your personality will demonstrate, to a large extent, your ability to associate and cooperate with others with a minimum of friction and opposition. Analyze your personality carefully and courageously. Take inventory and list all personal assets and liabilities. Philosophers teach men and women to know themselves. Self-analysis begins with a positive mental attitude and strict self-discipline, based on the sincerity to become a better you. Study the following stepping-stones to success.

1. *Don't Criticize, Condemn, or Complain.*
   Any fool can criticize, condemn, or complain—and most fools do. But it takes character and self-control to be understanding and forgiving. Instead of condemning others, try to understand them. Figure out why they do what they do. That's more profitable and intriguing than criticism; and it breeds sympathy, tolerance, and kindness.
2. *Show Interest in Others.*
   The individual who is not interested in his peers has the greatest difficulties in life and provides the greatest injury to others. It is from this camp that all hu-

man failures spring. You can generate more sincere friendship by becoming interested in others than you can by trying to get other people interested in you. When dealing with others, look for common ground. Identify the subjects you are both interested in, not just those *you* like or are particularly knowledgeable about. Conversations should be two-way. Listening is just as important as speaking.

3. *Integrity.*

Integrity develops a sound and dependable character. It also attracts others who believe in this trait. Practicing integrity provides you with a feeling of self-reliance and self-respect, and gives a clear conscience.

4. *Be Flexible.*

Flexibility is the art of being able to shift gears when necessary, in order to fit changing circumstances. Flexibility of personality enables you to meet changing and difficult situations without losing self-control. Flexibility of mind enables you to understand and sympathize with another's point of view.

5. *Tactfulness.*

You are tactful when you do and say the right thing at the right time. Tactfulness is a way of relating to others without being crude, embarrassing, or threatening to someone else's sensitivity. Be discreet about the subjects you choose to discuss. Don't discuss controversial topics such as religion, politics, or race at inappropriate times or places. Don't gossip or agree with someone who does. Always assume there are two sides to every story; you are only hearing one of them. Don't boast of your own achievements; deeds always speak louder than words. Tactfulness teaches the value of edification: building up those around you and never minimizing the achievements of others.

6. *Appropriateness of Attire.*

How you dress can also have a significant impact on how others perceive you. The best-dressed person usually is the one whose clothes and accessories are so well chosen and whose entire ensemble is so well harmonized that the individual does not attract undue attention. The award-winning fashion designer Willi Smith once remarked, "One of the peculiarities of people's attitudes toward clothing is that they won't dress for success *until* they have arrived. This is a mistake. People should start dressing for success *before* they're successful—not after!"

If your resources are minimal, neatness will provide adequate substitution. Notice the cut of your clothes, the style of your hair, the condition of your shoes and nails; always give yourself the once-over. Why? Because looking your best is one of the secrets of being the best.

7. *Keen Sense of Humor.*

The push for a higher goal or a change of position takes extra effort and energy. You must work harder and longer, take more risks, and adjust to change. The same traits that make you an achiever are also the most stressful. Humor helps defuse the pressure and restore equilibrium. Humor also improves the quality of life and makes the climb to success much more enjoyable. A keen sense of humor sends a good personality a longer distance than it could have traveled with a sorrowful face. Laugh and the world laughs with you; weep and you weep alone. A keen sense of humor will keep you from taking yourself too seriously—a tendency toward which too many of us are inclined.

8. *Punctuality.*

Time is your most precious tool. John H. Johnson of the Johnson publishing empire once told a friend that he regarded every hour of his time to be worth $1000. Time is worth everything to you, and even more to your associates. The common carelessness and indifference to the value of time is a real life tragedy. It was anonymously written that "promptness is a contagious inspiration.'' Whether it be an inspiration or an acquired trait, it is one of the practical virtues of an attractive personality.

Many a wasted life dates its ruin from a lost five minutes. ''Too late'' can be read between the lines on the tombstone of many a man who has failed. And it is a fact—a man who keeps his time, as a rule, will keep his word. ''Better late than never,'' is not half as good a maxim as ''better never late.''

9. *Effective Speech.*

The area in which a neglected education first appears is in self-expression, oral or written. It makes little difference how many diplomas or college degrees you may own. If you cannot use words to move an idea from one point to another, your education is incomplete. Not everyone may have the benefit of inherited wealth, but no one need be impoverished in language, nor need anyone be deprived of the distinction that comes from using words with strength and grace.

Effective speaking is a matter of desire, plus reading and study. Whether we care to admit it or not, when a person opens his or her mouth and talks, he announces to all within listening distance his level of thought. Every word we speak gives someone a chance to find out how much—or how little—we know. When we dress appropriately and arrive on time for an important meeting, and then ask, ''Where's he at?'' we have, with that simple, innocuous preposition, stripped ourselves to our underwear for all to see. There is correct speech and incorrect speech—neither can be hidden. Thirty to sixty minutes a day of serious reading and study will offset the poorest education.

Your personality is your greatest asset or your greatest liability. It embraces everything that you control—your mind, your body, and your soul. Your personality is *you*. It shapes the nature of your thoughts, deeds, and relationships with others. Visualize yourself as a loving friend to everyone, radiating sincere warmth, interest, and affection. This is the path toward achieving a pleasing personality.

For those who are sincerely interested in self-improvement, a list of the twenty traits of a pleasing personality is included. Study them for the next thirty days, making a more comprehensive list of those qualities that you already possess. After you have evaluated your finer points, make an additional list of traits you wish to improve. Take careful notes and reflect upon them as often as possible. You will discover at the end of this thirty-day period that you, too, can be a lamplighter, lighting the lamps of all those whom your personality touches.

Twenty Traits of a Pleasing Personality

1. A positive mental attitude
2. Visible interest in others
3. Integrity
4. Flexibility
5. Tactfulness
6. Proper attire
7. Sense of humor
8. Punctuality
9. Effective speech
10. Friendly smile
11. Control of emotions
12. Sincerity of purpose
13. Patience
14. Ability to listen
15. Respect opinions of others
16. Humility
17. Courtesy
18. Poise
19. Hope and ambition for success
20. Enthusiasm

Practically all success in life hinges on a pleasing personality. Analyze yourself against these twenty traits. Be open and honest. An accurate assessment might shorten your path to riches.

9

Enthusiasm!

"If it's hard, then do it hard."

—LES BROWN

"To become enthusiastic—you must act enthusiastic!"
—FRANK BETTGER

"Nothing great was ever achieved without enthusiasm."
—RALPH WALDO EMERSON

I don't know of any self-generated force that will do more for you than enthusiasm. Thomas Edison once said, "When a man dies, if he can pass enthusiasm along to his children, he has left them an estate of incalculable value." Experience proves that to be true. Enthusiasm is more than wealth; it is a zest for living.

Let me offer an example: Two men work side by side for the same employer and have identical tasks. One works in a half-hearted manner, is bored by his duties, and is pleased to see the clock approach the end of his shift. The other labors with gusto, finding his work exciting and rewarding, presenting new challenges each day. Now who do you think is going to do a better job? Which one is committed to excellence? *Which one is going to get ahead?*

When a young man begins thinking about career opportunities, he may ask, "What is a good field to get into?" A wise response would be, "The field that you can pour yourself into with the most enthusiasm. There is no future in any job, the future is in you."

The president of a railroad was on an inspection tour when he encountered a laborer in a section gang whom he had worked with for a number of years. He greeted his old friend warmly, remembering the "old days." The tired old laborer said, "John, you've gone a long way from the time we were laying tracks together." The executive shook his head and said, "No, Bill, that isn't quite correct. You were laying tracks—*I was building a railroad.*" Therein lies the difference. *Are you just laying tracks, or are you building a railroad?* No matter what conditions prevail, do you inject your task with enthusiasm?

Orison Swett Marden referred to enthusiasm as "the great force within us which is perpetually prodding us to do our best." Marden called enthusiasm an intense feeling of emotion known as a burning desire, without which words fail to carry conviction, deeds fail to impress, and actions fall short of their intended mark.

Napoleon Hill revealed his deep understanding of the power of enthusiasm when he stated: "One feels the noblest, and acts the best, when the inspiration of enthusiasm drives him onward toward the attainment of some preestablished goal."

Martin Luther King helps us bring the idea of enthusiasm into the context of our own experience. He preached, "If a man is called to be a street sweeper, he should sweep streets even as Michelangelo painted or Beethoven composed music or Shakespeare wrote poetry. He should sweep streets so well that all the hosts of heaven and earth will pause to say, here lived a great street sweeper who did his job well." *That is enthusiasm—the enthusiasm that motivates!*

Enthusiasm Is Power

What is enthusiasm and how do you use it? Loosely translated, "enthusiasm" means "the God within."

Webster defined it as the "strong excitement of feeling on behalf of a cause or subject; ardent zeal or fervor."

Enthusiasm is the expression of the dynamic vitality in your mental outlook—the way you walk, talk, and act. It is the result of your motivation and your physical magnetism and energy. It is the light in your eye, the timbre of your voice, the vigor in your handshake. It is the element that can kindle a fire under your chief aim and fan it into a burning desire. It is a quality that you must use as you march toward greatness.

Enthusiasm begins with definiteness of purpose. Your goals must be so firmly entrenched that they're a part of your being. Unless you have the courage of your convictions, it is impossible to enthusiastically sell your ideas, your hopes and desires to others.

Why should you want to know all you can know, learn all that you can learn, about the power of enthusiasm? Because more than any other quality or trait of human personality, enthusiasm has been the companion of success and every achievement. Enthusiasm is that inspiration that makes you wake up and live. It is the producer of confidence that cries to the world, "I've got what it takes!"

Enthusiasm is power! When that power is released to support definiteness of purpose, and is constantly renewed by faith, it becomes an irresistible force for which poverty and temporary defeat are no match. Enthusiasm is the magnetism of projected energy that can be caught by anyone. It's contagious, and when you've mastered its force and energy, you'll be amazed at the power you possess. Enthusiasm spreads like a prairie fire before the wind. It is the bolt of lightning that blasts every obstacle from its path. It is a state of mind that inspires and arouses you to put *action* into your tasks, and transmits the impetus to action as you inch closer to your goals.

Enthusiasm is emotion management. If you are able to transmit enthusiasm to others, you have the ability to control the emotional climate of any situation. When you

can generate true enthusiasm, you can break the preoccupation of those around you, making others take notice
and listen to your ideas. You can capture attention through
enthusiasm and guide that attention in any direction you
so choose.

Enthusiasm is a universal language. It is a state of mind
that we all recognize. Why? Because everyone is attracted by the magnetism of an enthusiasm that is genuinely felt and openly expressed.

One of the major reasons why so few of us know so
little about enthusiasm is that we frequently confuse its
signs with something quite different. At sporting events,
political rallies, and even religious services, we often see
a mass display of exuberance which we call enthusiasm.
Call it mass hysteria, group hypnosis, or crowd reaction
in its mildest forms—but it is not enthusiasm. At least
not in its formal definition.

The temporary "one-shot" excitement that comes
from attending a football game or backing a political
candidate is the result of group interaction and reaction.
It is neither true nor lasting. Genuine enthusiasm is as
enduring as any of our finer human qualities—love, sincerity, courage, or faith. And like these qualities, enthusiasm is the outward reflection of a deep emotion that
originates within.

There is a difference between *having enthusiasm* and
being enthusiastic. An instilled enthusiasm connotes a
positive mental attitude—an internal impelling force of
intense emotion. It always implies an objective cause that
is pursued with devotion. Being enthusiastic is a com-
pelling external expression of action. When you act enthusiastically, you accentuate the power of suggestion and
self-suggestion. Thus, the person who acts enthusiastic
by speaking in an enthusiastic manner develops genuine
enthusiasm.

When a salesman is imbued with a strong conviction,
he literally radiates his feelings with emotion. And so it
is with enthusiasm. It springs from the heart, and it is as

difficult to mask as is deep sorrow or abiding love. In fact, enthusiasm is the most important factor in successful selling. It converts the mediocre salesman into a master salesman. There has never been a top-notch salesman who didn't use the persuasive powers hidden in enthusiasm.

Another cause of confusion regarding the nature of enthusiasm is that many of us are embarrassed to express our true feelings. We either try to force our emotions or suppress our feelings by being sedate. In either case, the effectiveness, the real power of enthusiasm, is lost. The power of enthusiasm lies within its natural and unrestrained expression. It is not surprising, therefore, that Andrew Carnegie said, "Enthusiasm is a great leavening force in the mental world, for it gives power to your purpose. It helps to free your mind of negative influences and brings you peace of mind. Lastly, it inspires personal initiative, both in thought and physical action. It is very difficult for one to do his best when he does not feel and display enthusiasm."

There is no limit to what can be accomplished through enthusiasm. Take note of the following examples.

Armed with a fervent zest for scholarship and undying enthusiasm, George Washington Carver asked his Creator to unveil the secrets to the universe. "Little man," he was told, "your mind is too small to be burdened with such matters. It's best you choose just one of my creations and examine it in its entirety." Thus, Carver devoted his life to the full examination of the peanut, and revolutionized America's agricultural system in the process. He became the grand architect of America's $100 billion peanut industry.

Possessing nothing but an unrelenting enthusiasm, Arthur A. Schomburg still ranks as the foremost bibliophile and Afro-American archivist. In 1926, the Carnegie Foundation offered him the then incredible sum of $10,000 for his collection of books, prints, and manuscripts on the "dark continent." Attracted to African history since childhood, Schomburg had recorded every known fact he could find on the history of his people. His early research was to serve him well in debates and open discussions with white classmates, some of whom would declare that the black man had never achieved anything of note. On such occasions he was able to refute their ignorance. Known for his oratorical eloquence and memorable passages, Schomburg's enthusiasm for African history was apparent as he shared his knowledge to all who would listen.

Paul Robeson, both scorned and rebuked for his racial views, convinced an unbelieving world—through enthusiasm—that blacks could excel no matter the endeavor, no matter the odds. *And what better proof did he need than himself?* The youngest son of forbearing parents, Robeson was without peer. A world-class athlete, a distinguished scholar, an accomplished linguist, and a convincing actor, Robeson was culturally refined beyond his years. A member of Phi Beta Kappa, and later a Columbia Law School graduate, Robeson walked with kings but was loved by the common man. Regardless of the environment or the circumstance, Paul Robeson always managed to ignite his peers with a great deal of enthusiasm.

Matthew Henson stood literally on top of the world when he became the first man to reach the North Pole. Henson's unparalleled accomplishment holds a high place in the annals of what was previously labeled "impossible." Of course, the greater part of credit goes to Robert E. Peary, one of America's most courageous explorers. But Henson's role was so vitally important that it seems safe to say that had there been no Matthew Henson, Peary's impossible voyage might have ended like all the others—in failure.

History calls them scientist, historian, scholar, and explorer, and they were. But they were also enthusiasts in a less than enthusiastic world. They succeeded because they *projected enthusiasm* that sprang from the heart and the inner recesses of the soul.

The Source of Enthusiasm

You may ask, if enthusiasm springs from the heart, from within, how do I go about generating it? Frank Bettger, one of the world's best-known salesmen, spent a lifetime answering this question. For more than twenty years Bettger was among the top five salesmen—nationally—in the highly competitive insurance industry. During an illustrious selling career, he made more than 40,000 sales calls and developed many sure-fire techniques that helped thousands increase their sales volume. Because of his enormous sales success, he was called "Mr. Enthusiasm" by his peers. Frank Bettger said the key to enthusiasm can be reduced to five words: "To become enthusiastic—act enthusiastic!"

Many of us are cursed with mediocrity simply because we cannot, with simple honesty, become enthusiastic about our chief aim or purpose. Many of us have been taught, erroneously, since childhood, to contain our enthusiasm—to suppress or quell our zeal. Then, as adults, through this habit of repression, we become inhibited and try to hide our enthusiasm instead of expressing it naturally. Not surprisingly, few of us are award-winning actors, and that's what it would take to act out an enthusiasm that we do not feel.

Elmer Wheeler, who during the 1950s claimed the title "America's No. 1 Salesman" and had an almost legendary reputation for enthusiasm, stressed another facet of the same solution. Wheeler said, "If you want to become an enthusiastic person, align yourself with a product, idea, or purpose that you can become enthusiastic about." His statement, like Bettger's, points you in the right direction.

Effective enthusiasm must be based on an honest opinion. Contrary to popular belief, people are not born with enthusiasm. It is developed by the correct combination of three very essential ingredients:

INTEREST
KNOWLEDGE
BELIEF

I say correct combination because these qualities must be developed in this sequence and progression. *Interest*, *knowledge*, and *belief* are key words because of their close relationship. When they are combined with desire or purpose, they give one access to unlimited power.

Without interest, knowledge is lost—our minds simply will not comprehend the facts. Without knowledge there is no genuine or lasting belief, only superstition. And without belief, we never develop interest. If you combine both definitions—Bettger's and Wheeler's—you're given a clearer understanding of how to cultivate and maintain a newfound enthusiasm. Having done so, you will express an interest in ideas, products, or services about which you will have knowledge and belief. This generates the power of enthusiasm.

Interest—the First Step to Enthusiasm

Most people will agree that the first step to enthusiasm is interest. Certainly, enthusiasm is much easier to generate when it concerns something we like, something that draws our attention. But is it possible to be enthusiastic about something we don't like or have little interest in? The answer is both yes and no. If you mean genuine enthusiasm, the answer is an emphatic *no*. You cannot be genuinely enthusiastic about anything without being interested in it. At this point disbelievers seem ready to quit. They offer the following logic: "I could never be enthusiastic about my job, my company, my product, or my present circumstances, because I've lost all interest." On rare occasions I've advised individuals to make a change, either of vocation or location, simply because I felt they were in a place or field to which they were not well-suited. However, in the vast majority of circumstances, the only change that was really needed was one of attitude, not activity.

Imagine the pandemonium that would exist if everyone who was not interested in his or her work or occupation suddenly decided to make a change or seek greener pastures. What is most startling is that interest can be inspired. Somehow we get the idea that our interests are hereditary, that we're born with them in much the same manner that we are born with physical characteristics. This simply is not true. Interests are a social development of man, a by-product of our environment and experience, and like habits, they can be changed.

How can you develop an interest in something you care little about? Developing such an interest cannot be possible unless there is a reason why you should cultivate such an interest. Without motivation there is no purpose. Imagine that you're in a line of work in which you have lost complete interest, but you can't bring yourself to switch jobs, fearing that you will be forced to start over. You also realize that you won't advance any higher than your current level unless you somehow recapture your former interest and enthusiasm for your position.

You have good reason for developing an interest—that's motivation. And since you want to, you decide to do it—that's purpose. The rest is fairly easy. Interest is nothing more than unsatisfied curiosity. The reason you lost interest, initially, is because you satisfied your first wave of curiosity and neglected to maintain a fresh mental outlook. Subsequently, you stopped asking questions and seeking additional information regarding your situation or circumstance. But the moment your inquisitive nature resurfaces, you will immediately begin to rediscover interest.

The steps to this process are straightforward. First, define your purpose, thereby creating motivation. And second, search for unsatisfied curiosity that will help you discover interest. This is the key to developing the power of enthusiasm. Attitude is the motivating influence that will help you complete your task. By searching for the challenges and possibilities inherent in a goal, no matter the obstacles or odds, you can make the quest for its attainment just as exciting as your favorite hobby or recreation.

Knowledge—the Second Step to Enthusiasm

Just as interest is a product of man's social development, so too is knowledge a product of his intellectual development. This is the second step in developing the power of enthusiasm. Though few of us are relentless in our quest for knowledge, the pursuit of knowledge never has been and never will be impossible. Regardless of educational background, we can acquire knowledge on any subject if our interest is great enough.

Ask questions, search for answers, pursue ideas, until you are convinced of their significance. Age, health, social position, or present conditions have no bearing on your ability to learn. If you desire specific knowledge in the field of your choice, search for it, find it, and absorb it.

Knowledge is a crucial ingredient of enthusiasm because it determines direction in developing the power of enthusiasm. The degree of your level of enthusiasm is dependent in large measure on how much knowledge you possess on any particular subject. Why? Because knowledge is your only protection against the assaults of doubts, fears, worries, and indecision; without knowledge there is no real belief. Without knowledge, you will find your enthusiasm dimming with the first hint of weakness as you strive to reach your goal. And as you encounter other suspicions, your enthusiasm dies and interest is lost. Know all there is to know concerning your field—know the structure, the content, the advantages, the benefits and weaknesses of your product or service. Once you do, you'll find yourself on the threshold of belief.

Belief—the Third Step to Enthusiasm

You have learned that many lives have been changed because of belief and faith. Belief also plays a vital role in the development of enthusiasm. For example, though you know it is impossible to breathe underwater, you *believe* that man is not a fish only after you've felt your lungs almost bursting from lack of air.

It is impossible to be enthusiastic without belief and interest. It is emotional belief that releases the stored power of enthusiasm. Your belief, like any other habit or trait, can be learned. You can acquire the technique of emotional belief just as you acquired the ability to swim, play chess, or ride a bike.

None of us is born with a belief in anything. We learn to believe in our families, our friends, and our religions. Above all, we learn to believe emotionally in ourselves.

To create genuine enthusiasm we must combine a kindled interest and acquired knowledge with the emotional impact of sincere, unequivocal belief. Each of these qualities supports the other. The more interest you generate, the more knowledge you gain; and the more knowledge you gain, the greater your emotional belief. Consequently, you will reflect more enthusiasm.

There's no question that enthusiasm based on interest, knowledge, and belief is the critical difference between success and failure. Wherever you find an outstanding success in business or the professions, you may be sure that behind that success is an individual who has applied the principle of *enthusiasm*.

What Enthusiasm Can Do

Carter G. Woodson was respectfully called the "Father of Black History." As an elementary school teacher in his native Virginia, he contended that the black man had an important past. Born in the remote town of New Canton, Virginia, Woodson found his early schooling so limited and of such poor quality that he was later justified in saying that he never attended school at all. At seventeen he worked in West Virginia's coal mines. But so great was his love of knowledge that, despite the backbreaking labor, he managed to study such rigorous and demanding courses as Latin and Greek during the early morning hours in silent isolation.

After three years of self-education, he found his path leading upward. He received bachelor's and master's degrees from the University of Chicago, and a doctorate from Harvard. By 1965, fifteen years after his death, his *enthusiasm* for black history had spread. As the principal founder of Black History Week, Dr. Woodson expanded the consciousness of a nation, demanding that black history be taught in the public schools. As a result, educators developed programs and curriculums that filled an obvious gap in the literature, and America now sets aside one month each year to celebrate the contributions of Afro-Americans. Why? Because Carter G. Woodson *believed* in black history.

In 1893, Daniel Hale Williams validated his theories on abdominal and chest surgery by becoming the first surgeon to successfully operate on the human heart. In addition to his pioneering surgery, Dr. Williams organized America's first black-owned hospital, Provident Hospital in Chicago, Illinois. But it was his open-heart surgery and *enthusiasm* for new and innovative procedures that became the clarion call for treating heart disease. Why? Because Dr. Daniel Hale Williams *believed*.

The pointless remark "It's a man's world" is a myth, a mere assemblage of words. But generations of women have heard this old wives' tale, believed it, and thereby constructed unnecessary barriers in their lives. The ever-resourceful Suzanne de Passe proved that the world belongs not only to men, but to women as well. As president of Motown Productions, she describes the key to success in the following manner: "You have to keep your mind on what is truly important and focus your enthusiasms on your goal.''

Using resilience, belief, and by *focusing her enthusiasms on her goal*, de Passe grasped the true nature of her unique powers and pushed ahead until she reached her objective. She set her sights on the highly competitive entertainment field.

The product of a broken inner-city home, de Passe dropped out of college in 1966 to work as a talent coordinator for a New York nightclub. After several years of sporadic work, she grew disillusioned with the business and thought seriously of quitting. But success was hers to achieve, and after a fateful meeting with Motown founder and chairman Berry Gordy, she convinced him of her chief aim.

Two years after joining Motown Records, de Passe signed such artists as Lionel Richie and The Jackson Five. Her own talents expanded to writing, and she produced several TV shows and movies, including a Diana Ross special, *Motown Returns to the Apollo*, and *Lady Sings the Blues*, for which she was nominated for an Academy Award. With her instinct for discovering promising new talent and untapped film projects, de Passe is well on her way to becoming a major force in Motown in the 1990s. And let there be no confusion as to the power that carried her to the top—*enthusiastic belief!*

James Weldon Johnson condensed his thoughts on human rights for black Americans by writing *The Autobiography of an Ex-Coloured Man*. His book was widely read by Americans from all walks of life and became an integral part of the newly developing National Association for the Advancement of Colored People. Several years later Johnson made an even greater impact on the minds of black Americans by composing a spiritually moving song—''Lift Ev'ry Voice and Sing''—that today is called the Negro National Anthem. Like blacks of his day, he envisioned a land of freedom, hope, and opportunity. Why? Because James Weldon Johnson *believed*.

Enthusiasm flows contagiously from one mind to another. Success is attained by the application of a combination of the many powers of the mind. There is a saying that declares, "Everything a man needs comes to him when he is ready to use it." Begin now. Make the best possible use of the resources at your disposal—the power and freedom to direct your mind to whatever goal you so choose. Condition your mind to attract that which it needs. Having selected a definite purpose, use enthusiasm. Enthusiasm is a power that becomes an irresistible force for which poverty and temporary defeat are no match.

Enthusiasm Sells!

How does the power of enthusiasm sell? How do you make it work for you? Harvard psychologist William James answered these questions in the latter part of the nineteenth century with the announcement of a startling new theory. James noted that it had always been assumed that any given situation involving *action* provoked *emotion*. James, however, contended that the exact opposite was closer to the truth. He believed that emotion or enthusiasm drives the individual to action or accomplishment. And the individual's level of achievement is directly related to his or her level of emotion or enthusiasm. You may not be in the business of sales, but you've probably discovered that you're always *selling yourself*, converting ideas into action that can be transmuted into reality.

The master salesperson—housewife, doctor, lawyer, or student—has an abundance of enthusiasm that he or she can draw upon. It is a vital force that energizes all the forces of your mind and body. Enthusiasm brings the two minds—the seller's mind and the buyer's mind—into rapport or harmony. It allows the salesman to transmit to the buyer a feeling of need for the product or service, and an appreciation of its worth.

No better commentary could be made on the importance of enthusiasm and selling than the story of Don King. Pay close attention as you discover how one man used the power of this principle.

"I Don't Just Make Waves—I Am the Wave!"

He is known throughout the world. Outwardly flamboyant, a super-salesman, he is without question the world's greatest promoter. He is welcomed by heads of state, invited to White House dinners, and is on a first-name basis with many presidents, diplomats, celebrities, and world leaders. He is tireless, outspoken, innovative, and has accomplished what experts in his field had thought impossible. He has brought the boxing profession up from the count, and has transformed it from a bloodthirsty sport into a spectacle of style.

With the likes of the Alis, Fraziers, and Tysons, Don King took the heavyweight championship fights out of the limited arenas and staged them as extravaganzas in countries throughout the world, employing contagious enthusiasm and exuberant language, a thunderous roll blending black slang and eloquent soliloquy.

He has said it many times: "Only in America can a Don King happen. What I've accomplished could not have been done anywhere else." How did a poor black kid from the ghettos of Cleveland rise to such world acclaim? You need only read further to uncover his secret.

As a young child Don King held the same aspirations that were typical of those his age. He had hoped to be the first of his family to attend college and then, ultimately, law school. But the untimely death of his father altered his career plans. "My father died in 1941. A tragic accident in a local steel mill ended his life. My mother's monthly wages barely covered our needs. We moved from place to place, searching for anything she could afford."

Even as a youth King was successful at nearly everything he attempted. His outgoing personality and a hearty zest for life made him extremely popular. To offset his stifling poverty he hustled. "I remember selling anything I could get my hands on—fruit pies, peanuts, newspapers—just to earn a few dollars' spending change. My oldest brother said I was a born salesman and introduced me to the 'numbers game'—gambling. I was given a small territory in the heart of the projects. I quickly learned the ropes, earning enough money for a year's tuition at Kent State."

But fate intervened and gave him an unkindly shove. Against all odds, an unprecedented number of bets hit, and he had to use his savings to compensate his clients. He was devastated.

"Wouldn't you know it!" he reflected, "the numbers totaled $600—the exact amount I had saved. College, obviously, was placed on the back burner, and I started hustling full-time."

King's enterprise grew, and all those associated with this self-professed "black P.T. Barnum" shared his success. Though King as a businessman was strong and financially solvent, not all of his associates were as forceful. To put it bluntly, a colleague tried to cheat him. In 1967, one of his runners attempted to withhold money for himself, precipitating a fight that cost him his life. For his part in the altercation, King was sentenced to one to twenty years in the Ohio State Penitentiary in Marion. It was an experience that was to have an enormous impact on his life.

King remembers his first day at the facility. "I cried as I looked beyond those prison gates. I couldn't believe what had happened. I saw this calamity as a test of my faith. In that hard, dreary world of confinement, I reexamined my life, my direction and goals. I was determined to make the time *serve me*, instead of me serving time."

In order to kill time, King read books and materials on a wide range of subjects. What began as leisurely reading soon proliferated into an insatiable desire for knowledge. He became a sponge for information. As his reading habits changed, so too did his attitude. His voracious thirst soon led to correspondence courses from area colleges in business, economics, and philosophy. Within a four-year period King had read nearly every book in the prison library, transforming his goals and perception of himself in the process.

In 1971, King was paroled with no money and even fewer skills. Open to any ideas, he heard of the plight of a local hospital that was on the verge of shutting its doors for lack of funds. With his typical enthusiasm, King decided to get involved, though he knew little about fundraising. He toyed with the idea of staging a boxing benefit featuring then World Heavyweight Champion Muhammad Ali.

King's suggestion drew more than a mild reaction. Others involved in the project were skeptical and thought his idea foolhardy and impossible. After all, they thought, the heavyweight boxing champ doesn't give his time away. But believing that it made sense, King pressed on. Armed only with enthusiasm, without contacts or funds, King convinced influential backers to share the financial burden and persuaded the champ to donate his time to such a noble cause. Several weeks later, he staged the event as planned. King even surprised himself by raising more than $80,000. Through his efforts, the strapped institution was saved.

King used this experience to catapult himself into the fight game. By initially volunteering his services, he gained invaluable insight into what he liked doing and what he did well. He has a natural gift for motivating, promoting, and selling his ideas to others. Intoxicated with his success, King plunged headlong into professional boxing, beginning with many small-time bouts and slowly building his self-confidence.

Today the promotional company that he created, Don King Productions, includes more than sports entertainment. Under his auspices are record companies, athletic management, and public relations. In 1976, King was nationally recognized for his rags-to-riches achievements by the *Congressional Record*, where he was called ''one of the most astute entrepreneurs in the country.''

How does a black man from the inner city scale the mountain of success? Listen to this achiever reveal his secrets: ''My appraisal of myself is that I can do anything I want to do. I feel that if I am tenacious, work hard, persevere, and attack all obstacles with *enthusiasm*, I will be successful.

''What I've done can be done by anyone. If you set yourself on fire, the world will watch you burn. I came from the black hard core of East Cleveland. I didn't have rich parents, influential contacts, or a college degree. My father died when I was ten, and yes, I am an ex-con. But I did have, and still do possess, a great deal of *enthusiasm*. This is undoubtedly one of the keys to my success!''

Think back over this story. Realize that Don King's infectious enthusiasm enabled him to achieve his goal and establish a new career for himself in the process. Enthusiasm was the force that brushed aside the stumbling blocks that stood in his path.

Enthusiastic Momentum

Unfortunately, many of us generate enthusiasm for short periods of time only to see the fire of our power start to die down. Enthusiasm is like a fire: unless you continue to add fuel, it goes out. We're all familiar with the person who starts enthusiastically but in the long run dies out. This person lacks momentum; he is operating below a productive boiling point. Yet we all know that it takes but a single degree to transform water into steam. The same principle applies to achieving a goal or selling a product or service. Too often we try to sell ourselves and our ideas without that extra degree of power that is achieved with boiling-point enthusiasm. For the want of one degree of pressure, we fail to achieve our goals, because the enthusiasm we generate isn't consistent; it lacks momentum. It has no staying power.

What's the answer? Go back to the definition of purpose, to the goals you first outlined as your motivation for developing enthusiasm. To sustain enthusiastic momentum, you must deliberately rebuild your belief daily. This rebuilding comes about through a constant review of the goals you hope to achieve. Have those goals always in the forefront of your mind. *Write them down; burn them into your memory; make them an obsession.*

Enthusiastic momentum ensures a source of compulsive energy that never runs down and never wears out. It unlocks talents, abilities, and ideas sufficient to overcome any obstacle. Enthusiasm can help you realize more of your full potential and share in the excitement, the zest, and the enjoyment of lasting success.

The Power of Enthusiasm

When Ralph Waldo Emerson said, "Every great and commanding movement in the annals of the world is a triumph of enthusiasm," he was speaking not only in a historical context, but also of the common events of everyday life. Enthusiasm is the outward reflection of inner confidence. You can command every situation in life by taking each step with enthusiasm.

Enthusiasm isn't for sale—you can't buy it. But you can create it. And once created, it is your greatest single source of productivity. Consider enthusiasm's power points: It is a knowledge indicator; it registers in letters ten feet tall; it produces energy. Just as every living plant, through photosynthesis, draws increasing energy from the sun, so can the brilliance of your enthusiasm draw unlimited zeal and excitement. Self-projected enthusiasm is as much a part of your personality as your smile, your posture, or your handshake. No one can be exposed to its radiant force without being favorably affected. Enthusiasm can't be denied. *It is power—unlimited power!*

All of us have seen examples of direct opposites in our business and personal lives. One person, talented and well-educated, holds back and allows another, who is equally gifted, to press on, to win recognition and prestige. Why? The answer lies within the power of enthusiasm—one man has developed enthusiasm, while the other has not. One man has an insatiable desire for knowledge; the other is satisfied with what he knows. One man is excited by his outlook and the possibilities it presents; the other is bored and confined by his circumstances.

Have you grasped the formula for enthusiasm? If so, then take hold of it and form habits that will help keep your mind focused. Think *I can . . . I will!* Assure yourself that you *can* do it, and you *will* do it because you believe in yourself and the powers of accomplishment. Saturate yourself with confidence and belief. Fear and indecision can't possibly live in that kind of environment. When such belief is firmly embedded into your consciousness, you'll be a *true enthusiast*, a master of thoughts that breathe and words that burn.

10

A Message on Money, or Money Talks and You Would Do Well to Listen

"It is the first duty of every man not to be poor."
—George Bernard Shaw

"I've been rich and I've been poor—and rich is better."

—Sophie Tucker

"The only thing you can learn by studying poverty is how to be poor."

—Michael Novak

"Money doesn't talk, it screams!"

—Clara Luper

Nothing man has ever invented receives so much attention, is so widely sought, and generates so much controversy as this small item: It is a piece of paper that measures 2⅝ by 6⅛ inches, with a thickness of .0043 inches. It takes 490 of them to weigh a pound. It is both used and abused, worshiped and haggled over. Some say it liberates men; others say that it enslaves them. People sometimes become emotional over it, especially when there is too little of it. Sooner or later, it manages to become the focal point of all activity.

What is it? It's the dollar bill. The reason the subject of money almost invariably arises in a discussion of achievement is that the two so frequently go hand in hand—not always, but often. There are, of course, some types of success that have nothing whatsoever to do with money. But there are many others in which financial rewards follow great achievements, and the promise of those rewards sometimes inspires those achievements to start with. For the ambitious, the implications of seeking and attracting large sums of money are often more than abstractions. Money or wealth is an issue about which we hear contradictory opinions, and one that we must ultimately sort out for ourselves. The purpose of this lesson is to get down to the basics, to clear the air surrounding the entire subject of money and to explain exactly what money is and what it isn't.

The desire for material gain is fundamental in human nature. Men and women have been concerned about prosperity and wealth since the first coin was fashioned in Asia Minor around 750 B.C. Many have said that money is like good health: Man is concerned about it to the extent that he doesn't have it. True happiness consists not in the possession of things, but in the privilege of self-expression through the use of material things. You must have money in order to enjoy freedom of body and mind.

A person cannot really be free if he is chained to a routine job most of his waking hours and receives a mere subsistence in return. If a person has to pay that much for existence, he is paying too high a price. This chapter will teach you a proven way to rid yourself of self-imposed limitations and enjoy your fill of life's riches.

To begin, it is terribly important that you bury, once and for all, the myth that *money is bad or unimportant*. Money is not bad. As the Bible says, "the love of money is bad." In fact, money is important—it's terribly important. It's just as important as the food and clothes that it buys, the shelter that it affords, the education that it provides, and the bills that it pays. Money is important to anyone living in a civilized society, and to argue that it's not important is absurd. Let anyone who imagines that he does not need money try to get along without it. Let us be realistic enough to face the facts of life, and demand from life the best that it can give. *Nothing will take the place of money in the area in which money works.*

It's Your Right to Be Rich

Money is a great motivator. Increasing your net worth, accumulating wealth in order to help others, and earning money for the advantages it can offer you and your family are worthwhile objectives. The availability of money frees your mind to concentrate on achieving your goals. If you know that your expenses are covered and you are relieved of the worry that comes with meeting your debts, you can devote all of your time and energy to achieving your objectives. And achieving them becomes easier. You feel relaxed and at ease; you attract others because they are attracted to you.

There is also a peace of mind that comes with financial security that allows you to set your own agenda for your life. A healthy investment portfolio eliminates many of the "what ifs" associated with money worries. You no longer haggle over unexpected expenses that could throw your business or family budget into a tailspin. You can make career and business decisions based on merit rather than expediency, and you can take a chance on an idea that has great potential if you know you are protected against disaster. A healthy cash reserve is the best protection against financial ruin.

But most people, unfortunately, don't bother to build cash reserves. Perhaps one of the greatest shocks I ever received was one that I encountered when I began lecturing on success. I soon realized that many who attended my lectures were still trying to resolve the inner conflict of *whether they should actually desire prosperity.* Of course, they wanted prosperity—it's human nature. But they secretly questioned whether they should seek it, especially from a spiritual point of view. Surprisingly, many businessmen and -women seemed to feel guilty about the whole idea of prosperity, though they were working quite hard to become prosperous, day in and day out, in their respective professions. But the question remained in their minds: *Is poverty a spiritual virtue or a common vice?* This discord in their thinking was creating a tug-of-war in their affairs, which neutralized their efforts to succeed, no matter how much work they put forth.

It became apparent that it would take the expression of some bold, even shocking ideas on the subject of wealth to blast these individuals out of their confining beliefs, which had chained them to the anchor of mediocrity. That is why this chapter is so important.

As highlighted earlier, it is shockingly right instead of shockingly wrong for you to be prosperous. Obviously, you cannot be very happy if you are poor, and *you need not be poor*. Poverty—or the lack of wealth—is a form of hell caused by man's ignorance of the mental laws governing prosperity. Poverty is a dirty, uncomfortable, degrading experience. It is a form of disease, and in its acute phases seems to be a form of insanity. Poverty fills prisons; it drives men and women to drink, to drug addiction, and sometimes to suicide. It can lead potentially fine, talented, intelligent children to delinquency and crime. It can make people do things they otherwise would never dream of doing.

Be done with the thinking of poverty as a virtue—it is a common vice! If you've been living in this hell on earth, you've literally been blinded to the abundance that lies at your feet. *This is the shocking truth about poverty.*

"What I Learned from America's Most Successful Black Entrepreneurs"

Nearly five years ago, as a part of my graduate requirements for a doctoral degree, I found myself in the unenviable position during my oral examination of trying to convince a group of seemingly unconvinceable scholars as to my command of the causes of wealth and poverty among Third World nations. Halfway through the grueling ordeal one of my committee members asked, "How does a nation choked with poverty reverse its course and create wealth?"

In my anxiety to answer his question and gain the committee's approval, I cited various reasons why a country would experience poverty or prosperity. I quoted reams of government statistics culled from numerous sources that were sure-fire antecedents of growth and stagnation. A deafening silence elapsed before this body of scholars confronted me with another barrage of questions.

Though I was eventually awarded a doctorate, that same question continued to surface: *How does a nation prosper?* Or better yet, *how does an entire race or an individual create success?* An idea began to take hold. For the next five years my focus dramatically shifted. I sought out individuals who could provide answers to my probing questions, high-achieving black men and women who had asked these questions themselves. As a result, I combed the nation interviewing successful black businesspeople—from John H. Johnson of Johnson Publications and Earl Graves of *Black Enterprise* magazine to fight promoter Don King and computer entrepreneur Alicia Paige—35 in all, and at a personal expense of $25,000.

It was in this laboratory that I saw for myself the qualities and characteristics that are peculiar to economic advancement. Armed with a three-page questionnaire, I observed these giants up close, charting their every move. From this research I identified principles that revealed two separate paths—*one to prosperity, and the other to poverty.*

Man has been taught that wealth is basically material, and therefore ultimately finite. The cornerstone of this thinking is the philosophy that there are only two ways to promote equality in terms of wealth: *You either make the rich poor or the poor rich.* This illusion is shared by countless Americans. Their general idea centers on life as a zero-sum game: that one's gain comes at the expense of another's loss.

According to this view, there are only so many jobs to go around, only so much energy to be used, and only so much opportunity to be taken advantage of. A fixed amount of prosperity, and a fixed amount of poverty. And it is the "luck of the draw" as to who will prosper or hunger. Throughout the ages, mankind has been afflicted with such limited thinking and its adherents.

But this misconstrues wealth's true nature. Wealth is neither physical nor limited. Wealth takes on contrasting forms—vision, discipline, work, faith, initiative, resilience, desire, ideas, and thought—all unlimited and infinite. Wealth is embodied in a web of enterprise that retains its worth only through constant work, sacrifice, and service. Oftentimes it comes from doing what others consider insufferably boring. Wealth's most salient characteristic is that it's available to all, *and is primarily metaphysical—not physical.* Consequently, the creation of wealth lies within *you*—the individual.

Government Cannot Provide the Answer

No government or institution could ever produce a Barbara Proctor, John Johnson, or Don King. Why? *Because the precepts of wealth run contrary to the very nature of bureaucracies.* Wealth develops within the individual. Under a capitalist or open society, wealth is less a stock of goods than a flow of ideas. Wealth comes from a consciousness that unfolds within. In practical terms, wealth is a characteristic of thought.

Man's foremost quality is his rational faculty. The skills of living successfully are acquired through knowledge. Knowledge is available to each of us, and when properly applied, is power. The antithesis of knowledge is ignorance. Our degree of ignorance will determine our place in society. Though each of us is born ignorant and must for a time live in ignorance, those who remain ignorant have only themselves to blame.

Since knowledge, thinking, and rational action are human qualities, and since the choice to exercise this faculty rests with each of us, society's survival requires that those who *think* be free to do so without interference from those who don't. If some men *choose not to think*, they can survive only by imitating and repeating a routine line of work contrived by more resourceful men. Every man or woman is free to rise as far as he or she is able or willing; but it's only the degree to which he or she *thinks* that will determine the degree to which *he or she will rise*. Wealth always starts in the mind with a prosperity consciousness.

Until mankind reorients its thinking about wealth's true nature, the wreckage of the ghetto and unnecessary failures will continue to mount. The key to any condition of lack is mental principle. Poverty is not corrected by a redistribution of wealth, but by ideas. You can give a man begging for coffee or food a dollar, but before that day is out he will be hungry again. Unless there is a change in consciousness, unless all parties awaken to wealth's true nature and get in tune with the infinite supply of ideas, nothing will change.

As I pen these thoughts, my mind drifts back to the words Wally Amos shared with me several years ago. Wally succinctly expressed a great deal of wisdom when he stated: "In order to overcome poverty, one needs only to raise his level of vision. The cure for lack of any type is found within a change of thinking."

What Is Money?

Money is a warm home and healthy children; it's birthday presents and a college education; it's a family vacation and the means to help the less fortunate. Money is the harvest of our giving; it is what we receive for our production and services, and in turn it can be used to obtain the production and services of others. Quite often we can accurately gauge the extent of our production and services by counting the money we receive for our efforts. In this respect money is a yardstick, a rule or standard that is completely negotiable and can be used by each of us. You'll hear people say, "Money won't bring happiness," but the earning and possession of money has brought much more happiness than has poverty.

Money is an extension of you—your thinking. It is a symbol of either limitation or limitlessness, according to your thoughts. If you think favorably about money, it increases in your midst; but if you criticize or condemn it, it will dissipate as you approach it. The good news is that regardless of our present circumstances, each of us can change or alter our thinking to coax wealth into our lives.

Black America, You Are Already Rich!

To nine-tenths of the world's population, the average black American is already rich! There is a larger gap between the standard of living of most of the world's population and the average black worker than there is between the standard enjoyed by America's average black worker and the wealthiest member of our society. In case you have fallen for the nonsense that blacks are poor, consider this not-so-well-known fact: Black Americans earn $350 billion in annual income (estimated at $900 billion by year 2000) and spend $225 billion a year on goods and services. *This dollar figure is equivalent to the gross national product of Canada or Australia, two of the ten largest nations in the free world.* Black America's problem is not a lack of money; its problems stem from what it does with the money it has.

Black Americans possess just about everything the wealthy possess—*only in smaller amounts*. They have homes, cars, stereos, televisions, savings accounts, and debts—only in smaller quantities. Their food is just as tasty and as plentiful; their beds are just as comfortable, and their homes are just as cozy. They have exactly the same amount of time and just as much freedom.

With only a fraction of the world's population, American blacks possess 10 percent of the free world's total monetary income. Or, to draw a clearer picture, *Black America's combined income is slightly greater than that of Western Europe, and greater than that of Israel or South Africa. As a people, Black America is already rich.*

Now, how much do *you* want? How much money do *you* need to live the way you want to live? To accomplish the goals you've set for yourself?

Most people think they need more money than they really do, and they settle for a lot less than they could earn. The world will pay you exactly what you bargain for—exactly what *you earn*, but not a penny more. That old dictum is so true: "I bargained with life for a penny, and life would pay no more." You'll receive not what you idly wish for, but what you justly earn. Your rewards will always be in exact proportion to your service. If you are unhappy with your income, you must devise ways and means of increasing your service.

How May I Serve?

Economic security is not attained by the possession of money alone. *It is captured by the service one renders.* Useful service may be converted into all forms of human needs, with or without the use of money.

A successful businessman has economic security not because he controls vast amounts of money, but for the better reason that he provides profitable employment for men and women, and through them, provides goods and services of great value to countless others. The service he renders attracts the money he controls, and it is in this manner that all enduring economic security must be obtained.

Your service must come from *you*, your mind, your ability, your talent, and your energy. A *strong* individual cannot make a *weak* person strong. But a weak man or woman can become strong through his or her volition by following a specific course of action. And one who is already strong can become much stronger.

Put in metaphorical terms, a diamond is more valuable than a lump of coal, yet that's exactly what a diamond was at one time. And just as a lump of coal can be transformed into one of the world's most valuable gems, a human being can vastly increase his or her own value to the world. To paraphrase Earl Nightingale, who had a knack for graphically verbalizing a point: *The amount of money you receive will always be in direct proportion to the demand for what you do, your ability to do it, and the difficulty of replacing you.*

One who is highly trained is worth more money in our economy than a person who is low-skilled and who can easily be replaced. This is not to say that one person is any better or more important than anyone else. Remember, this lesson centers on money—nothing else. A janitor is just as important a human being as a brain surgeon, but the amount of money each will earn will be proportional to the demand for what they do, the ability to do what they do, and the difficulty of replacing them.

Anyone can be trained to clean and maintain a building in a few days, and replacing this person is not difficult. A brain surgeon, however, spends many years learning his profession, often at great personal sacrifice and cost, and he cannot easily be replaced. As a result, the surgeon might earn as much money in an hour as a janitor might earn in a month.

Now these are extreme cases used only to show the relationship of income to demand, skill, and supply—and this is as it should be. This is why there are few limitations on a person within his or her company or occupation. *Your* income will be in exact proportion to the demand for what *you do*, the ability to do what *you do*, and the difficulty of replacing *you*. This proposition also explains why the whole notion of trying to receive something for nothing is absurd, and is based on sheer delusion.

A star athlete, for example, may earn millions over the course of a career. You might say shooting a basketball or lugging a football 100 yards serves no useful purpose, but the demand is there, useful or not. It's the same with celebrity status. A Hollywood starlet's income will very accurately reflect the demand for what she does. If more people understood this line of thinking, they would see why preparing for a career is crucial. Luck has been defined as what happens when "preparedness meets opportunity"; a great opportunity will only make the unprepared, the unqualified, look foolish.

Now, how do you measure up? While this may sound elementary, you would be amazed at the number of people who desire material riches but who do not take the time and trouble to qualify for them. And until they qualify for them, there is little chance for them to earn them. It's like the farmer who stood in front of the fireplace trying to get warm; he soon realized, however, that until he gathered wood and started a fire, he would freeze.

Parents—Do Not Shield Your Children from Serving

It has been said, and with reason, that a rich man's son often does not display the qualities of his father. Many children of affluent means are robbed of important traits because they inherited their parents' wealth. By and large, the father or mother worked for every penny he or she earned. The father's earnings came to him side by side with the development of his insight, his talents, and his ability. He was not given riches by *his* father; he was given riches by *his service*!

Now, let us look at his son. All his life his son has

lived in the midst of luxury and the many comforts that money provides. The son knows he is going to share and eventually acquire great amounts of wealth that he has not earned. Assuming that his son does have the inherent willingness to serve—what happens to that willingness? In many cases it is replaced by a desire to obtain something for nothing, and thus he never learns one of life's basic lessons: *the practice of service first and profits second*.

Great fortunes or comfortable means are a blessing only when they are used to benefit others. No father benefits his son when he robs him of initiative. If you wish to shield your children from the bad parts of life, you are to be praised. But beyond that, do not shield them from their *ability to serve*—for this is true wealth. Allow them to have the priceless opportunity of building better lives with their own self-taught wisdom and lessons.

Peace of Mind Is Wealth

Napoleon Hill tells a fascinating story of his visit with John D. Rockefeller, Sr., the oil magnate. During their meeting Rockefeller, easily the world's richest man at the time, asked the young reporter if he would like to change places with him. Without hesitation Hill politely told him that he would not, that he valued his health and freedom, neither of which Rockefeller, for all of his opulence, had or enjoyed. Many years later after his death, Hill reflected on that eventful meeting.

"What did Rockefeller really want?" Hill questioned. By consulting with those who knew him, Hill firmly believed that the multimillionaire wanted nothing more than what he had missed in his tremendous money-making career—*peace of mind*.

Peace of mind is an essential ingredient of prosperity and covers a surprisingly broad field. In every way you use it, peace of mind aids you in your quest for riches—both material and spiritual—and success. Peace of mind helps you live your life on your own terms, in values of your own choosing, so that every day your life grows richer and greater.

Is there a connection between wealth and peace of mind? Maybe. There certainly are poor people who have peace of mind; but not as many as we are taught to believe. You need not be a millionaire or even financially independent, but without sufficient money, you are cut off from much in life that sustains the spirit. If you are continually worrying about feeding your family or keeping a roof over your head, you will have no peace of mind. Money brings the finer things of life and many times the bare necessities.

While it is no surprise that many wealthy people enjoy peace of mind, there are members of this touted class who do not. If the main purpose of wealth is to make its possessor worry about keeping his fortune, peace of mind will forever elude him.

One of my favorite real-life stories that illustrates the power of peace of mind and how it can be used to benefit the spirit is the experience of Oprah Winfrey.

"My Life Is at Peace"

Oprah Winfrey has become one of America's most watched television talk-show hosts, as well as a promising actress. She was honored for her 1985 screen debut in *The Color Purple* with nominations from both the Academy of Motion Picture Arts and Sciences and the Golden Globe Awards. In 1987, the syndicated *Oprah Winfrey Show* won an Emmy Award for television's best talk show, and Oprah received an Emmy for best talk-show host. In 1986, she formed her own production company, HARPO Productions, which has already become a major creative force in the entertainment industry. In 1990, deals for made-for-TV movies and licensing fees from her talk show have netted her nearly $40 million in revenues, making her the wealthiest black woman in

America. To say that Oprah Winfrey lives life to its fullest while radiating an inner harmony would be a gross understatement. For she is a woman at peace with herself, her life and world.

But there was a tense period in Oprah's life when she sought inner solitude but couldn't find it. Instead, the sheltered little girl from a small southern town found a troubled world.

Oprah Winfrey was born on a farm in Kosciusko, Mississippi. Her unwed parents had intended to name her "Orpah" after Ruth's sister-in-law in the Bible, but a midwife transposed the letters on the birth certificate, and she was named Oprah instead. Soon after her birth, her parents separated. She would be nearly six years old before she would know her father.

Raised under her grandmother's protective wing, Oprah was a precociously bookish child. She learned to read at three years of age. When she enrolled in kindergarten, she intuitively wrote a note that pointed out in no uncertain terms that she belonged in the first grade. An astonished teacher recognized her ability and had her promoted. After completing the academic year, Oprah skipped directly to the third grade.

At age six she was sent north to Milwaukee to join her mother and two half brothers. Her mother had since found a marginal existence, trying to make ends meet by supplementing a fifty-dollar-a-month domestic's salary with whatever welfare was available. Deprived of the wide-open farm life of Mississippi and her grandmother's love, Oprah turned inward. Acts of sexual abuse by a series of trusted men violated her innocence, first by an older male relative, and later by a "friend." Each incident left her guilty, confused, and afraid to report the offense.

Lashing out at the world, she constantly rebelled. She began staging dramatic, if minor, acts of delinquency. Trying to escape an abusive environment, Oprah ran away several times, only to be caught and returned home. When she was thirteen her beleaguered and distraught mother dragged her to a detention center that was already full. With few options left, her mother decided to turn her over to her father.

Vernon Winfrey had found a better life in Nashville, Tennessee, as a barber, businessman, and community leader. Living with her father and stepmother gave Oprah protection and security, while reaffirming her grandmother's early teachings in excellence and pride. Oprah's father was a strict disciplinarian who provided his daughter with guidance, late-night discussions, and books. Privileges were withheld unless she could add new words to an already expanding vocabulary. But he didn't stop here. He demanded weekly book reports, combing each report for correct grammar usage and proper sentence structure. Under his stern regimen, the once-rebellious child began to excel—both in and out of the classroom.

With renewed vigor, Oprah made two solemn promises: First, she would begin to apply herself fully and take total responsibility for her life; second, she would close the door to her troubled past and reconstruct her life on the solid foundation of divine guidance. Adhering to both promises, she set her mind at ease.

The child who'd learned to read and who had made her first speech in church at age three found outlets for her talents. In high school she presided over the student council, joined the drama club, and distinguished herself as a public speaker. When she was sixteen she won an oratorical contest that awarded a scholarship to Tennessee State University. A year later she was invited to the White House with other young achievers.

During her freshman year at Tennessee State, Oprah continued to blossom. She entered and won the Miss Black Nashville contest; later she captured the title of Miss Tennessee. In 1971, she ran for Miss Black America and sought a career in broadcasting. To her surprise, she was hired as a reporter while still at Tennessee State, first by a local radio station and later by a CBS affiliate. By 1976, she was working in Baltimore for ABC-TV as a feature reporter and co-anchor of that city's six o'clock news.

But suddenly Oprah started having trouble at work. As a reporter and co-anchor, she found that she had "to fight back tears" when covering stories that tugged at her heart. In fact, the station manager threatened to discharge her if she failed to question a distraught woman at the scene of a fire in which the woman had lost her family. Reluctantly, Oprah complied, but apologized later during a live news broadcast.

Her difficulties at work were compounded when the same station manager altered her reporting style and format. "They tried to make me into something I wasn't," Oprah remembers. This left her self-esteem battered and her career sidetracked. Hoping to steer her in a new direction, the news director moved her to the station's morning talk show. Though viewed by many as a demotion, the move was a blessing in disguise. After her first day in the new slot, she exclaimed: "This is what I was born to do. This is like breathing!" The once-lackluster show's ratings rocketed. Within five months it was the third-highest-rated show in syndication—*and the number-one talk show in Baltimore*! Based on that performance, Oprah was offered the host slot of WLS-TV's *A.M. Chicago* show in 1984.

The rest is much-publicized history. For eight years Oprah Winfrey has tackled nearly every topic under the sun. By 1986, she had reached true celebrity status as "daytime TV's reigning queen," *worth an estimated $40 million*!

Many have called her lucky, and because of her "instant success," some say she is a financial genius. But whatever the reasons for her accomplishments, peace of mind certainly plays a part.

"Life is quite simple," she confesses. "So simple that most people miss the point entirely. They either think I'm lucky or I get all the breaks. The truth of the matter is that I am spirit-led. My life is actually better than it appears because of my inner peace. I used to be my own worst enemy. But that has changed. If you allow yourself to get out of the way, grace will come to you.''

I share this story with you because your goal in life, presumably, is to achieve success. Oprah Winfrey's logic is so simple everyone can understand her message. Her message is clear: *To be successful, regardless of personal wealth, you must find peace of mind.* Oprah Winfrey found peace and harmony through daily spiritual guidance. Your methods may differ. But regardless of the source of your power, you must find and maintain inner tranquility. Why? Because those who work for money alone, and those who receive nothing but money for their efforts, *are always underpaid—no matter how much they receive.* No amount of money could possibly take the place of peace of mind. *To get more out of life, you must first give more.*

She Gives Back More Than She Receives

Wealth comes to the individual who sees a potential for wealth. As previously noted, you cannot carry others along the highway of success; but you may point the way by helping others to help themselves. A large sum of money in the hands of a man or woman generally does not create as much prosperity as does capital that circulates, provided those who handle its circulation are interested in creating wealth. The virtue of money consists in its utility, not its quantity.

Although Oprah's lifestyle in some ways fits her financial status—a splendidly decorated home, jet-set travel, and a bejeweled and fashionable wardrobe—in some ways it doesn't. More often than not, Oprah seems quite unaffected by her success. Many times she is equally as comfortable simply relaxing at home with a good book. There's more to her agenda than building a business, making movies, or generating additional income. She wants to make a positive change in people's lives.

Philanthropy is an important responsibility. There is always the possibility that a financial gift to an institution or an individual can do more harm than good. Misplaced intentions have people dependent upon something for nothing, robbing them of their dignity and any opportunity to develop their best potential.

But Oprah knows better. For example, she gave four-year scholarships to ten students attending her alma mater. She selected the winners from a list of incoming first-year students, assessing their needs and scholastic abilities. The scholarships included tuition, room and board, books, even spending money. But like all good stewards, Oprah placed a condition on her philanthropy. She required each student to maintain at least a B (3.0) average.

When her scholars were about to begin their sophomore year, two of her students let their grades slip. As a result, she sent each of them a letter that said, in part:

> I understand that the first year is really difficult and there were a lot of adjustments to be made. I believe in you. We all made an agreement that it would be a three-point (B) average, not a 2.9. I know you want to uphold your end of the agreement, because I intend to uphold mine.

By requiring her scholars to adhere to the letter of the agreement, Oprah has transferred principles such as responsibility, persistence, and self-discipline that are far more valuable than any material riches. These qualities play key roles that will lead to peace of mind.

Can you increase your wealth without achieving happiness? Or peace of mind? Or by sharing your happiness and riches? Yes, of course you can. But whether you will enjoy the fruits of your efforts remains to be seen. Service, as you will see, is another matter.

We Are Here to Serve Others

The greatest idea in the world is the opportunity to be of service to others. There is an entire world crying for help, for ideas, for endless products and *services*. The extent of your opportunity to be of service is often the extent of your imagination coupled with knowledge. And the best place to begin is where you stand.

There is much to be said for the old cliché "service with a smile." If your attitude is positive, and you go the extra mile, giving added service over and above that which is required, then you are well on your way to rich and worthwhile relationships. The habit of giving more and better service brings rewards in many forms—both in the heart and in the pocketbook. Bread cast upon the water will return to sustain and strengthen the man who is rendering more service and better service than he is paid or expected to do.

Lee Dunham has served all his life. As a young boy reared in Kannapolis, North Carolina, the son of share-croppers, Lee balanced his time between chopping cotton and raising hogs. After school he hustled—shining shoes at his own shoe stand, selling newspapers, and delivering groceries.

"My parents pointed out the value of work," Dunham said. "I was taught at an early age that everyone has the ability to serve, and by serving others, I could be successful."

In 1951, Dunham joined the Air Force and was immediately sent to its food service school. There he sharpened skills that he would use in later years. Dunham became such a proficient cook that he was soon transferred from the enlisted men's mess to the officer's dining hall. He left the military after a four-year commitment and worked in a number of restaurants, among them the dining room of the plush Waldorf-Astoria Hotel in New York. Two years later he decided to serve in a different capacity and joined the city's police force.

Dunham was a policeman for fifteen years before a chronic back ailment forced him into early retirement. Regardless of the beat or the assignment, he thoroughly enjoyed his work. "If I had to do it all over again," he says with sincerity, "I would still be a cop. There was something about public service that attracted me. Working on the force was the greatest thing in my life." But Dunham knew the food business equally as well, and had similar feelings. Deep inside a dream gnawed away. He hoped to open a family restaurant in the heart of New York, catering to a select clientele.

In pursuit of his dream, Dunham had expected financial help from a number of sources created to support minority enterprises. But he and these agencies haggled over the specifics, and several deals fell through. Left with no other immediate sources of financing, Dunham turned to franchising instead.

In 1971, he queried a few companies, among them Kentucky Fried Chicken, Holiday Inn, Chicken Delight, and McDonald's, about business opportunities. McDonald's was the first to write back inviting him to an interview at its Boston office. The chain told him he would need nearly $200,000 to purchase an outlet, and proposed a location in inner-city New York—the first of its type. Understandably, Dunham was hesitant. Through he was anxious to get started, McDonald's had absolutely no experience marketing hamburgers in the black community. The last thing he wanted was to be a guinea pig.

After many sleepless nights, Dunham blasted forward, investing his life savings—$35,000—and borrowing the balance from a bank. He became one of only a handful of black owner-operators nationwide, *and the only operator with an outlet in the inner city!* The odds against his success were frightening. His family and friends questioned his judgment, and even he had moments of doubt. But in his mind he had a plan that would eventually ensure his success.

Lee Teaches Others What He Already Knew

When Lee Dunham opened his McDonald's franchise in March 1972 on Harlem's main thoroughfare, the soft smile on his face slowly faded. The fast-deteriorating neighborhood was rampant with crime. His first three months in business resembled a chronicle of war as he faced violent confrontations almost every day. Fights were far too frequent, guns were fired on occasion, and the mere presence of jacketed gang members drove customers away. The safe in Dunham's corner office was routinely blown open. Furthermore, he lost whatever profits he made as employees stole food and other supplies, as well as money from the registers.

Normally, field agents from the McDonald's home office would visit new franchisees to help with management problems. But in Dunham's case, representatives were too apprehensive to go into the inner city. Dunham would have to solve his problems himself. He also knew he had to make his intentions of succeeding on Harlem's 125th Street crystal clear to the area's thugs and stickup men. Nearing the end of his rope, he had to develop a plan— *and fast!*

"My experience as a cop was just as important to my success as the training I received in the home office. Without it, the criminal element would have run me out in one week."

Refusing to back down, Dunham made significant changes. He viewed the shambles of the neighborhood and the wrecked human lives. He saw the need for someone to inspire and offer positive solutions; *he saw the need to serve*.

Dunham spoke openly and honestly with gang leaders, helping them find more useful ways to channel their energies. He sponsored athletic teams, awarded scholarships, and employed gang members, teaching them the principles of discipline, responsibility, and the value of service. He began spot checks on all cashiers and fired anyone caught stealing. He improved working conditions and gave time off to full-time employees. Dunham told anyone who would listen—in no-nonsense terms—that his store offered a way out of a life of confinement, offered hope and opportunity—and that he would do anything to keep it. Even if that meant meeting force with force.

But most important, after thorough and careful review, he developed faster and more efficient methods to serve the customer. Dunham examined and timed the entire ordering process, searching for flaws. He surveyed customers and asked for their input. He stressed the basics—quality, service, cleanliness, and value—and required each employee to give his or her personal best and go the extra mile to satisfy customer needs.

The tactics worked. By the end of the first year his investment began to pay off as profits soared. This McDonald's franchise with the questionable location began attracting 3500 people each week, and 5000 on the weekends. Because of his phenomenal success, McDonald's offered Dunham a second store, which he opened a year later.

Word quickly spread as Lee Dunham and his employees began to collect company awards and honors. The Harlem operation became McDonald's most profitable franchise worldwide, earning more than $1.5 million a year. Company officials flocked to the New York unit to uncover Dunham's winning secret.

What Is His Secret?

A modest man, Dunham attributes much of his success to his employees and *to the one key principle that he learned as a child.* Every Tuesday evening, at his company's New York headquarters and at his own expense, he unveils this secret in a management development course that he teaches to employees.

"Kill them with service," he says with simplicity. "All of us can serve—we can give faster service, cheaper service, and go the extra mile. Serving others is *the* reason for our business—not an intrusion on our business!''

Dunham pauses, and further explains the secret that put him over the top. ''The underpinnings of prosperity have been studied and analyzed. Unequivocally, growth and profits are a by-product of service. Everyone must be his own salesman of personal services. You must give your very best, and commit yourself to excellence. You must give customers more than they expect. There is something infinitely better than making a living—*and that's making a contribution.*''

Dunham is adamant about making a contribution and serving his community. When asked to define success, he advises: ''You just can't take, you must give something back. I'm not in business just to make money. The greatest service that I can render is to motivate our youth.'' Through his success philosophy, Dunham has seen young men and women change the course of their lives for the better.

Today, Lee Dunham is the owner-operator of eight McDonald's franchises that employ 520 workers—mostly black teens—and generate more than $14 million a year.

Read and reread the above story. *Give your best; work at making your service better; and give more than is expected with the right attitude.* Do what you do so well that you'll always guarantee you're receiving a larger share of any available business. Human beings have wants and needs, and it is by meeting these wants and needs that we serve others.

Albert Einstein embodied the idealism of service when he was asked, ''Why are we here?'' to which he replied, ''We are here to serve others.'' Lee Dunham is correct; we all have the ability to serve. And if we don't serve, we don't reap a harvest. The extent of our sowing will determine the size of our harvest, our action and reaction.

Millions have misunderstood this principle, thereby forcing themselves into a quandary. You've heard people say, "So-and-so worked hard every day of his life and has nothing to show for it." If this is true, this person has made some serious mistakes. In reality, he should be quite well-to-do by now. He was either in the wrong field or failed to seize the opportunities around him.

We see millions who are starving in Africa, and the world responds by sending money and donations. The drought, the closed, inefficient governments, the lack of freedom and education—all contribute to the inability of these people to serve. Because they are unable to serve, they receive nothing in return.

Lee Dunham receives hundreds of letters each week from people asking for a portion of his wealth; yet few of these poor, ignorant souls understand that Dunham's *real wealth* is not measured by the dollars in his bank account, or by the franchises that he owns, but by the reputation and satisfaction he has gained through rendering the best possible service.

Service Is the Rent You Pay

How can you gain such a reputation? Certainly not by offering as little service as possible. Service is the rent you pay for the space you occupy while on this earth. You'll never get rich except by enriching the lives of others; and you'll never prosper except by bringing prosperity to your fellowman. An ancient parable illustrates this point.

Many years ago, in a kingdom far away, lived a man whose official title was "Server of the Kingdom." One day, as he was walking through the forest, he was approached by a genie. And, like all genies, this one offered to grant the young man a wish. "Any wish?" he exclaimed.

"Anything," replied the genie.

The young man pondered his good fortune for a moment, then told the genie how all of his life he had served others. "I know what I want," the man blurted out. "I want people to *serve* me for a change!"

The genie said, "Granted!" and vanished into the forest. Eager to test this newfound power, the young man walked back to the castle. As he approached the gate of the royal palace, a servant presented himself and opened the gate for him. That night after he finished his dinner, a servant stepped forward to wipe his mouth and clear his table. When the young man retired for the evening, a servant appeared to pull back his bed. The next morning he was greeted by another servant who retrieved his slippers and prepared a royal breakfast.

Though he valiantly tried to perform his duties as the king's cup bearer, somebody was always there to perform the chore for him. Throughout his life all he had ever done was serve others. It wasn't long before he realized that he couldn't do anything for anyone, and he began to feel its effect.

For the first thirty days the novelty of his fortune was interesting; for the next thirty days it was irritating; and by the last thirty days, he couldn't stand it any longer. With a thundering fury, he looked diligently for the genie. After a three-day search, he found him in the forest.

Reduced to tears, the young man told the genie, "I am so glad I found you. I've changed my mind. I want to go back to serving others."

Without any emotion the genie said, "I can't help you."

But the young man reiterated, "You don't understand. I am willing to do anything to dedicate my life to my fellowman."

Again the genie stated, "There's nothing I can do."

But the king's servant wouldn't quit. He pleaded, "Kind sir, I would rather be in hell than *not* be able to *serve* my fellowman!"

And to this the genie replied, "My dear man, where do you think you've been for the past ninety days?"

You have the greatest vehicle for service in America.

In our country you no longer sell a product, you render a service. The greatest thing in the world is the opportunity to be of service to others. The customer wants the most for the least amount of money, and will decide where he will spend his earnings. There is a world yearning for new ideas, products, and services.

How can you be of service? How best can you serve? Joseph Karbo, the author of *The Lazy Man's Way to Riches*, was fond of saying that most people are too busy earning a living to make any money. What Karbo meant was that the average person never seems to find the time to work on the really important things, the creative projects that produce big payoffs. It is creativity, more so than hard work, that lies at the heart of success in any field or endeavor. And in order for a person to have the time to engage in creative thinking, he must learn to work efficiently. Refer back to lesson two. Remember, all you need is one good idea.

How Much Money Do You Want to Earn?

Take a few moments and answer the following questions: What have you got to sell? What will the world offer for what you do? How many people do what you do? And in the field in which you serve, where do you stand in its hierarchy of value? Not as a human being, but as *one who serves others*. As you answer these questions, you might realize why some people earn more money than others. They have made themselves more valuable as servers of others—more in demand.

People who are unwilling to do more than they're paid for will seldom be paid for more than they're doing. You may have heard someone say, "Why should I knock myself out for the money I'm making?" It is this attitude, more than anything else, that keeps men and women at the bottom of the economic pile. They have yet to understand the correlation between value and income: As you grow in value as a person, you will receive the income you seek.

If you try to stand still in life, and millions do, you will never know the rewards or the joy of accomplishment, the personal satisfaction and peace of mind that comes only to the person who strives to achieve. There are two steps that you must take: First, you must decide how much money you really want—not a vague figure, but the exact amount. Second, you must release your preoccupation with the money and concentrate on improving what you now do. Improve your service. Expand your service. And most important, go the extra mile. This is the format by which you will qualify yourself for the amount of money that you expect to earn.

Once you have rendered adequate service for the amount of money you've decided upon, you'll soon find yourself earning it. In addition, you'll also discover that with your new forces and abilities, your tasks are no more difficult—perhaps even *less* difficult—than what you have been doing for the money that you are currently earning.

Now, ask yourself: *How much money am I willing to earn?* There are really three amounts you should decide upon: first, a yearly income you wish to earn now or in the future; second, the amount of money you wish to have saved in the near future; and third, the amount of money you would like to have as retirement income, whether you retire from active work or not. Write down these three amounts.

Most people stumble at this point. *They never decide on any of these three amounts.* If you will answer these questions honestly, and review what you've written periodically, you will have automatically placed yourself in the top five percent of wage earners, as discussed in the third chapter. You will have a plan and a blueprint for your future financial success. You will know where you are going, and if you are determined, you'll most assuredly reach your objectives.

How One Man Rose to the Top

Whoever you are—regardless of race, age, or education—you can increase the amount of money you earn. After reading such a statement, you may think of me as brash and off-base. However, to earn all that you wish is possible. How? The key is provided in the following illustration.

A. Barry Rand, president of the marketing division of Xerox, makes an imposing presence as he strides through the company boardroom. He's on the job promptly at six A.M. Like clockwork, dozens of senior executives assemble for strategy sessions as "Team Xerox" begins to unfold. Within the next hour Rand will conduct sales meetings in his spacious office, return to the boardroom for a critical conference with a market research group, and catch a corporate jet to go to a meeting about mapping future strategies. While commuting to the airport he dictates letters and memos on his car phone to his secretary. When his day finally winds down, he describes it as routine.

Rand does not take a matter-of-fact approach to his position as president of Xerox's $5 billion operation. Charged with setting the strategic direction of the organization's marketing efforts, Rand is responsible for a work force of 33,000 that handles direct sales and service of Xerox products and systems. In a very real sense, the future of this multibillion-dollar corporation rests in his hands. *How did this black man assume such a position of authority?* His story should provide some insights.

Barry Rand hails from a middle-class family where achievement was the order of the day. Both parents are college graduates, and he inevitably grew up in an environment of high expectations. His parents hoped their son would pursue a career in medicine, but having whet his appetite with a part-time sales job while still in high school, he switched majors in college from premed to marketing. "I was convinced," says Rand, "that sales offered me the best opportunities. I felt that I could literally sell anything to anybody.''

Rand joined Xerox in 1968 as its first black sales trainee in the Washington, D.C., area. By 1970, he earned the title of ''Regional Sales Representative of the Year'' and placed among the top three sales representatives in the nation. For his efforts, he was given special recognition. Unknowingly, this would be his first lesson on the importance of establishing clear financial goals.

''With great anticipation I took my award home, beaming from ear to ear. I shared my good fortune with my dad. He took one look at the plaque and shook his head. 'Son,' he said, 'that's a nice prize for your efforts, but where's the money?' I stood in front of him dazed by his question. 'Don't ever let anybody fool you again.'

''The reality of his words struck like a bolt of lightning. I immediately began to set specific career and income goals. Though it was a painstaking process, I knew this would be the only way I could plan my life. I fastidiously recorded the dates in which I would reach the first level of sales management. Moreover, I developed a timetable in which I would return to school to complete an MBA degree. Finally, I recorded my income goals with a specific time frame for achievement—all to be accomplished by my thirtieth birthday! Mind you, these were not wishes or pipe dreams, but goals that I reviewed each day. I was aware that my income was directly linked to my area of responsibility and service to the organization.''

With clearly defined goals, Rand rapidly progressed up the corporate ladder—from corporate director in 1980, to vice-president of eastern operations in 1984, to his current position as marketing president in 1986. Inch by inch Barry Rand stalked his goals, as promotions, pay raises, and recognition followed according to plan.

You, too, can benefit from the lesson that Barry Rand learned.

The sad fact is that 95 percent of all workers have no

major purpose other than working for a daily wage. The overwhelming majority will never decide upon specific, planned financial goals. Therefore, no matter how much work they perform or what effort they put forth, they will never eke out more than a bare living. They neither expect nor demand more.

But the man of affluence and success demands riches in definite terms. He has a specific plan that he carries out, giving useful service equivalent in value to the wealth he demands. Life pays the successful man on his own terms, and equally compensates the man who asks for nothing more than daily wages. The wheel of fortune reacts to the mental blueprints each man sets up in his mind, *and brings him in physical or financial form the exact equivalent of that blueprint.*

Attitudes Toward Money

There are two attitudes toward money. There's the attitude held by the majority who trim their wants and desires to fit their incomes; and there's the attitude held by the minority—free spirits who make their incomes fit their wants. *Which of these attitudes represents your present thinking?*

When you write down the yearly income you plan to earn, you undoubtedly know whether or not it's average for your present line of work. Chances are that the figure you decide upon will be above average. *Ask yourself, who in my line of work is now earning this amount of money?* If you know, you'll have a clear idea what you'll have to do in order to earn it. It is through this process that men and women of average abilities advance through the ranks into positions of prominence, positions with corresponding incomes. Regardless of your field, your business needs new leaders. It needs men and women to keep the industry expanding. It needs new servers.

Many of today's top black executives were once accountants, shipping clerks, struggling lawyers, service station attendants, sales people, mailroom clerks, and mechanics. There isn't a position from which men and women have not climbed to the top. If you understand what I am about to say, you will attain the riches you desire: *It's not the position, it's the person. It's not your present circumstances that count, but the circumstances you create that are important.* The only limit on your income is *you.* And the income you decide upon can be achieved within the framework of your present work, industry, or profession, where you already have a start and a place.

All that is needed is a plan, a road map, and the courage to press on to your destination. You must know in advance that there will be disappointments and setbacks—but you must also know that nothing on earth can stand in the way of a well-thought-out plan backed by persistence and determination.

With your income goal firmly planted in your subconscious, spend a part of each day thinking of ways in which you can increase your service. Know that you have only to manage this, and the income will take care of itself. Since the money you want to earn is more than you're now receiving, you should try to find ways of increasing your service until the gap has been bridged. Look at your card or paper with the three amounts written on it. By setting a financial goal, you're demonstrating faith. You'll find that you will begin to become what others call lucky. You'll begin to get good ideas, and you'll take far more interest in your work and your company. You'll see opportunities that until now have gone unnoticed. In fact, you'll soon discover that you're no longer the same person.

Be realistic about your financial goals. Trying to jump too far too soon can often result in confusion, tension, and worry. Take your growth in sensible, logical steps, remembering that the main idea is that you *know what you want* and that you realize your rewards will match your service. Reflect on the mental laws—cause and effect—that control our universe. The cause must precede the effect or the effect cannot occur. You can have whatever you desire—*you need only make up your mind*.

Have faith in yourself and the quiet, firm inner knowledge that you can and will accomplish your goals. Know that the answers you seek will come to you in their own time if only you keep searching for them. Above all, realize that money cannot be directly sought. Money, like happiness, is an effect. It is the result of a cause. And the cause is valuable service. Keep money in its proper place—it is a servant and nothing more. Too much emphasis on money reverses the entire picture—you then become the servant and money the master.

It's good to have money and the things that money can buy, but it's good, too, to occasionally make sure that you haven't lost the things that money *cannot* buy. Personal prosperity means more than wealth.

Read this chapter as often as possible. Seal your plans in your mind, then relax. Right now, you may have no idea how the additional income you seek is going to come; or how you are going to save the amount you planned; or how you can possibly arrange for the retirement income you've decided upon. Remember, the means are not important. The only important idea is that you *know* what you *want*. *Whatever your mind can conceive and believe, you can achieve!*

11

Three Magic Words

"Man is not in the world to set it right, but to see it rightly."

—ERIC BUTTERWORTH

". . . And cast now your nets on the right side."

—JOHN 21:6

"The color of the rose lies within us, not in the rose."

—JOHN KEATS

No matter who you are—
  No matter where you are—
  No matter how many times you have failed in the past—
  I've got good news! What single quality do we find in all men and women of high achievement? They raise their sights and tap into their inner power by using the "three magic words."

Experts call them the three most important words in life. Before approaching the idea upon which this lesson is based, keep in mind that the same theme runs throughout the entire text. The purpose of this lesson is to aid you in unlocking and expanding your mind so you can think with accuracy and attract the results you desire. In addition, you will be able to pry open the door that leads to the power you will need as you complete your search for riches.

Recently, I counseled a friend who was in deep despair. When I refused to join in his lament and expressed my faith that there are no unsolvable problems, that in the higher realms of his mind he could find the answers to any apparent obstacles, he promptly dismissed me with, "That's that same ol' positive stuff. You've got to face the facts."

Though his remarks seemed reasonable, the problem is that we don't always have all the facts. Many times we confuse facts with theories, outward appearances, or worse yet, assumptions. For instance, a quick glimpse at a morning's daybreak may lead you to believe the sun is rising. And yet, precisely at the same moment at another point on earth, someone else may be facing a beautiful sunset. The truth is that the sun neither rises nor sets; and we should give thanks that it never does, or the entire solar system would be tragically disrupted. The sun shines eternally. Its rising and setting are simply views from our limited vantage points. The sunrise and sunset are changing experiences; but the sun is a changeless reality.

Think of the process we call sight. Since infancy we've used our eyes in progressive degrees of perceptiveness. Through the process of sight, objects fall on the retina of the eye upside down, as in a camera. Through nerve endings that are light sensitive, a picture is distributed over several recording points. But by the miracle of vision, we do not see those individual points; these tracings are transformed into one solid view. Furthermore, what the *mind* sees *is not* the solid picture that is communicated to the brain, but what our experience has conditioned us to see. To put it plainly, seeing is not believing—believing *is* seeing. *We* see things not as they are, *but as we are*. Our perception is shaped by our previous experiences.

You see in your life essentially what you believe. Oliver Wendell Holmes, the learned Supreme Court justice, said, "Man's mind, stretched to a new idea, never goes back to its original dimension." The principles discussed in this book may require you to stretch to new ideas. Should you take these words and apply them to your life, you will feel the stretch marks in your mind, and you will never again return to the person that you were before.

This personal transformation from the "old" you—a person bogged down with impossibilities and powerless—to the "new" you—a person who realizes that he is more than just a body, able to think and feel and use his mind in any way that he chooses—will help you tap into the part of you that cannot be understood through the physical senses. This new you is a part of a universal consciousness guided by principles and forces that are always at work. These forces are, in turn, guided by *three magic words*.

The words that I speak of are *right mental attitude*. A right mental attitude is defined as the correct position or bearing in terms of action, feeling, or mood. And it is our actions, feelings, or moods that will determine the actions, feelings, or moods of others toward us. It is our attitude toward life that will determine life's attitude toward us. Now, what does this mean?

Your Attitude Sets the Stage

Our attitudes set the stage for what will occur in our lives—good attitude, good results; fair attitude, fair results; poor attitude, poor results. Each of us shapes his own life; and the shapes of our lives will be and are determined by our attitude.

The person who goes through life, as millions do, saying, "With my luck, the whole thing will go right down the drain!" goes down the drain, over and over again. His attitude sets the stage for failure. If we expect failure and dwell on its possibility, then we will undoubtedly fail again and again. "When there is fear of failure," warned World War II hero General George Patton, "there will be failure." Your mental attitude is a two-way gate on the pathway of life. It can be swung one way toward success, or the other way toward failure.

A right mental attitude, on the other hand, is the habit

of keeping your mind busily locked on your desires and goals. With this attitude you can keep your mind tuned in to those things you wish to experience, and off the things you do not want.

The majority of people go through life with their mental attitudes dominated by fears, anxieties, and worries, seeing only the appearance of failure, which somehow has a way of becoming a reality. Millions of people continually crash on the rocks of bad consequences, often suffering irreparable damage, because they allowed themselves to get caught in rough waters without staying focused. A right mental attitude is the fixed compass assuring that every experience, whether it is pleasant or unpleasant, yields some form of benefit. Only a right mental attitude pays off in the affairs of our everyday living.

You Hold the Key

A number of years ago a haggard-looking, beaten old man entered a posh executive's office in downtown Chicago. Without a formal introduction, the tattered stranger said that a mutual friend recommended that he make the visit with the hope of turning his life around. He went on to say that he had decided to end his life if he failed to get help.

From all outward appearances, the executive's guest was a failure. He had that dull stare of defeat in his eyes, and the drooping shoulders of a man worn down by life. Yet someone must have recognized some degree of worth in him or surely he would have not been sent to the executive's office. The smartly clad businessman stood aghast as he pondered what to do for this unfortunate soul. His imagination raced until suddenly he stumbled upon an idea!

In the rear of his private office was a full-length mirror which was concealed by drapes. The downhearted visitor was asked to stand in front of the curtain while an experiment was being performed. He was told that very little could be done for him, but he would be introduced to someone who might be able to help him regain his self-confidence and overcome his misfortune.

After building up to a dramatic climax, the gentleman jerked the drapes apart and the dejected old man was allowed to meet himself face to face in the mirror. His jaw dropped. He looked at his own image, stunned and speechless. *After a lengthy scrutiny, he realized the solution to his problem.* With sincere thanks, he hugged his compassionate friend, turned and went on his way.

Psychologists know that poverty-stricken people maintain a *poverty consciousness*, some of them from early childhood throughout life. They think in terms of poverty; they fear poverty; they talk poverty; *and prophetically, they expect poverty*. But they have been given the power to intervene and affect the odds in their favor. James Allen, the English essayist and author of the masterpiece *As a Man Thinketh*, was unequivocal on this point when he stated, "A man can only rise, conquer, and achieve by lifting up his thoughts; they themselves are makers of themselves. The mind is the master weaver." No man has ever attained the higher brackets of success without a right mental attitude.

According to Napoleon Hill, a right mental attitude is "the habit of searching for the seed of an equivalent or a greater benefit which comes with every failure, defeat, or adversity we experience."

This seed often germinates into something beneficial. A right mental attitude is the habit of evaluating all problems and distinguishing between those you can master and those beyond your control. The person with a right mental attitude will solve the problems he can control and shun those he has no control over, so they do not influence his mental outlook. A right mental attitude is the habit of acting with a definite purpose, with full belief in the soundness of that purpose and in the ability to achieve it.

For most of us, learning new habits takes time. But once positive habits are mastered, life takes on a new meaning. Those with poor or negative attitudes toward learning, for example, won't learn very much. If you assume an attitude that you cannot reach your goals, you generally will not. With an attitude of despair, you're defeated before you start. What you achieve or fail to achieve is due, in large measure, to your overall attitude.

In order to develop a right mental attitude, you must develop the right mental attitude toward yourself. It can't be repeated too often: *It is the attitude that you have toward yourself that will determine your attitude toward your world.*

Your Attitude Reflects the Real You

It's strange that we're so familiar with ourselves that we tend to take ourselves for granted. We tend to minimize the things that we can accomplish as well as the goals we can reach. For some equally strange reason, we believe others to be more capable of success, and dwell on our ineptness. There remains an enormous gap of undeveloped potential in all of us—a great reserve of talent and ability that we habitually fail to use.

Look at today's black achievers who have reached amazing heights. No matter their endeavors, wherever you find men or women of distinction, you will find a person with the right mental attitude. You need only to think of your friends and acquaintances to prove this. The successful take the attitude that they *can* accomplish whatever they set their minds to. They have a healthy attitude toward themselves, and as a result, toward life. Subsequently, they aim high and come to be called successful, outstanding, and achievers. Quite frankly, they are no more brilliant or outstanding than the majority of people with whom they come in contact. It's their *attitude* that makes the difference.

"The Least Likely to Succeed"

In the winter of 1968, Willie Davis was at an impasse.
Davis was an All-Pro standout with the World Champion
Green Bay Packers, a man possessed who could single-
handedly dominate a football game. At the height of his
career he was arguably the best defensive player in the
game. Despite his on-the-field heroics, however, Davis
was falling far short of his off-season pursuit—to complete a master's degree program at the University of Chicago.

Davis had been toiling away for a number of years, but
the routinization and rigor made him miserable. He was
ready to throw in the towel. After all, he figured, he
could make a decent living in business without a graduate degree—so why bother? This particular morning was
tougher than most. Almost instinctively, Davis cut his
classes and drove to Green Bay, Wisconsin, to discuss
his problems with then head coach Vince Lombardi. For
the first time in his life Willie Davis thought of quitting.

"I thought you had classes today," Lombardi said to
Davis after greeting him.

"I had some personal business to attend to" was Davis's sheepish reply. After seeing that Lombardi wasn't
buying his story, Davis opened up and shared his concern
with his coach. After listening intensively, the usually
fiery Lombardi ignored Davis's self-pity and used a clever
analogy to help solve his problems.

"I've been meaning to tell you, Willie, that we reviewed last year's game films, and the entire staff agrees
that you were at your best in the final quarter of every
game. For the average defensive end, the fourth quarter
is sheer torture. Many players just quit. They don't realize it, but it shows in their performance and it shows
in their lives. But not you, Willie. You're a winner.
You've never quit anything in your life. *Have you*?"

"I guess not, coach," Davis said ashamedly.

Later that afternoon while driving back to Chicago,

Davis reflected on his conversation with Lombardi. The farsighted yet humble head coach had a worthy message. Davis began to think about the many hardships he had experienced during his life. He had encountered the typical problems that many blacks had confronted in a hostile, southern environment: the problems of poverty and withheld opportunities, the problems of low self-esteem and shallow dreams. But Willie Davis was a fighter. Lombardi was right. He had never been a quitter, *and he wasn't going to start now!*

Renewed and refreshed, he began to apply the same *attitude* that he possessed on Sunday afternoons to his studies. For the next two sessions at the university's prestigious business school, Davis barely missed the dean's list by only a fraction of a point, before making it in his final quarter!

Willie Davis was accustomed to tough, uphill battles. For example, in his senior year at a tiny, segregated high school in Texarkana, Arkansas, Davis was voted the "least likely to succeed." Four years later, bent on proving his classmates wrong, he was the only male from his class to graduate from college.

After graduate school and a teaching stint in Cleveland, Ohio, Davis subconsciously began seeking fresh challenges. In 1964, his bid to land an off-season sales job with the Schlitz Brewing Company was unsuccessful. He saw the brewery as a unique opportunity, and hoped to cut his marketing teeth within a major firm. After several attempts he finally convinced the company to hire him in its sales and public relations department. A marketing major in college, Davis was in his element. Once on board, he learned all he could before venturing off on his own. By 1970, he transferred his skills and became the owner and operator of Willie Davis Distributing in Los Angeles—Schlitz's largest beer distributorship on the West Coast. Two years later he rejoined the parent company and served on its board of directors.

In addition to his distributorships, Davis owns a wide

array of enterprises. He branched out from distribution to broadcasting, buying five highly profitable radio stations within varied markets. From there he maneuvered his way into trucking, using his company to transport his beer across the country. In addition to his outside activities, he still finds time to serve on the boards of many of the nation's most successful companies, including Mattel, Fireman's Fund Insurance, and MGM Studios. Paradoxically, the man who was voted the least likely to succeed nearly thirty years ago has become one of the most likely to succeed within corporate America.

Sit up and take notice as he gives you a hint to his secret to success:

I'm often asked, "What was the turning point in your life?" In response, I would have to point to my junior year in high school as the catalyst. During that year, I lacked direction and wrestled with a poor self-image. With no idea of my capabilities, more than once I considered dropping out. As I look back, that would've obviously been a terrible mistake.

But one day while walking home from school, my outlook changed for the better. As I passed a city work crew digging ditches, I noticed from their weary and worn faces their disdain for their jobs, as well as their low self-esteem. Their attitudes were poor, and it reflected in their half-hearted effort. I shuddered at the thought of switching places with them. I didn't want to dig ditches—but if I had to—*I would be the best ditch digger in town*! Only then did I realize that *attitude* meant *everything*!

I knew that my attitude, more than any other factor, would determine my success or failure. Subsequently, I returned to school with a deeper sense of commitment and purpose.

Don't let his message get lost. Willie Davis has more than just a good attitude toward life, *he has the right mental attitude*. He possesses a deep, fundamental belief that whatever the difficulties, no matter the obstacles, he will reach his goal.

The great majority of people begin their days in neutral as far as their attitude is concerned. They depend on external stimuli to determine their attitudes for them. If things go well, their attitude is fine; but if things go poorly—watch out—their attitudes will reflect these circumstances. Beware of the most dangerous and destructive force on earth—*a negative mental attitude!*

Attitudes and Goals

The role your attitude plays in goal achievement cannot be overestimated. Goals without the right mental attitude are not goals at all. There is no sense in pursuing them, for there is no way to reach them. The right mental attitude says, "I can and I will." And when failure strikes—as it most assuredly will—the right mental attitude has a fall-back position from which it will rally again.

Unfortunately and unnecessarily, too many highly skilled people with impressive academic backgrounds stay on the lower rungs of the ladder of success. Above them can be found a surprising number of men and women with less education and schooling. What is the difference? The three magic words. *Right mental attitude is more important than knowledge!*

Jesse Jackson believes the right mental attitude will help you reach any star. No matter how adverse your circumstances, how you react (your attitude) is up to you: "Even in the worst situations, you still have the choice between the high road and the low road. It doesn't take money to buy character, integrity, and decency."

Incredible breakthroughs happen once you face your obstacles with the right mental attitude. In 1969, Dempsey Travis was on the verge of tears as he received a B.A. degree from Chicago's Roosevelt University. Several years later this scene was repeated when he concluded his graduate studies at Northwestern University. Travis's accomplishments are well-known and documented. But the road to success has not always been smooth.

Dempsey Travis was born on Chicago's South Side, the son of a stockyard laborer. After completing high school, he joined the Army and was honorably discharged. Young, energetic, and eager to get ahead, he immediately sought a career in business, but felt inadequate. Why? Because in his own words, "I was such a poor reader. I could barely hold a decent conversation."

Hoping to launch a business of his own, Travis saw his lack of college training as a hurdle that he doubted he would ever clear.

Travis remembers his moments of doubt. "After high school I wanted to go to college, but my reading skills were so poor I thought, what's the use? Even if I started, I didn't know if I would ever finish." He sat quietly and weighed his options. As he came precariously close to dropping the idea of a college degree, the right mental attitude helped him set the record straight. Travis met his challenge head on and went into action.

Dempsey Travis read. And read, and read—relentlessly— five, six, and sometimes seven hours a day *after work* to sharpen his reading skills and enhance his vocabulary. Through it all, he maintained the right attitude. Within a short period the self-assured Travis was reading a book a week and began to master many of literature's most scholarly works. *And then he overcame the final barrier—he took the plunge and enrolled in college.* He says it was the turning point of his life.

Today, the man who was "such a poor reader" is the president of the Travis Realty Company, the Sivart Mortgage Corporation, and a publishing enterprise. Over the course of his professional career, Dempsey Travis has received many honors, including the International Black Writers Award, for his literary skills.

Dempsey Travis has learned the secret of success. He

has discovered that nothing is impossible if you program yourself with the right mental attitude: if you eliminate the word "impossible" from your vocabulary, if you re-program yourself to think positively and view your problems "rightly," and if you look for the possibilities. A right mental attitude enabled him to obtain the desires of his heart.

Problems are inevitable, yet through the power of your mind, you can exert a great deal of control over your destiny. When Napoleon Hill first penned such statements as "Anything the mind can conceive and believe, it can achieve," and "When you're ready for a thing, it will make its appearance," he based his beliefs on centuries of empirical evidence drawn from human experience. The great illusion called misfortune, when viewed "rightly," is just that—an illusion. Misfortune and setbacks are often illusions because we fail to connect the long-term benefits to the negative occurrence.

Whenever you are faced with a knotty dilemma, you always have a clear choice in how you will deal with it. If you brood over the disappointment, you simply magnify your problems out of proportion. It's like taking a pebble off the beach and holding it close to your eyes. This small stone, when held close, can completely block your view. But if you hold it at a proper viewing distance, it can be examined and properly dealt with. If you drop it at your feet, it becomes a stepping-stone.

Dr. Eric Butterworth, a Unity minister and one of the most learned minds of this century, summed up this idea beautifully in his book *Discover the Power Within You*: "Man is not in the world to set it right *but to see it rightly*, and right seeing is the passport from illusion to the heaven of accomplishment. If you want to change the world, or to be influenced for such a change, you must begin within yourself by changing the way you see the world. *I keep my thoughts centered upon only those things that I want to see manifest in my life*."

"America Isn't Ready for a Black Talk Show"

Arsenio Hall's time had come! He had stepped onto center stage in the game of life. Hall had just gained national prominence by signing a two-year, multimillion-dollar contract with Paramount Pictures. In June 1988, his first movie, the box office hit *Coming to America*, was released. His good fortune continued with the promotion of yet another comedy, *Harlem Nights*, again featuring him and his longtime pal Eddie Murphy, that would be released the following summer. Due to Hall's enormous success, Paramount approached him with the idea of hosting a late-night talk show—*something he had waited for his entire life*. But now that his chance had come, he surprisingly turned the studio down—*not once, but twice!* Why? Many sleepless nights ensued as Hall searched for answers and questioned his sanity.

By the time Arsenio was twelve, he had already developed a laserlike focus. Every evening he sat on the edge of his bed, long after his mother had fallen asleep, attentively watching his idol perform. He wanted to follow the path blazed by Johnny Carson and become the next great late-night talk show host.

Hall's admiration for Carson goes back even further. As a child reared in Cleveland, he set up chairs in the basement of his home and pretended to host some of the most starlit names in Hollywood. Even in college, nearly a decade later, he announced in a speech class that he would one day replace the show-biz legend. After graduating from Kent State, where he majored in speech communications, Hall suppressed his desires and worked as a sales rep for a pharmaceutical company. The pay was good but the monotony was sheer torture.

One night, after watching a *Tonight* show segment, he decided to pursue his dream. Against his mother's wishes, he quit his job the next day.

As an entertainer, Hall delighted in his work. Unfortunately, it didn't pay the bills. At least not immediately.

Following a series of breaks as a stand-up comic in Chicago's nightclubs, he left for Los Angeles to perfect his craft. Once he was in California, his skills began to flourish. Through numerous auditions and a little luck, he had established himself as a hot young comedian and promising actor. But in between bit parts and much shorter layoffs, Hall never relinquished hope of one day entertaining late-night viewers.

And now that his moment had arrived, you would think he'd be poised and prepared to make the commitment. Amazingly, he was hesitant.

"Everyone was telling me," Arsenio recalls, " 'it's hard, too hard to crack into the late-night ratings. Television isn't ready for a black talk show host. This is America,' they said, 'and you can forget it.' I began to listen to this nonsense."

Does He Make the Right Decision?

Uncertain as to whether television was indeed ready for a black talk show, and advised by those close to him to reject Paramount's offer, Hall hesitated.

Place yourself in Hall's position. Unfortunately, we live in a negative world, a world in which we continually meet people who try to convince us that what we want to do can't be done. In truth, every successful person in history has been told—many times—that what he wanted couldn't be done. *The important question is whether or not you or anyone else will allow negative inputs to prevent you from taking action.*

Thankfully, Arsenio Hall thought clearly and considered the facts. And then fate intervened. On July 21, 1988, while promoting an upcoming movie, Hall appeared as a guest on the *Tonight* show. Here he was, at last, sitting in the chair to the right of the man, Johnny Carson, who had inspired him for most of his life. "It was eerie," he remembers. "I sat there watching the master at work. I soon realized the opportunity that was before me. It was my goal! Right then, I decided to accept Paramount's offer. I said the hell with 'too hard'! I had to trust my own judgment. All my life, I've wanted to do what this man does."

In order to make the correct decision in any situation, you must be able to think clearly and accurately, and approach all the "facts" with a healthy skepticism. Achievers who possess the right mental attitude learn to trust their own judgment and are cautious, no matter who tried to influence them. The accurate thinker recognizes all the facts, both the good and the bad, and assumes the responsibility of separating and organizing the two, choosing the facts that serve his needs and rejecting all others.

The majority of people who fail to accumulate riches sufficient to meet their needs are easily influenced by the opinions of others. They permit newspapers or friends or relatives to do their thinking for them. Opinions are the cheapest commodities on earth. Everyone has a flock of opinions ready to be heaped upon anyone who will listen. If you are influenced by opinions when you reach decisions, you will not succeed in any undertaking.

The Meaning of the Right Mental Attitude

The measure of success that you achieve in your lifetime—personal, financial, or otherwise—will be governed more by your attitude than by any other single factor. There are no physical, intellectual, or spiritual limitations that cannot be overcome with the right mental attitude.

It is your inner conviction, the fire in your guts, that keeps you going long after everyone else has decided it isn't worth the effort. It is the persistence to follow your plan, your hunch, your intuition, when everyone you know is telling you that you are making a foolish mistake.

When you've lost a skirmish or even a major battle,

the right mental attitude is the little voice in your head that whispers, "I'll never make that mistake again." It's knowing that the painful lessons learned from temporary setbacks will make you a stronger and better person. It is the assurance that defeat is, after all, only temporary. You'll simply dust yourself off and charge back into the fray, only slightly the worse for the wear.

When desire for a purposeful life becomes a fixed habit, it consumes so much of your time, attention, and energy that there is no place for a negative outlook. Here, then, is the starting point for the development of a right mental attitude. Though successful people come in all shapes and sizes, and in widely varying degrees of intelligence, background, and education, they nevertheless have one thing in common: *They expect more good out of life than bad; and they expect to succeed more often than they fail.*

As you seek a worthy goal or ideal, take the attitude that there are more reasons why you *can* reach your objective than reasons why you cannot. Set out to earn it; go after it, ask for it—and nine times out of ten you'll get it.

Your environment is really a mirror of your mental attitude. If you don't like your environment, you first have to change your attitude. The world plays no favorites; it is totally impersonal. It cares not who succeeds or who fails. Your attitude toward life doesn't affect the world and its inhabitants nearly as much as it affects you. It would be impossible to estimate the number of jobs that have been lost, the number of promotions missed, the number of sales blown, or the number of marriages ruined, by poor attitudes.

Unfortunately, there is no protection against those who, either by design or ignorance, poison the minds of others with negative suggestion. Just look about you. Look at those who enjoy their work, their families, and their lives; *now look at those who don't.* What's the difference between the two? *Happy and satisfied people control their mental attitude.* They take a positive view of their world. When something isn't to their liking, they look first to themselves. They constantly learn more about their lives through personal self-development, which ultimately results in higher self-esteem and greater satisfaction.

But those who are unhappy clutch the wrong mental attitude tightly. Indeed, it is almost as if they want to be unhappy. They search for everything about which to complain—their jobs, their spouses, their family, their lives. This form of mental self-destruction often destroys one's chances of acquiring riches or attaining one's goals.

Studies made of the lives of thousands of successful people have shown that they radiate confidence and assurance; they expect success, and they receive it—in abundance. You can spot people who possess a right mental attitude by their walk, their speech, and their outlook toward life. You can feel their presence when they enter the room. Whoever you are, you too can attract success.

The Pursuit of Excellence

Human beings at the highest level of evolution have three forces at work: instinct and its development, called intuition; the unique capacity to pass on information; and the ability to take past knowledge and project it into the future. The progress of man is the result of these evolutionary factors. Mankind's substantial leap upward is generally built upon the accumulated knowledge of the past, and this progress is sometimes called the "divine urge."

Implanted within you is the need to continually improve your condition—a desire for fulfillment, a stirring ambition. These drives motivate you to seek and to find; to look within yourself and to seek without; to attain a way of life that will produce for you that new, better, more developed level of existence.

Each time you desire a greater good, have a need for

achievement, the divine urge impels you into action. It is right mental thinking for you to be fulfilled. It is right for you to have success and prosperity in your experience. But it is up to you to determine the nature of this fulfillment and the time frame.

The pursuit of excellence must be pursued through thought, reason, and conscious acts. Man has special instincts that can be called the action of the human spirit. However you describe it, these instincts drive the human being toward accomplishment. Striving for the greater, the better, the noble, is a valid quest.

The Right Mental Attitude Leads to Personal Excellence

Words motivate, especially when they are offered in the spirit of a right mental attitude and come from someone whom we love and respect. As a young man, Jesse Hill was moved to personal excellence by his mother. A proud black woman with a formal education only through the eighth grade, she had a Ph.D. from the school of hard knocks. She would share her years of wisdom with her son.

"I stand on the shoulders of those gone before me," says Jesse Hill, president and chief executive officer of the Atlanta Life Insurance Company. "As much as I welcome compliments, I am not a self-made man. I cannot forget those who have sacrificed on my behalf.

"I was fortunate to experience the loving guidance of a mother who, although she never attended high school, worked hard to pave the way for me and my sister to secure an education. She stressed two key principles: *One, give praise to God, from whom all blessings flow; and two, always pursue excellence and give your best no matter what the task.*" Like many achievers, Hill lived by these and similar words—words that wiped out poverty and disappointment, and emboldened his heart for future conquests.

As a young boy in St. Louis, Missouri, Hill received

an early dose of business training while working for his grandfather, who sold fruit, coal, and wood from a horse-drawn wagon to keep food on his family's table. Hill's modest earnings enabled him to attend Lincoln University, where he graduated with honors in mathematics and physics. A year later he continued his education and earned a master's degree in business from the University of Michigan.

After college Hill set his sights on Atlanta, Georgia, having heard many favorable reports. Among the more interesting items was the news that an ex-slave, A. F. Herndon, had built a hugely successful insurance empire there that stood as a shining example to black enterprise. Hill's emotions raced as his professors told intriguing tales of Atlanta's sky-rocketing growth and development. They thought a young man like himself might be able to make a decent start. Based on these conversations, Hill was hooked. His attraction became twofold: first, to Atlanta in general; and second, to Atlanta Life, the black institution that was the source of his inspiration. Hill hoped to make a contribution to both.

Hill possessed raw energy that could penetrate. Upon his arrival, he convinced Atlanta Life officials of his deep sense of purpose and commitment. In order to learn every phase of the business, he toiled faithfully at the bottom in an entry-level position, spending his time searching for ways to make the firm more profitable and efficient. From there he moved to planning, then sales, and finally management—leaving his imprint on every department.

His civic involvement grew equally as fast. During his first three years at Atlanta Life, Hill spent nearly every evening serving Atlanta in a variety of capacities. For example, he taught Sunday school at his local church, served as secretary of the Atlanta Negro Business League, and even volunteered as a scoutmaster to provide leadership and direction to young black boys. In subsequent years he held similar key positions with the NAACP, the Community Chest, and the Atlanta Urban League.

To his surprise, his early community involvement did not go unnoticed. At twenty-five Hill became one of Atlanta's youngest citizens to be honored for his tireless efforts in the city's black community.

In 1973, after a promotion to vice-president and chief actuary officer, Hill was selected by Norris Herndon, the son of the founder, to succeed him upon his retirement. Herndon appointed Hill president and chief executive officer. Hill's first bold iniatiative was to direct a new strategy that focused on acquisitions. Next, he launched a Career Sales and Management Academy for once-overlooked business students of Atlanta's predominately black colleges. The academy, which is based at Clark-Atlanta University, is geared to place promising young candidates on the managerial fast track.

Under Hill's tutelage, at a time when black insurance companies were facing severe economic hardships from larger, more competitive firms, Atlanta Life has continued to flourish and became a beacon of hope to other black institutions. In 1989, its net worth exceeded $130 million.

Today, Jesse Hill is as much a key figure in the civic, political, and economic mainstream of Black America as he is at Atlanta Life. He has earned a national reputation for his business savvy, serving on the corporate boards of Delta Air Lines and Knight-Ridder Newspapers while directing the efforts of the Martin Luther King, Jr. Center for Nonviolent Social Change. From administrative assistant to company president to civic directorships, Hill's involvement has been vast and wide. His many talents prompt—no, impel—others to do their best.

What was Hill's secret? *That success arrives only through the pursuit of excellence and the right mental attitude.*

We are not all born with a drive for excellence like Jesse Hill. That quality comes only from learning and experience. But we are born with exuberance and curiosity, and when these qualities are combined with great expectations, we can expect marvelous results. We try harder and put more of ourselves into what we do when we expect the best.

An expectant attitude—an attitude that expects positive things to happen, that expects success—has an uncanny way of shaping future events and bringing together the most astonishing coincidences—whether it's people, if you need people; or money, if you need money. Remember, life is nothing more than the sum total of many successful years; a successful year is nothing more than the sum total of many successful months; a successful month is the result of successful weeks; and so on. That's why practicing a right mental attitude is the surest way to win over the long term.

Make It a Habit

It's been said that life is dull only to dull people. It's equally as true to say that life is interesting only to interesting people; or life is successful only to successful people. One of the sad realities of our world is that most people are unhappy in their work. Many people believe that if they could just make more money, they would enjoy their work. Ironically, it's the other way around: If people viewed their work with the right mental attitude, they would probably make more money. You have to enjoy your work naturally; work must be an end in itself. But how?

First, from an attitude standpoint, you must become mentally that which you wish to achieve. You must *act*, *look*, and *feel* successful *before* the success you seek will come. How does a person develop the right mental attitude? By forming the habit of developing a good, positive, expectant attitude toward life. Why? Because actions trigger feelings, just as feelings trigger actions.

Chances are that you know people who seem to be what others call "lucky" or "get all the breaks." These achievers give the impression of happily sailing through life, having a joyous time reaching one goal after another. If you will conscientiously undertake what I recommend, and focus on this principle, you'll find yourself joining this small, happy, and extremely productive group. You'll find yourself becoming lucky, and most of your problems will take care of themselves.

For the next thirty days approach the world—everything and everyone with whom you come into contact—with an attitude that represents the kind of results you want to achieve. That is, if the outcome you wish is more success in your present line of work, act as though you already possess it. If you want others to treat you with admiration and respect, treat others with admiration and respect first. If you desire more from others—more love, more support, more time—then give of yourself first. Give your love. Give your support. Give your time—first. For the next thirty days treat every person you come in contact with as the most important person on earth.

Do this for two reasons. First, as far as that person is concerned, he or she *is* the most important person on earth. You may never get him to admit this, but that's the way he feels. Second, do it because this is the manner in which human beings ought to treat each other.

But *everyone?* you ask. Why should we treat the cab driver or waitress or delivery boy with the same respect and courtesy that we show to our family and friends? Again, for two reasons. First, by treating everyone in like manner, we form correct habits. Every man is where he is and what he is because of his habits. By repeating these thoughts and deeds, you are forming habits that will carry on automatically once they have been set in motion. Second, no one is more important than anyone else. By approaching everyone with the same warmth and generosity, you will touch all hearts with which you come in contact.

There's nothing in the world that men, women, and children want and need more than the feeling that they're important; that they're needed and respected. They will give their love, their affection, their respect, and their business to the person who fills this need.

A Lesson from a Child

One Saturday morning a minister was busily trying to prepare his sermon under the most difficult conditions. His wife was out shopping. It was a rainy day, and his young son was restless and bored, with little to do. Finally, in desperation, the minister picked up an old magazine and thumbed through it until he came to a large brightly colored picture. It showed a map of the world. He tore the page from the magazine, ripped it into little pieces and scattered the scraps all over the living room floor with the words, "Son, if you can put this page together, I'll give you a quarter."

The preacher hoped this might take his son most of the morning, but within ten minutes there was a knock on his study door. His son had completed the puzzle. The minister was amazed to see that the boy had finished the project so soon, with the pieces of paper neatly arranged and the map of the world back in order.

"Son, how did you get that done so fast?" his father asked.

"Oh," said the boy, "it was easy. On the other side there was a picture of a man. I just put a piece of paper on the bottom, put the picture of the man together, put a piece of paper on top, and then turned it over. I figured that if I got the man right, the world would be right."

His father smiled, and handed his son a quarter.

"Not only have you earned that quarter, but you've given me my sermon for tomorrow. *If a man is right, his world will be right!*"

There's a great lesson in this tale. If you are unhappy with your world and want to change it, the place to start is with yourself, using the three magic words—right mental attitude. *If you are right, your world will be right.* Your attitude is the one thing over which you have absolute control. This is one of the most significant and inspiring facts known to man.

Attitude control is the result of self-discipline and habit. Either you control your attitude or it controls you; there is no compromise. The most practical way to control your attitude is to develop the habit of staying focused on your goal. This is the starting point for the development of a right mental attitude. Study the record of any man or woman who has achieved success, and you will observe that he possessed the right mental attitude and directed his mind toward the attainment of definite objectives.

They Possess the Right Mental Attitude

Call it desire, perseverance, determination—but it was the *right mental attitude* that provided General Colin L. Powell, the son of Jamaican immigrants, the springboard to rise to the position of chairman of the Joint Chiefs of Staff, making him the number-one military officer in all the armed forces and the first black ever to occupy that post. Said the press of General Powell's appointment, "He is the model of a major staff officer—universally popular and respected within the White House. The President seems to be very comfortable with him."

It took persistence, faith, and the right mental attitude to propel Robert Maynard from the streets of Bedford-Stuyvesant to the office of editor-in-chief of the *Oakland Tribune*. Maynard has become the first black editor, publisher, and owner of a major metropolitan daily newspaper.

"Much of what I have learned," Maynard says, "has come by watching my father, who was a successful businessman in his own right. He established a pattern of excellence in education matched only by hard work, and he felt anything could be accomplished by approaching it with the right attitude." Today, Robert Maynard is a man with his shoulder to the wheel. His mission is to continue to produce a quality newspaper that Oakland can be proud of.

Family and friends tried to convince Donnie Cochran that his dream of becoming a member of the Navy's prestigious flight squad, the Blue Angels, was impossible. "After all," they warned, "no black had ever been selected to the precision flying team." Fortunately, Cochran turned a deaf ear and refused to listen to their advice. "I will reach my goals!" he exclaimed. The only question was *when*—not *if*—and that was answered in 1978, when he enrolled in aviator training school.

Eight years later the barriers had fallen. Lieutenant Commander Donnie Cochran mesmerized the Navy, as well as the naysayers in his native Pelham, Georgia, when he took command of the sleek, sky-blue A-4 Skyhawk aircraft. The right mental attitude enabled him to tame the skies.

In 1940, while working in a feed mill for twenty-five cents an hour, Eddie Robinson was told by men with negative minds that he wouldn't amount to much. Undeterred, Robinson ignored his critics and concentrated on his first love—coaching football. Robinson had all the tools; he was an effective motivator and a good judge of young men. Deep within his heart he felt that if he was willing to pay the price with hard work, determination, and the right mental attitude, his chance would come.

Robinson was right—his chance did come! Tiny Grambling University offered him his first and only coaching job. Since 1941 he's been a fixture along the sidelines. Robinson's persuasive style and leadership attracted top national talent to the small black college tucked into the Louisiana foothills. Five decades later Eddie Robinson became college football's all-time winningest coach. When probing sports writers asked for his key to success, the head coach said, "It's been said that no one can really motivate anyone else; all you can do is instill a positive attitude and hope it catches on."

In the 1960s Mary Frances Berry meant to have a full

say in ending the racial and sexist myths of her day. Throughout her fabled career, Mary Berry has been an apostle of self-help, a fighter for dignity, and an unrepentant lover of her race.

Even as a poor black child raised in the South, she dared to question and challenge the social norms of the day. Mary Berry would not be barred from making a difference. "My mother would say to me, 'You, Mary Frances, you're smart,' " she recounts. " 'But you have a responsibility to use your mind, and go as far as it will take you.' " Due in part to the influence of her mother, Mary Berry refused to believe that women were born with innate limitations, and set out to prove her worth.

While studying both law and history during the day at Howard University, she worked full-time as a lab assistant in a D.C. hospital. It was a grueling schedule that lasted four years. More than once she was tempted to drop out because of the stress and work load. In those times of difficulty, Mary leaned against her mother's words and strong teachings. Her favorite homily was the words written by Paul in Romans: "Glory in tribulations, knowing that tribulation produces perseverance; and perseverance, character; and character, hope. And hope does not disappoint."

"Struggle takes a long time," she says. "In order to succeed you must be armed with the right mental attitude. Because sometimes when it seems like you're losing, you're really winning."

Over the years, Dr. Berry has hit all her targets. As past chairman of the Commission on Civil Rights; professor of history and law; member of the bar; scholar with many published books to her credit; Assistant Secretary of Health, Education, and Welfare; and, at thirty-eight, the first black woman to head a major college—the University of Colorado—she has been awarded more citations and honorary degrees than her office walls can hold.

Let it be remembered that the sole difference between

Mary Berry and her trying circumstances was this: Dr. Berry had a mind and controlled it through the use of a right mental attitude. This alone gave her strength and the wings to carry her to success.

Change Your Attitude and Change Your Life!

When a person develops the right mental attitude, he has already placed himself on the road to what he seeks. He has prepared the ground and planted the seed. He has made himself the embodiment of what he wants to become, and is using one of life's most precious gifts. The story of Bill Demby illustrates how it works.

As a young man Bill Demby didn't seem to have the stuff of which success is made. He grew up poor on Maryland's Eastern Shore and was a country boy at heart. A basketball fanatic in high school, he hoped to play professionally, but when a guidance counselor told him he wasn't college material, he took a job making batteries at a nearby manufacturing plant. In 1970, he was drafted.

A year later Demby's basketball hopes came to an abrupt end. On March 26, 1971, on a road outside Quang Tri, a Vietcong rocket blew up the truck he was driving. The twenty-year-old Army private from Price, Maryland, never saw it coming. "It was like a quarter hit the side of the door—there was a 'ping' sound," he recalls. "All I remember is smoke filling the truck, and I saw my left leg on the floor."

Demby was helicoptered to the 95th Evacuation Hospital. There, minutes later, his left leg already severed below the knee, doctors amputated his right leg after seeing that his foot had been so badly crushed as to make the leg useless.

In the helicopter on the way to the hospital, Demby remembers wondering "how my family would react, whether they would accept me. I knew I wasn't going to change inside, but society judges you physically. If my family held up, so would I."

But he did change. Back home he spent a year at the Walter Reed Army Hospital, and when he left, he began drinking heavily as well as experimenting with drugs. One night, after one such binge, he hit rock bottom when he passed out on his mother's couch.

"When I woke up," Demby said, "I found my mother and sister clutching each other and crying. They told me I had said I was going to kill somebody. That's when I decided to turn my life around."

Sports became Demby's rehab. He learned to ski while at Walter Reed, and in 1974 took up wheelchair basketball, playing in area tournaments. He found that participation in athletics gave him the self-confidence he needed to move ahead in other areas as well. And then it all came together. He was in Tennessee in 1987 at one such tournament sponsored by the U.S. Amputee Athletic Association when he was invited to audition for a Du Pont commercial.

The chemical firm had expanded its research into highly resilient plastics, the type that are used in prostheses, making artificial limbs lifelike. Demby became one of the original testers of a new prosthesis called the "Seattle Foot," developed for the U.S. Veterans Administration. The foot, made with Du Pont Delrin acetal resin, was more flexible than the limbs Demby used previously. Because the new prostheses work in the same manner muscles move—storing and releasing energy as a real foot does—they gave him the freedom to move and jump. This cleared the way for Demby to play stand-up basketball again.

Du Pont sent representatives of its advertising agency to the amputee tournament. Demby and four other disabled men wearing prostheses played basketball, with personnel from the ad agency looking on. After a series of informal interviews, Demby was told that he had been selected from the five to be the star of the Du Pont spot.

However, Demby was far from thrilled. Hesitant at first, he had never exposed his artificial limbs to the public, and seemed genuinely embarrassed. But in the end he consented. The TV commercial was shot on a basketball court in New York City. It showed Demby holding his own in a rough-and-tumble game with able-bodied players and took a day to produce. The agency quickly put the commercial together while Demby—totally exhausted—flew back to Maryland. A month later the spot aired on the national networks and changed his life forever.

Bill Demby can't jump as well as he did when he was averaging 16 points a game for his high school basketball team in 1969. Nor can he dribble past would-be defenders as he did against other eighteen-year-olds. But through steel-like determination and the right mental attitude, Bill Demby has changed lives. One such magic moment happened on the streets near his home: "One day a stranger approached me. He told me that he had fallen onto bad times and explained the details of his difficulties. He had lost his job, and his family had left him. He said that life had turned its back and he had given up hope until he saw my story on TV. Seeing me in that commercial, he said, turned him around. He thanked me for changing his life.

"Though it happens all the time, I never get used to it. I walked away so he wouldn't see me cry."

Demby's inspiration and motivation have since become sought after. Ironically—after being told he wasn't college material—he enrolled in college and finished. He has grown accustomed to the public recognition, lifting spirits wherever he goes. He has also expanded his athleticism to include other sports—running, track and field, and drag racing. Perhaps one of his most commendable activities is his involvement in programs like the "disAbility Awareness Project" and the National Handicapped Sports and Recreation Association. He brings much-needed attention to the *nation's largest minority group—disabled Americans*.

Fortunately, not everyone is faced with problems as

severe as Bill Demby's. There is a lesson in his story. No one will ever know the number of lives he has touched. Thousands are facing their rehabilitation efforts with greater determination and courage because of his inspiration. Let each of us look inward to make sure that we give of ourselves. We must give our time, our support, our love, and our attitude.

Before metal can be cast into a desired shape, the mold must first be fashioned; before a building can be erected, the excavation must be constructed and the foundation put in place. Before a person can achieve the kind of life he desires, he must become that kind of individual. He must *think, act, talk, walk*, and *conduct* himself in all of his affairs as would the person he wishes to become—*in the spirit of a right mental attitude*. He is then actually that person, and the things that person would have and do will naturally come to him.

What Lies Ahead?

It's true: A right mental attitude takes effort, patience, and practice to gain and maintain. But a definite purpose, clear thinking, creative vision, action, and persistence, all applied with enthusiasm and faith, will go far to help you achieve and maintain a positive and upbeat attitude. Remember, *if the man is right, his world will be right!*

What lies ahead? All that you desire. Begin now to acquire the right mental attitude by using the following mind conditioners.

1. *It is your attitude toward life that will determine life's attitude toward you.* Feed your mind with positive, nourishing thoughts just as you feed your body with nourishing food. Program your mind with *faith, hope,* and *enthusiastic expectancy.* Replace every doubt with a faith stronger than doubt.
2. *Overcome negative thinking or negative mental attitudes.* Your basic thought should be: "I can, if I know

I can.'' Negative thoughts will produce negative results, while positive thinking draws positive experiences into your life.

3. *Before you can achieve the type of life you desire, you must become the type of individual you desire to be.* You must think, act, walk, talk, and conduct yourself in your affairs as would the person you wish to become. *Overcome any sense of inferiority.* An inferiority complex is, after all, only a mental outlook on life. It is a merely a denial that there is a power greater than you, a power great enough to overcome any obstacle.

4. *Radiate the attitude of well-being and confidence.* The person who knows where he is going will soon find that good things just seem to happen.

5. *Make prayer and affirmative meditation a part of your life.* Prayer is not something that should be reserved for life's emergencies. Your entire life should be a prayer. Pray as if everything depended on God, and act as if everything depended on you.

6. *The deepest craving of human beings is to be needed, to feel important, to be appreciated.* Give appreciation and others will return appreciation to you.

7. *Part of the right mental attitude is to look for the best in new ideas;* innovate, create, and search for new ideas.

8. *Don't waste your time discussing personal problems;* it probably won't help you, and cannot help others.

9. *For the next thirty days treat everyone with whom you come in contact as the most important person on earth.* If you'll do this for thirty days, you'll do this for the rest of your life.

12

Outer Space: Your Great Discovery

"What makes the great great? It is a sense of destiny!"
—PETER DANIELS

"The mind is the standard of the man."
—PAUL LAWRENCE DUNBAR

"You can be anything you want to be, if only you believe with sufficient conviction and act in accordance with your faith; for whatever the mind can conceive and believe, the mind can achieve."
—NAPOLEON HILL

The great savannahs of the African continent are ancient and seemingly changeless. It's a place where the wind blows and the days pass as they did millions of years ago. It is a land rich and beautiful, but mysterious. Here life abounds, though death is never far off. In this unforgiving place nature and time brought forth a creature unlike any before; upright and curious, confident and adept, this creature saw the world unlike anyone before him. Forced from the jungle into the savannah, it emerged a fierce competitor. Armed with a brain of unparalleled power, it was not only able to adapt to its world, but have its world adapt to it. A new being had stepped forth. A human being. *A black man!*

We are newcomers against the vast backdrop of the past. We are human beings with a brain. A brain that would soon reshape the very world that brought it forth.

318

Within this brain burns an invisible cellular flame that controls its world. It struggles with the most human of questions: "Who am I?" and "Why am I?" This human houses a steering mechanism that can refashion positive and negative thoughts as artfully as it could fashion flame and food and shelter for its survival.

The human brain is a three-pound mental guide wire that is comprised of one hundred billion soft, wet, fragile cells, small enough to balance in the palm of the hand. Here resides the architecture of our experience, the mindscape of human thought. But how does this mass of tissue weave the human mind? How does its crackling fires stop time in memory? Though it does not generate enough energy to illuminate a light bulb, the brain is still the most powerful energy source on earth. It is the center of every insight and invention, every vision and idea, every symphony, painting, and poem. To paraphrase William Shakespeare: *This is truly the stuff of which dreams are made.*

This cellular network holds the record of who and what we are and the experience we call life. And through it flow the forces that have accomplished all that our species has brought to the planet. No mammal enters the universe more helpless than the human being, but none shows so much promise. While creatures are blessed with greater speed, size, and strength, they lack the power of the human brain.

By now you realize that all that man achieves or fails to achieve is the result of his own thoughts. A man can rise, conquer, and achieve only by lifting his thoughts. He will remain weak, spiritless, and miserable by refusing to do so. Before a man can achieve anything, he must lift his thoughts above slavish animal indulgence. The higher he lifts his thoughts, the more upright and righteous he becomes, the greater will be his success and the more blessed and enduring his achievements.

The universe does not favor the greedy, the dishonest, the lazy, although on the surface it may sometimes appear to do so. Instead, it helps the honest, the persevering, and the virtuous. A strong man cannot help a weaker man unless the weaker man is *willing* to be helped. And even then, the weaker man must become strong himself; he must, *by his own efforts,* develop the strength that he admires in another. *No one but he can alter his condition.* There is nothing in the universe that limits him. The great masters of the ages have declared this in varying forms. To prove this maxim, a man needs only to persist in making himself more virtuous by lifting his thoughts.

Achievement of any kind is the crowning effort of self-discipline. With the support of the aforementioned principles, a man ascends; through neglect that same man declines.

The Ultimate Resource

When asked to describe man's greatest resource, James Allen, the English essayist, told the following tale.

One day, two successful businessmen were standing on the bridge overlooking Niagara Falls, impressed by the breathtaking view. One turned to the other and said, "Behold the greatest source of undeveloped power in America."

"No!" replied his friend. *"America's greatest source of undeveloped power is the soul of man."*

In our country thousands of people of all races try desperately to excuse themselves for their lack of achievement. Millions turn their attention toward poverty and failure, and are receiving both in overabundance. Try to uncover any reason for this inactivity and you will hear the following arguments: "It's society's fault," or "The circumstances are beyond my control," or better yet, "You either have it or you don't." These people view themselves as victims of an unforgiving system rigged for their eventual demise. When you study the unheralded accomplishments of the thousands who have walked out of the ghettos into greatness, you uncover the truth: *These poor, despondent victims are actually volunteers who are ignorantly cooperating in their own failure.*

Many men and women idle away their lives, waiting for something to turn up or for someone to give them a boost. The greatest evil lies within the minds of those who believe that the world owes them something, or that somebody must help them before they ever start. Let me hasten to remind you of those valuable words spoken by Theodore Roosevelt, who emphatically stated, ''Begin where you stand!''

The greatest resources of the world today are not those that lie beneath the earth. Natural resources such as oil, iron, platinum, and yes, even gold, when compared to the resources that each of us has at our disposal, are virtually worthless. The greatest resources are *human* resources—that is, *the need of the human soul to desire, to produce, to be self-reliant.*

Langston Hughes, the prolific and acclaimed writer, knew the true meaning of this ultimate resource. Few American writers have had such rich and varied experiences, and few were so indiscriminate in selecting materials for their works. A broken family and a segregated society appeared to offer him little. When life seemed to close its doors, he turned to writing and discovered a different world. Never one to forget his cultural past, Hughes wrote with a passion concerning the plight of Black America in the 1930s. So talented was he that the literary world referred to him as ''Shakespeare in Harlem.''

Though Hughes was a victim of discrimination, his deepest allegiance and hope for the future was distinctively tied to the country of his birth. He wrote:

All over America there has been an economic color line against the Negro. Since the Civil War, we have been kept, as a racial group, in the lowest economic bracket. Look around you on the main street of any American city. There are no colored clerks, no colored street car conductors, no colored girls at the switchboards of the telephone company. Even in Harlem, nine times out of ten, the man who comes to collect your rent is white. Yet America is a land where, in spite of its defects, I can write this article. Here, the voice of democracy is still heard.

Being black and poor did not distract Hughes from realizing his ultimate resource—*hope for the future!*

Stand Up and Step Out!

Unfortunately, too many of my race cannot define or specify what exactly keeps them back. All too frequently they feel there's "something"—whether they call it fate, hard luck, or "the system"—that binds them to lives of misery and poverty. Perhaps this is the most bitter irony of all. Some even tell of what wonderful things they *could* accomplish *if only* they could cut the cords that tie them; *if only they could* sever the shackles that hold them to insufferably boring lives. They feel *if only they could* rid themselves of their impediment, they could soar into achievement.

Do not hypnotize yourself with the idea that you are not in possession of this ultimate resource. Do not talk of such nonsense. *There is nothing in the universe that limits you,* or that could or would desire to limit you. As long as you *think* you are inhibited, you will never rise above those boundaries. The man who acknowledges that he is only a menial laborer will never become a leader of others—unless he changes his conviction. He is simply paralyzed by his inability to recognize and put into action his ultimate resource.

The world stands back and takes notice of the exceptional man or woman—regardless of color—who can step out from the crowd and do things in an original way, who can facilitate new ideas. The world is looking for leaders, always searching for aggressive and progressive men and women—those who identify with success and can show others how to attain it. Booker T. Washington makes the point crystal clear. "I have begun everything with the idea that I could succeed, and I never had much patience with the multitudes who theorized why my goals were impossible. I've always had a high regard for the man who could tell me how to succeed." There is no shortage of human robots who will do just enough to hold their places within the ranks. The world craves creativity, individuality, and successful methods. Supply a waiting world with these needs, and it will beat a path to your door. *Black America, this is your responsibility!*

The Person You Are Meant to Be

About a year before his death George Bernard Shaw granted a rare interview to a well-known journalist. The reporter's questions were designed to lead the famous English playwright to reminisce. One of the journalist's probing questions was "Mr. Shaw, you have known some of the greatest men of our time—statesmen, artists, philosophers, and writers—and you've outlived most of them. Suppose it were possible for you to talk with one of them again, whom would it be? Which man do you miss the most?" Without hesitation, Shaw, whose biting wit had made him internationally known, retorted, "The man I miss most is the man I could have been."

One need not be a renowned philosopher to be able to look back at "the man I could have been." But retrospect without purpose has little value. When you compare yourself to what you were yesterday, what differences do you find? Is life a challenge? Do you have a sense of personal fulfillment? *Who is the person you were meant to be?*

Have you ever heard a person say, "I'm sorry, but I can't help it, that's just the way I am?" This person is indeed to be pitied. And if such a person truly believes he has no more control than that over the one person for whom he has been given complete control, he can't possibly believe his life is run by anything more than chance, whim, or circumstance. The truth is, he *can* help it; and if he chooses not to change the way he thinks or acts, he is delinquent in his most basic, moral responsibility—*his responsibility to himself.* As you begin to gain self-control, you will also acquire self-knowledge. You will discover your true self.

Though it's true that we are all different—some of us are strong, industrious self-starters, while others are not—all of us can be successful to some extent. But far too many of us don't know we can control our lives, our futures, our destinies; that we can discover the persons we were meant to be.

If you wish to uncover your true self, examine your surroundings—your home, your community, your peers. These are a reflection and extension of you, just as much as your image is a reflection in the mirror. Do you like what you see? Remember, it is just as easy to see yourself a success as it is to see yourself a failure—and far more interesting. What about the attitudes of your friends? Do you enjoy their friendship? Do they treat you with respect and admiration?

Seek to know yourself. When you do, then and only then will you discover the process of building the *inner* person.

The Master Key to Riches

What does this process need more than anything else? *It needs self-discipline.* What is self-discipline? In the philosophy of success taught by Napoleon Hill, self-discipline might be described as the counterbalance of enthusiasm. Self-discipline is the principle that channels your enthusiasm in the right direction. Without it, enthusiasm resembles the unharnessed lightning of an electrical storm; it may strike anywhere, leaving death and destruction in its trail.

Like so many of the principles of success, self-discipline must constantly be practiced before it can be mastered. If you force yourself to meet prescribed deadlines, to go the extra mile, to stay with a task until its completion, to replace negative habits with positive ones, then you are on your way toward developing self-discipline.

In simplest terms, self-discipline is taking control of your mind, your habits, and your emotions. Until you master self-discipline, you cannot be a leader of others, and success will evade your grasp. Self-discipline is the ability to *do what you should do, when you should do it, whether you want to or not.* We all have our moments of supreme dedication, whether it's fidelity to others or loyalty to an ideal. But how many of us can carry out that resolution when the mood has left and the tide of temptation comes sweeping in? Self-discipline means the development of inner strength, conscious willpower, overwhelming desire, and the determination to reach any goal. If you want to change your thoughts into realities, your desires into achievement, the all-important key is *self-discipline.*

In his best-seller *Creating Wealth,* Robert Allen writes, "In the locker rooms and lunch halls they will talk about success, and hitting the jackpot, and luck. 'One day my ship will come in.' 'One day I'll strike it rich'; not a second thought about the years of preparation that goes into most successes. The sacrifices. The planning. The coordination. The sleepless nights. The prices paid. The self-discipline."

William Hazlitt, the noted English essayist, had a refreshingly positive sense of what is at play. Hazlitt simply said, "Those who can command themselves, command others." The person who is not the master of himself may never become the master of anything outside of himself. He who masters his earthly destiny becomes, to paraphrase Henley, the master of his fate, the captain of his soul.

We all go through life searching for freedom—personal freedom, religious freedom, financial freedom—yet most of us never find it. Why? The Creator provided the means by which men could be free. He gave every man and woman access to these means; and He inspired every man and woman with impelling motives for the attainment of freedom. Then why do men and women go through life imprisoned in jails of their own making—the jail of poverty, the jail of fear, the jail of ignorance—when the keys to the door of freedom are easily within their reach? *Because the door to freedom can only be unlocked with the key of self-discipline.*

Many individuals search their entire lives for power, fame, fortune, and "acres of diamonds." However, most never reach their goals. Why? Because they fail to realize that their real source of power lies within. The mechanism of the mind is a profound system of organized power that can be released by only one means—*strict self-discipline.*

The disciplined person is inner-directed toward definite ends, and is an irresistible power who recognizes no obstacle as permanent defeat. He converts his setbacks into victory. He makes stepping-stones out of stumbling blocks and reaches for the stars, using the force of the universe to carry him to his every desire. *The person who masters himself through self-discipline will never be mastered by others!*

Self-Discipline in Action

Principles such as a pleasing personality, faith, imagination, persistence, freedom from fear and failure, right mental attitude, and desire are attainable only through self-discipline. Self-discipline is the key quality by which you may voluntarily shape the patterns of thought to harmonize with your aims and chief purpose.

In the field of salesmanship, for example, all master salesmen know that the successful salesman is the persistent salesman. And persistence is a matter of strict self-discipline.

Maynard H. Jackson has always been a master salesman. In the late 1950s, fresh out of college, he sold encyclopedias door-to-door. Starting with a modest territory and a strict self-discipline, he worked his way up to sales manager, earning as much as $30,000 in commissions. In 1973, after earning a law degree and entering politics, Jackson sold himself to Atlanta voters and became the first black mayor of a major southern city.

"Discipline has been one of my greatest strengths," Jackson said. "Through persistence, faith, and self-discipline, small opportunities have blossomed into great enterprises."

In the field of athletics the same rule applies. The most successful athletes carry on with unyielding self-discipline, repeating their efforts day after day, year after year, with unabating regularity. Superstar athletes have convincing evidence that this may be the only strategy that produces winning results.

Debi Thomas started skating in secondhand skates so tight her feet ached. To finance her training and constant travel, her mother was forced to skip mortgage payments. In order to reach her goal of competing in the Olympics, Debi made her own costumes, choreographed her own routines, repaired broken skates with Elmer's glue, and for twelve successive years adhered to the same six-hour-a-day practice routine. Thomas was the first black female to make the U.S. Olympic figure-skating team. She was also the first American female skating champion in thirty years to attend college while competing.

Raised by her mother, Debi has always relied on relentless willpower and strict self-discipline. Listen as she describes her secret of inner strength:

I've learned that being good at anything—sports, school, or whatever—means devoting time, energy, and effort. It also means making some difficult choices and sacrifices. For me, becoming a world-class figure skater meant long hours of practice while sometimes tolerating painful injuries. It meant being totally exhausted sometimes, and not being able to do all the things I wanted to do when I wanted to do them. But my dream came true. It took some talent, a fair share of luck, a good measure of persistence, but most of all it took a great deal of self-discipline.

Thus, we see that a successful individual gets his or her start through the application of self-discipline, in pursuit of a definite purpose. He carries on until he attains that purpose, with the aid of that same principle. Self-discipline is a self-acquired trait. It is not a quality that can be appropriated from the lives of others, nor can it be taught. It is an asset that must come from within by the exercise of one's power of choice.

When Debi Thomas said that being good at anything means devoting time, energy, and effort, and means making difficult choices and sacrifices, she doubtlessly meant that mastery of any endeavor can be attained in only one way: by the constant, persistent application of all the principles mentioned in this text. These are principles that must be woven into daily habit, applied in all human relationships and used in the solution of all personal problems.

Study men and women of greatness, and you'll find evidence that the power of self-discipline, organized and persistently applied, is the dominating factor of their success. Further, you will discover that successful men and women commit themselves to a stricter system of self-discipline than any that is forced upon them by circumstances beyond their control. They focus on their goals with an intensity that sweeps aside trivial things so they can concentrate on the matters at hand, and they remain steadfast until they succeed.

High achievers go the extra mile, and if need be, another, and still another, never stopping until they have reached their objective. They move on their own personal initiative because they direct their efforts by the strictest form of discipline.

Self-discipline is training that corrects, molds, strengthens, and perfects. Your behavior and your attitudes are expressions of your thoughts. Much of our thinking seems to be uncontrolled, random thinking, or is on a semiconscious level. From time to time we are aware of our feelings. Feelings may indicate that we have been thinking strongly on certain subjects. Self-discipline teaches us to direct the energy generated by our thoughts into feeling—and action—that will be invaluable as we move forward. Self-discipline will help direct your energy into the most useful, successful channels.

The term self-discipline refers only to the power of thought, because all discipline of self must take place in the mind. You are where you are and what you are because of your thoughts, and your thoughts are subject to your control! You can mold your thoughts to fit any circumstance, positive or negative. You can keep your mind trained on that which you desire, and receive just that—or you can feed on thoughts of things you do not desire, and your thoughts will, unerringly, bring you that also.

The World's Heaviest Man

How do you develop such discipline? Hopefully, the story of a man who used the power of self-discipline to achieve a lifelong goal will explain.

At age six Walter Hudson weighed 125 pounds. When he was twelve, he'd reached 375 pounds. Thirty years later it took firemen, police, and a trained emergency team nearly five hours to lift him after he fell on his bathroom floor. *By then, Hudson weighed an estimated*

1200 pounds! When his story reached the local newspapers—even the *Guinness Book of World Records* wanted to cite him—the headlines across the country proclaimed him to be "The World's Heaviest Man."

Because of his obesity, Hudson had forced himself to live a life in seclusion. He had ventured outdoors only once in twenty-seven years, and that was when his family moved from Brooklyn to an adjoining suburb. For sixteen years, Hudson was unable to lead a normal life.

His days were spent in bed, covered by sheets, wearing only colored ribbons in his braided hair. Propped against a wall of pillows, Hudson was an accumulation of flesh six feet long and more than nine feet around. Held at his sides, his arms pushed out across his double bed, each one the size of two bushel sacks connected by a dimpled elbow. In this condition he lived in a first-floor bedroom, going through the daily routine of watching television, reading magazines, and anticipating his next meal.

Hudson began each day by giving himself a sponge bath from a pail of water—cleansing the folds of his body with a washcloth wrapped around a long stick—followed by eating. Breakfast consisted of a pound of bacon, two pounds of sausage, a dozen eggs, coffee, orange juice, six doughnuts, and potatoes. For lunch he would eat three hero sandwiches and a box of cupcakes, washed down with a liter bottle of soda. For dinner he would gorge on two chickens, vegetables, and, of course, dessert. His weekly food bill ran as high as $300.

He recalls, as a boy, how he outfoxed his mother's attempts to slim him down. "She dragged me to doctors and clinics, admonishing me to stick to the diet. But sooner or later I would sneak off to the kitchen on one of my uncontrollable binges."

The seventh son and youngest of nine children from a broken home, Hudson remembers the day he stopped going outdoors—eighteen years ago. "I went for a short walk with my mother before I got exhausted," he said. "My legs couldn't carry me another step. I confined myself to my house and refused to go out—not even to attend my mother's funeral.

"After I lost my mother I really started to put on the weight. I prayed for God's help. Deep down inside, I wanted to die, and I would have if it wasn't for my brother. He told me that I was my worst enemy, and that only I could save myself."

Filled with shame and condemnation, Hudson poured himself into the Scriptures, seeking answers to his problem. He desperately wanted to be thin—to be normal. "Why can't I control my emotions?" he questioned—emotions that led to a food addiction. Day in and day out he waged war with himself. Then, after months of prayer and solitude in the quiet of his bedroom, his answer came. Inadvertently, he reached for the nearest book, opened it to a dog-eared page. It read: "But those who wait on the Lord shall renew their strength; they shall mount up with wings like eagles, they shall run and not be weary, they shall walk and not faint."

Hudson read it again. *And again!* He had read that verse hundreds of times but with little meaning. This time, however, the words sunk in. After more meditation, *he had renewed his strength*. With a simple prayer he would face his challenge head on.

After expressing a desire to meet Dick Gregory, Hudson was contacted by the comedian and civil rights activist whose protest fasting had led him into the nutrition movement. After a detailed analysis of his medical history, Gregory prepared a menu and exercise plan. Soon Hudson's meals consisted of orange juice and powdered nutrients, supplemented by light exercising. Within five months he had lost 375 pounds. Calls and letters came in from celebrities and supporters the world over, wishing him well. His very soul glowed with the satisfaction of his imminent success. After eight months he'd lost more than 500 pounds, *and something else. He had lost his fear!* For the first time in nearly two decades he took his first steps outdoors.

What changed his life? How did Walter Hudson overcome his greatest obstacle? In spite of his mother's constant pleas, after all the tears, heartaches, and lost battles—what turned the tide in his favor?

Walter Hudson was ready! Once he made his irrevocable decision to lose weight, he had peace of mind. His new lifestyle proved it. After forty-two years of gross obesity, he now felt his life had meaning. "I want to get well," he said. "I know I have the willpower. There are things that I want to do with my life. I want to walk through the snow and play in the autumn leaves. I want to feel the rain on my face. But most importantly, I want to help others overcome their adversities, no matter what they are."

When hardest hit, Walter Hudson turned on his willpower to its full capacity. It sustained him through those moments of temporary defeat, and set him on the path to victory. Willpower is needed most when the oppositions of life are the greatest. And self-discipline will provide willpower for every such emergency, whether great or small.

Unleash the Power of Self-Discipline

How do you unleash the power of self-discipline? By habit. And you develop a habit through repetition. "Sow an action and you reap a habit; sow a habit and you reap a character; sow a character and you reap a destiny," said the psychologist and philosopher William James. Through self-discipline, Walter Hudson converted his greatest sorrow into his greatest asset, for it revealed to him the presence of that "other self" that he found in his Bible readings.

There is one unbeatable rule for the mastery of self-discipline: Resolve yourself to change those habits you dislike, and once changed, *never let an exception occur.* This is a rule that has no equal. This is self-discipline of the highest order. Freedom of the body and mind, independence and economic security, are the results of personal initiative expressed through self-discipline. By no other means may these desires be assured.

The late Albert E. N. Gray, insurance tycoon and philanthropist, perhaps put it best when he spoke of success before the annual convention of the National Association of Life Underwriters. Gray said:

> The common denominator of success—the secret of success of every man who has ever been successful—lies in the fact that he formed the habit of doing things that failures don't like to do.
>
> It's just as true as it sounds and it's just as simple as it seems. You can hold it up to the light, you can put it to the acid test, and you can kick it around until it's worn out, but when you are all through with it, it will still be the common denominator of success, whether we like it or not.
>
> The things that failures don't like to do are the very things that you and I and other human beings, including successful men, naturally don't like to do. In other words, we've got to realize right from the start that success is something which is achieved by the minority of men, and is therefore unnatural and not to be achieved by following our natural likes and dislikes nor by being guided by our natural preferences and prejudices.

Self-discipline is the first rule of successful leadership. Whenever you find a person who is succeeding, you will find a person who has exercised tremendous self-discipline.

Where Does Self-Discipline Lead?

Self-discipline leads to self-actualization. Abraham Maslow, father of third-force psychology, defined the self-actualized person as "a person who makes full use of and exploits his talents, potentialities, and capacities. Such a person seems to be fulfilling himself and doing the best he is capable of doing." Maslow further explained that "the self-actualized person must find in his life those qualities that make his living rich and rewarding. He must find meaningfulness, self-sufficiency, effortlessness, playfulness, richness, simplicity, completion, necessity, perfection, individuality, beauty, and truth." This is the whole person—the rich, fulfilled inner person combined with the well-organized, complete outer person.

The self-actualizer is not a spectator to life, but a participant in it. He determines what it is he wants out of life and then boldly sets out to attain it. He carefully and thoughtfully determines what he desires; he evaluates the cost of achieving it; then he moves ahead with unfailing determination to possess it. He never forgets that a price must be paid.

The Most Valuable Person in Society

Self-discipline also leads to the most cherished of all skills: leadership. All organizations, from the smallest to the largest, require leadership. Wherever you find a successful, growing organization, you'll find behind its success an outstanding leader. This is the most valuable person in society.

In industry, leaders make the wheels turn and the entire operation click with clockwork precision. This is the man or woman who has been responsible for the growth of nations and their positions in the world. You'll find the "most valuable player" exercising his self-discipline by starting early and staying late; and when not toiling away, he or she is usually thinking and planning.

A Call for New Leaders

Anyone who will be honest with himself realizes that he has been happiest and most satisfied after having successfully completed a difficult task. A leader is the person who can help others overcome any challenge. A leader is the parent who shows by example that any job worth doing is worth doing well. A leader is the student who studies to learn, and not just to receive a grade. A leader is the neighbor who sets a positive example in his or her community. A leader is the employee who has the sense to realize that he gets the most out of any job by giving loyalty and dedication to the firm that pays his wages. A leader is the person who realizes the importance of becoming a bigger and better person with each passing day. A leader takes the responsibility for his own growth through self-discipline.

How can you become such a leader? Easy. Fix your eye upon your goal, visualize it with every ounce of your being, and courageously set out toward it. Know and have faith that what should come to you *will* come to you. Everything in the universe works on the side of the person who works within nature's laws.

How to Get the Job You Want

Earl Nightingale tells a moving story of one man's search for work in the heart of the Great Depression, a story that accurately defines the word "leadership." Pay careful attention to the lesson that is about to unfold.

During the Depression in the 1930s, the phrase most often heard by employers was "I'll do anything—just give me a job." Millions were unemployed. Hundreds of businesses had closed their doors, and employment offices were besieged by people looking for work. Tens of thousands of people had migrated to southern California, only to find thousands more searching for employment that didn't exist. However, one young man—unintimidated by what he saw—made a startling discovery. Amazing as this may sound, he found that he could go to work almost anywhere he chose.

It dawned upon him one day that businesses of every type were just as anxious to succeed as were the people seeking work. The owners of these firms were also preoccupied with the country's hard times, and many of them were looking and hoping for someone to come to their aid. This "knight in shining armor" would somehow show up on their doorstep and solve their company's problems. But all they had heard was the same old demoralizing theme: "I'll do anything. Just give me a job." Simply speaking, these beaten hired hands were asking for unearned paychecks from companies that were bordering on financial ruin.

As "No Help Wanted" signs appeared in storefront windows, this enterprising young man decided to become a *part of the solution, rather than part of the problem.* His was a simple idea with positive results. With pad and pencil in hand, he selected a business and industry in which he thought he'd like to work, and one in which he could build a career. He then spent weeks researching and analyzing all he could about that particular field.

He met and talked with people in the same area—listening intently and constantly probing for additional answers. He wanted to know the benefits and the opportunities, as well as the pitfalls and drawbacks, of that particular industry. He asked what bold developments were on the horizon, and what were the leading technologies. Most important, he wanted to know what business owners felt was *needed* to place their firms back on solid footing. While others were knocking on doors begging for work, this enterprising young man could be found in the library scanning every available piece of information, thinking and planning ways a business might be improved.

When he was ready to approach companies in the field that he had selected, he didn't ask for a job. With his briefcase in hand, and a head full of knowledge, the young man said to the owner something like this: "Sir, I believe I know several ways in which your business can be greatly increased, and I'd like to talk to you about them."

Imagine, here stood someone selling the one thing on earth in which his prospect was most interested—*improving his business*! The fact that he knew a good deal about the industry permitted him to talk intelligently. He took the right mental attitude and expressed a willingness to pitch in and be of service. And the result? The possibilities mushroomed and he got several job offers.

While millions of jobless workers were asking for work, one man found a way to be of help. Ask yourself, what had he done? First, he decided exactly on the job and industry he wanted. Second, he specialized; he had selected a particular line of work and decided that was where his future would be. Third, he researched and studied his field of interest. Fourth, he knew his strengths and weaknesses, and emphasized his strengths. And fifth, he set out to prove himself. This he did most diligently.

This process may involve investing your time and efforts, but the difference in income and advancement can eliminate years of hard work at shamefully low wages.

Personal initiative is a trait much admired, and if carried out with discretion and logic, it can quickly place you ahead of the crowd. Initiative built on a definite understanding of what must be achieved puts you in harmony with your peers. If you have a goal in mind, then opportunities for personal initiative are easy to find.

The jack-of-all-trades and master of none was the man who suffered during the Depression. People who knew what they were doing and where they were going sailed through those Depression years like a vessel sails through a storm. It wasn't as comfortable as it could have been, but at least the crossing was a success. And thousands of businesses actually prospered and grew larger during those lean years.

Become Indispensable

Ask any achiever the secret of his or her success and you are likely to get an answer something along these lines:

"Well, I was fortunate. I worked hard, didn't make too many mistakes, and happened to be in the right place at the right time."

This is true, as far as it goes. The real truth, however, is that in most cases these modest people made their own breaks. They became indispensable to the enterprise or to their clients and customers because they developed invaluable personal attributes. Management, clients, and customers alike trust, rely, and can't seem to function without their support. These peak performers take the initiative, assume leadership roles, and can often be found volunteering for difficult or unpopular assignments.

Others envy and admire these indispensable types. They seem to have a better understanding of themselves than most; though they like group dynamics, they work equally well alone. This is a person of quiet confidence; this is an individual who is aware of his ability and has intimate knowledge of his position and industry. Indispensable men and women have the enthusiasm to inspire, and the self-discipline to stick to the job until it's complete.

The best way for you to develop the security that lasts a lifetime is to become outstanding at one particular line of work. Why? Because in the event of any ripple or economic slowdown, as long as you are among the top producers in your field, you will always be in demand. The man or woman who becomes truly outstanding at what he or she does will always be in demand. Ask yourself this question: "Am I now such a person?"

Only you know the answer. If you answer yes, you are among the most fortunate people in one of the smallest and most elite groups on earth. If your answer is no, it can be turned into a yes in a surprisingly short time.

Think for a moment. What gets thrown overboard when a ship is in danger of sinking? Anything that is not absolutely essential to the operation of the vessel and the safety of its passengers. It's the same with a business or organization. Who gets laid off during an economic slump? Those individuals who are not absolutely essential to the operation of the enterprise or organization. Those who insist on doing no more than they must can expect to be jettisoned when things get rough. Nobody, particularly the captain, likes to see cargo thrown over the side. Nonetheless, if it will help save the ship, there's nothing else to do. The same is equally true in business. More often than not, layoffs or cutbacks have nothing to do with personalities, management, or labor relations. Once smooth sailing has been reached, additional workers can always be employed. But it is up to you to decide whether you want to be part of the cargo or an indispensable member of the crew.

Readers Are Leaders

There has long been a general misconception regarding the meaning of the word "educate." The word has its roots within the Latin word "educo," which means "to develop from within, to draw out, to grow through use." An educated person is one who knows how to acquire the resources he needs in the attainment of his main purpose.

Cato, the Roman statesman, once said: "Wise men profit more from fools than fools profit from wise men, for wise men try to avoid the faults of fools, but not so many fools ever try to emulate the good example of wise men."

"No man's education is ever finished," said Napoleon

Hill. "A man's reading program should be as carefully planned as his daily diet, for that too is food, without which he cannot mentally develop." "My move upward," says Governor L. Douglas Wilder of Virginia, "started with the great books. There is nothing more gratifying than satisfying the desire to know." And Pulitzer Prize–winning author Alice Walker says, "More than once did I hesitate between eating and buying a rare book."

John Wesley, the founder of the Methodist movement, told his pastoral students, "Either read or get out of the ministry." As a reader seeking the true path to riches, I say to you, *Either read or learn to fail gracefully.* All major breakthroughs come as the result of taking in new information. A good book on self-improvement is like a friend who can help in an hour of need.

Every achiever highlighted in *Think and Grow Rich: A Black Choice*—past or present—is or was an avid reader. Having realized that they would be classified by what they said and how they said it, they kept company with many of the masters of literature. You would be wise to follow their example. Take the time to spend your evenings with Maya Angelou, Zora Neale Hurston, James Weldon Johnson, James Baldwin, and other great writers and masters of prose. Read and study Toni Morrison, John Hope Franklin, Carter G. Woodson, and Langston Hughes, as well as Milton, Cicero, Emerson, Thoreau, Shakespeare, Steinbeck, Browning, W. Clement Stone, and, of course, Napoleon Hill. Reserve specific hours for reading and meditation. Read with a dictionary and thesaurus at your side.

The case for reading can be summed up in a quote from a past U.S. President: "Men die; devices change; success and fame run their course. But within the walls of the smallest library lie the treasures, the wisdom, and the wonder of man's greatest adventures on earth."

"There Is No End to Learning"

John Morton Finney is a very special man. One hundred years old and the son of a former slave, he served in World War I, became fluent in six foreign languages, earned eleven degrees, taught school until he was eighty-one, and still practices law. His was an unquenchable thirst for knowledge that has never abated. In his sixties he enrolled in college all over again, earning his fourth bachelor's degree at seventy-five. Today he attends law school seminars with the wide-eyed eagerness of a freshman.

A very humble man who insists there's nothing extraordinary about his accomplishments, Finney reads three or four books at a time, making copious notes. In his book-lined study in his house, Finney is at peace as he reads Homer, Cervantes, Pericles, Du Bois, Shakespeare, and Chaucer. Why does he read so desperately? "I can get interested in so many things," he says. "There is so much to know in this world. And it is such a pleasure for me to learn. Besides, a cultivated man would never say 'I finished my education' because he graduated from college. *There is no end to learning.*"

In his childhood Finney learned about his ancestors, who migrated from Ethiopia to Nigeria. Enslaved and brought to America, the family was bought, sold, and separated, only to be rejoined after the Emancipation Proclamation. Finney was born in 1889, in Uniontown, Kentucky. The son of a barber, he was an inquisitive child who loved reading history and poetry. The first book he'd ever purchased was *Webster's Dictionary*. It cost 35 cents—every cent he had—but it proved to be a wise investment.

When his mother died, he was sent to Missouri to live with his grandfather and continue his education. The nearest school for blacks was six miles away. Each day, John Finney walked that endless road past a school for whites that was only half as far.

In 1914, he joined the Army and served in Europe. After the war, he immediately enrolled in college and earned bachelor's degrees in mathematics, French, and history. Several years later, when Indiana began to segregate its public schools, Finney taught Greek, Latin, German, Spanish, and French at all-black Crispus Attucks High School, where there were more teachers with advanced degrees than any other school in the state. Here, he passed on his love for learning and a demanding level for scholarship, while continuing to further his education. Every semester, and each summer, he would take a course.

"I had set this ideal," he said. "No child could ask me a question that I couldn't answer or did not know how to find the answer." Soon Finney had earned master's degrees in education and French from Indiana University. In 1935, he finished his first law degree, *to which he would add four more*!

When asked to reveal the secrets of his lifelong pursuit of education, Finney tells the story of a bookseller who came to him seeking an order. He was white. The salesman apparently did not think too highly of Finney teaching black children Latin and Greek.

"I don't believe in a black man getting a white man's education," the salesman said rather curtly.

"And what is a white man's education?" Finney retorted. After trying to respond to his answerless question, the salesman shrugged his shoulders and left.

"Education is education!" Finney snapped.

Take John Morton Finney's teachings to heart. Read widely in your chosen field. The public libraries are free. They offer a wide array of organized knowledge on any subject. Attend lectures by respected authorities. Take courses, if available. As the above story illustrates, *education is a lifelong process and should only end when you do*. Think deeply about what you've learned. Digest information for your subconscious to act on. But most importantly, *read!* Stand out from the crowd. *Readers are leaders.*

The Future Belongs to the Dreamer

Black America, the entire world needs and is demanding a group of pioneers who have the capacity to conceive bold new plans, new ideas, and new visions; black men and women who have the courage and the initiative to blaze new trails. "Beware," said Emerson, "when the great God lets loose a thinker on this planet. Then all things are at risk." These new leaders will establish roots in every profession—the arts, education, business, politics, and religion. What you will witness will be the golden age of mankind.

Banish forever the thoughts of poverty, of limit and scarcity. Poverty is *not* the enemy. *The enemy is the man who not only believes in his own helplessness but actually worships it.* His main article of faith is that there are mammoth forces at work against him which he cannot possibly comprehend, much less alter or direct. He expends his energies in attempting to convince others that there is nothing either he or they can do. *He is an enemy because of his proximity of helplessness to hopelessness.*

Banish forever the idea that you must be poor! To begin with, you are never seeing poverty, but the representation of an idea of lack. Both poverty and prosperity are states of mind. If you desire to erase the thought of poverty, you must occupy your mind with the thought of success, prosperity, and achievement. You must confront the revealing truth that poverty is a lack of knowledge of who and what you really are.

Remember the secrets you uncovered in "Acres of Diamonds." That story demonstrated one of the great secrets of life—that you have acres of diamonds *within you!* These diamonds within are called potential and ability. There are plenty of these gems inside you waiting to be mined.

The future will require dreamers who can put their dreams into action. Achieving men and women will know the four fundamental steps taken by all who succeed:

1. The choice of a definite goal.
2. The desire to develop sufficient power for goal attainment.
3. A plan involving the accumulation of specialized knowledge for attaining that goal.
4. Action, which includes persistence in carrying out the plan.

"If You Say to That Mountain, Move . . ."

The dreamer will succeed in this progressive age. Any person who cherishes a lofty ideal or purpose and holds fast to it will see that dream manifest into reality. This is the age that is favorable to practical visionaries. The world is no longer scoffing at the dreamer, nor calling him impractical. Instead, it beckons him to bring forth his ideas and plans, and rewards him justly.

If you view yourself a failure, nothing short of a dream and action will change your circumstances. The world never forgives failure; it hungers for and worships success. It has no time for shortcomings or a half-hearted approach. Though the achiever may have sympathy for the man who has failed, he or she will not permit another's failures to contaminate his or her own thinking. The achiever knows that it would better for him or her to suffer loneliness and exclusion than to associate with those minds that are overrun with thoughts of failure and distress. Success requires no explanations; failure permits no alibis.

If you are trying to get a start in the world but feel unable to remove the many barriers that block your path, do not be discouraged. The obstacles that look so formidable at a distance will grow smaller and smaller as you approach your goals. Have courage and confidence in yourself, and the road will clear before you advance. Study the life stories of great men and women, who from humble beginnings have cleared their pathways of obstructions. Magnify your faith and you will minimize your obstacles.

The entire science of success consists of the vigorous, persistent affirmation of your determination and ability to do that which you have set your heart upon. It consists of facing your goal, turning to neither the left nor the right, though many may tempt you, while disaster threatens your every move.

If your determination and persistence are easily deflected, if any persuasion can separate you from your objective, you may be sure that you are on the wrong track.

If ill health or affliction holds you back—though there are numerous instances of success in spite of them—then assess your objectives. You may lack grit or initiative. Success in anything worthwhile is the result of wholehearted faith, tremendous persistence, and *work—steady, unremitting, conscientious work!* Light, half-hearted efforts, indifferent, intermittent toil, has never accomplished anything—and never will.

In his classic work, *The Prophet,* Kahlil Gibran says, "When you work, you fulfill a part of earth's furthest dream, assigned to you when that dream was born, and in keeping yourself with labor, you are in truth loving life, and to love life through labor is to be intimate with life's inmost secret."

Emerson says, "Men talk of victory as of something fortunate. Work is victory. Wherever work is done, victory is obtained." Get busy and work with all your might! There is no such thing as failure for the willing, ambitious worker. Work, which many have called a curse, *is really the salvation of the race.* It is the greatest educator. It is the most effective mentor. There is no other way of developing power, summoning resources, and building stamina of character. All achievement begins in thought but ends in work. *Work is the savior!*

Don't hide behind such silly excuses as "I have no chance" or "No one is willing to help me or show me the way." If there is something within you, if you are worth your weight, *you will make a way if you cannot find one!* You belong to the world minority who live in a free society. This alone offers you the opportunity to become whatever you wish.

It Can Be Done!

I am constantly asked by ambitious men and women whether I think they really have what it takes to achieve success. Without fail, my answer is a resounding yes! "Success is the most natural thing in the world," stated philosopher and writer Elbert Hubbard. "The person who does not succeed has placed himself in opposition to the laws of the universe."

I *know* you have the ability to succeed, but I don't know *if* you will succeed. That rests entirely with you. *You can, but will you?* It's one thing to possess the ability to do something distinctive—something outstanding—but *doing it* is a different matter. There is a tremendous surplus of unproductive ability within the ranks of the mediocre. Why don't more men and women use this ability? Many of them could lead prosperous, productive lives. They have the opportunity to do so. *But why don't they?*

You say you desire to make your life count; that you are ambitious. Then why don't you? What are you waiting for? What holds you down? Who is keeping you back? Answer these questions and you will have taken a major step toward achievement. There is only one answer: *you!* The man or woman who waits for favorable conditions or favorable circumstances will do nothing but wait.

Time Is Running Out . . .

Now is the time for personal inventory. Now is the time to find out who you are, where you are going, and how you are going to get there. If you are not where you wish to be or what you wish to be, there is only one reason. Now is the time to find out why.

A time bomb is in your possession. It is ticking away, moment by moment, bringing you closer and closer to the day when either success or failure will be written beside your name. The time bomb is your life span. How you utilize your time will determine either success or failure. Your knowledge and your ability to make the most of your time is the vital factor that determines what you will achieve on this road called LIFE. *And time waits for no one!*

Blacks Are Growing Rich

Reason now with a man who understands and has achieved riches. He is proof that *blacks are growing rich!* Rich, not only in material terms, but in all the great riches of life. He has mastered the principles of *desire, imagination, faith, persistence, self-image, self-reliance, personality, enthusiasm, money, right mental attitude,* and *self-discipline.* He now possesses all this great land has to offer. Perhaps no individual has shown more understanding of the principles in this book than George E. Johnson, founder of Johnson Products, and a distinguished businessman.

Here are highlights from a speech he delivered before a local black civic organization in his native Chicago, Illinois:

No one can explain why we sometimes find ourselves in what proves to be the right place at the right time. No one, at the time, can accurately assess the value of being exposed to positive, dynamic and creative thinking, which challenges the imagination, quickens the energy and instills a desire to succeed.

As I look back over my childhood, I realize my brothers and I were blessed, for we were never poor—*we just didn't have any money.* But our mother saw to it that there was never spiritual impoverishment in our home or in our lives. It is the presence of the spiritual element that provides the individual with the drive we call incentive.

My life's experiences have taught me the value of many principles that I would like to emphasize. *First, education is a paramount prerequisite for improving the lot of the individual and the group that he belongs to.* Black America has discovered through experience that the system does not always work in its behalf and must be changed. I agree. But, I emphasize that the American system is intricate and frequently deceptive. And no one is qualified to change a system he or she does not understand. Education brings understanding.

Second, be curious. Discover all you can about yourself and this world you live in. Be curious at school, at work, in the community. Learn from others: your family, your teachers, and friends. Everyone has something to offer.

Third, decide what you want out of life. Set your sights high and don't be afraid to dream big dreams. Some downgrade dreaming, but I don't. *I know that he who never dreamed never had a dream come true.* Strike out boldly for the things you honestly want.

Approach each new problem, not with the view of finding what you hope will be there, but to get the truth, the realities you must grapple with. You may not like what you find—in that case, you are entitled to try and change it.

Fourth, be ready to take advantage of ALL opportunities. Not only when opportunity knocks at your door—but be ready to knock on opportunity's door. Be different. Though it's sometimes dangerous to do so.

Fifth, do not hate. Hate is unproductive. It creates nothing of value and has a much more corrosive effect on the hater than the hated.

And above all, have faith in yourself. Be a person of worth and know it. Believe in yourself. Hold in your consciousness a vision of the life you desire. Move through each day with a vision of yourself as strong, yet loving—flexible, yet in charge. Act as though failing was impossible. *Within you are limitless possibilities waiting for birth. Go ahead, give life to them!*

Yours is a grave responsibility. Each generation must pick up where the last has left off. This is no time for the weak-kneed, indecisive, compromising, and crawling men and women. *If ever we needed strength, courage, character, and determined will backed by unfaltering faith, it is now!*

Let me leave you with this final thought: When these principles are a part of your life, you will have developed a philosophy you can live with and one of which you can be proud. *If you are in touch with your divine potential, you have WEALTH and POWER. Each of us is created to do something special with our lives.* We have an individual mission and a collective contribution to make toward uplifting this world. *The only limitations of life you need ever fear are those which you place on yourself.*

Black America, the Decision Is Yours

You have just studied an outline that can help you walk in the light of accomplishment. In the preceding chapters you have been exposed to success formulas that others have used to lift themselves to great heights of personal achievement. You have been introduced to the methods by which successful black men and women have learned to direct their minds and control their thoughts while performing seemingly miraculous tasks. I have shared with you what may be merely words, or great wealth and contentment—depending on how you use them. *But the decision is yours.*

Each one of us has a divine inheritance of good and a unique path to follow in life to realize that good. Your path is *your path*. It is particular to you. Though the general outcome of your life and your specific goals may be similar to those of others, the circumstances, events, and obstacles you encounter will be distinctly your own.

Each one of us is a unique creation in the mind of the Almighty. What's right is what is right and appropriate for you, for all that you are and all that you want to become. What's right is what is consistent with your spiritual identity; who and what you really are. What's normal is what it takes for you to proceed on your path smoothly, confidently, and intelligently. What it requires is for you to live compatibly and charitably with others—and still be able to achieve your goals and work out your destiny in your own way. You are given as your richest birthright the privilege of controlling your own thoughts. Therefore, treat this divine gift with the profound respect to which it is entitled. *DO NOT ALLOW anyone to do your thinking for you or influence your thinking in any manner except by the principles discussed herewith.* Learn to *think* for yourself and to trust your inner voice. It will guide you unfailingly.

What Is Needed

The crying need of the hour is *HUMANITY—not organizations, not legislation, but MEN AND WOMEN— BLACK MEN AND WOMEN!* Men and women who can stand in the presence of their God and truthfully say, "The place I occupy does not need reforming." Men and women who are ready and willing to bring the reformation of the world into their hearts. *Men and women who can say to their struggling brothers and sisters, with love, "FOLLOW ME!"* We need to send this message of love throughout the world; but first, let it start with us, in our community. Speak it in every pulpit, every school, and engrave it on our hearts. Embedded in the hearts of all mankind—love is the answer.

I am confident that you will succeed in your efforts if you concentrate on that which you desire and persevere. And when you do succeed—because you surely will—my joy will be unbounded.

> *Come to the edge, He said.*
> *They said, we are afraid.*
> *Come to the edge, He said.*
> *They came.*
> *He pushed them . . . and they flew.*
> —GUILLAUME APOLLINAIRE

Index

ABC-TV, 269
Academy Awards, 247, 267
"Acres of Diamonds"
    (Conwell), 1–2, 343
Air Force, U.S., 87, 201, 221,
    273
Alabama Coal Iron and Steel
    Company, 44
Alberto-Culver, 143
Aldridge, Ira, 153
Ali, Muhammad, 251
Allen, James, 291, 320
Allen, Robert, 158, 325
A.M. Chicago, 270
American Academy of
    Achievement, 92
American Bankers Insurance,
    228
American Medical Student
    Association, 69
Amos, Wally "Famous," xiii,
    xiv, 87, 201–2
Amputee Athletic Association,
    U.S., 314
Amway, 88
Anderson, Marian, 88, 146
Andrews, Markita, 227–29
Angelou, Maya, 340
Apollinaire, Guillaume, 298
Apollo Theater, 205
Aristotle, 108
Armstrong, Louis, 154
Army, U.S., 197
As a Man Thinketh (Allen), 291
AT&T, 228
Atlanta Benevolent and
    Protective Association, 61

Atlanta Life Insurance
    Company, 62, 304–6
Atlanta Negro Business League,
    305
Atlanta Urban League, 305
Auburn University, 146
*Autobiography of an Ex-
    Coloured Man, The*
    (Johnson), 247

Baldwin, James, 340
"Banked Blood" (Drew), 127
Barnum, P. T., 250
Baxter, Coralee, 140, 143
Beamon, Bob, 126–27
Beethoven, Ludwig van, 145,
    236
Bell, Alexander Graham, 7
Berry, Mary Frances, 311–13
Bethune, Mary McLeod, 36–38
Bethune Cookman College, 38
Bettger, Frank, 235, 241–42
Black Enterprise, 149, 198, 259
Black History Week, 246
Black Power, 48
Blotnick, Srully, 57–58
Blue Angels, 311
Booker T. Washington Business
    College, 45
Booker T. Washington
    Insurance Company, 43–
    44
Book of Genesis, 51
"Born to Lose," 74
Boyer National Laboratories, 83
Brooke, Edward W., 87–88
Brooks, Gwendolyn, 89

Brown, Les, 235
Brown, Ron, 10, 206
Browning, Robert, 340
Bryant, Paul "Bear," 163
Bureau of Labor Statistics, 10
Bureau of the Census, 11
Burke, Edmund, 165
Burke, Selma, 146
Burke Mountain Academy, 122
Burrell, Thomas, 204–5
Burrell Advertising, 204
Butterworth, Eric, 287, 298

Caesar, Julius, 81
Camus, Albert, 78
Career Sales and Management
    Academy, 306
Carlisle, Darlwin, 146
Carnegie, Andrew, 6–7, 194,
    239
Carnegie Foundation, 239
Carnegie Hall, 216
Carson, Benjamin, 160–63
Carson, Johnny, 299–301
Carver, George Washington, 63
    background of, 110–11
    enthusiasm of, 239
    goal-setting system of, 110–13
    persistence of, 156
Carver, Moses, 110
CBS, 269
Central State University, 215
Cervantes, Miguel de, 212, 341
Challenger, 136
Charles, Ray, 71–75
Chaucer, Geoffrey, 341
Chicago, University of, 246,
    293
Chicken Delight, 274
Chisolm, Elizabeth, 216–17
Christ Universal Complex, 14
Churchill, Winston, 145
Cicero, 340
Clark-Atlanta University, 306
Coast Guard, U.S., 117, 118
Coca-Cola, 142, 205

Cochran, Donnie, 311
Cole, Johnetta, 10
Coleman, Johnnie, 14
Collier, Robert, 84, 93
Collins, Marva, 92–93
Colorado, University of, 312
Color Purple, The (film), 267
Color Purple, The (Walker),
    205–6
Columbia University, 127, 240
Columbus, Christopher, 81
Coming to America, 299
Commission on Civil Rights,
    312
Community Chest, 305
Confucius, 167
Congress, U.S., 24, 112
Congressional Record, 252
Conwell, Russell H., 1–2, 343
Cookie Kid, 227–29
Coolidge, Calvin, 145, 156
Cornell University, 68, 123
Cosby Show, 10
Cousins, Norman, 80
Cox, Danny, 209–10
Creating Wealth (Allen), 158,
    325
Crispus Attucks High School,
    342

Daniels, Peter, 318
Davis, Al, 137
Davis, Willie, 293–96
Daytona, Fla., Bethune's work
    in, 38
Daytona Educational &
    Industrial Training
    School, 38
Declaration of Independence,
    23
Declaration of Personal
    Responsibility, 209–10
Delta Air Lines, 306
Demby, Bill, 313–16
Democratic National
    Committee, 10, 206

de Passe, Suzanne, 246–47
desire:
 for achievement, 80–116
 belief and, 124–25
 for fame, 87
 fueling of, 100–101
 goals for, 101–3, 105–16
 and miracle of motivation,
  93–94
 persistence and, 155–56
 and power of motives, 85–93
 right mental attitude and,
  289–90
 rules governing principle of,
  82–83
 self-discipline and, 327
 to teach, 92–93
 top five percent theory and,
  103–5
 and walking to beat of
  different drummer, 107
 for wealth, 82–85, 87–88, 113
Detroit Tigers, 46
disAbility Awareness Project,
  315
Discover the Power Within You
  (Butterworth), 298
Discovery, 67
Disraeli, Benjamin, 34–35, 93,
  211
Don King Productions, 251
Don Quixote (Cervantes), 212
Douglass, Frederick:
 flight from slavery of, 23–24
 self-reliance and, 185–86,
  203
Drew, Charles, 127
DuBois, W. E. B., 341
Dunbar, Paul Lawrence, 318
Duncan, Bert, 179–80
Dunham, Lee:
 background of, 273–74
 McDonald's franchises of,
  274–78
 management development
  course taught by, 276–77

 service to others provided by,
  273–78
Du Pont, 314

Earl G. Graves, Ltd., 149
Ebony, 200
Ebony Fashion Fair, 200–201
Edison, Thomas, 7, 63
 Carver and, 113
 on enthusiasm, 235
 on failure, 157
 positive mental attitude of,
  133
Einstein, Albert:
 on imagination, 55
 persistence of, 146
 on service, 277
Emerson, Ralph Waldo, 35, 57,
  340, 343, 345
 on enthusiasm, 235, 253
 on love, 97
 on persistence, 145
Emmy Awards, 119, 267
enthusiasm, 235–54
 belief and, 245, 251
 interest and, 242–44
 knowledge and, 244
 momentum and, 252–53
 power and, 236–40
 self-discipline and, 326
 sources of, 241–45
 what it can do, 245–48
Epicharmus, 117
Epictetus, 147
Essence, 65
Estée Lauder, 200

faith:
 in ability, 125, 129–30
 for achievement, 120
 fundamentals of, 133–39
 God and, 130–34
 as mainspring of soul, 119
 persistence as form of, 152
 and power of prayer, 134
 as prerequisite to power, 117–44

and pushing aside self-limiting beliefs, 125–29
right mental attitude and, 133–34, 316
risk and, 139–40
self-discipline and, 327
self-suggestion and, 135–38
as trust and believing without proof, 133
what it can do, 130–31
Famous Amos Chocolate Chip Cookies, 87, 202
Fashion Fair products, 200–201
Finney, John Morton, 341–43
Fireman's Fund Insurance, 295
Fitzhugh, H. Naylor, 90
Flipper, Henry, 10, 21
Ford, Henry, 7, 63, 113, 186
Foreign Service, U.S., 206
Foreman, George, 70
France, Anatole, 51
Franklin, John Hope, 340
Frazier, Joe, 134, 249
Fuller, R. Buckminster, 17
Fuller, S. B., 17, 82–85
  background of, 83
  desire to achieve of, 83–84
  persistence of, 156
  on power of prayer, 134

Gandhi, Mahatma, 108, 113, 134
Garvey, Marcus, 80, 186, 209
Gaston, Arthur G., 47
  background of, 44
  persistence of, 156
  success formula of, 43–45
General Motors, 142
George Foster Peabody Broadcasting Award, 154
Georgia, University of, 154
"Georgia on My Mind," 74
G. Heileman Brewing, 143
Gibran, Kahlil, 345
Gibson, Althea, 23
Gloster, Hugh, 22–23

God, 32, 130–34
Godmind, 57
Go for It (Kassorla), 158
Golden Globe Awards, 267
Golden Rule, 214–18
Gordy, Berry, 247
Gospel According to Saint John, 287
Grambling University, 163, 311
Grammy Awards, 88
Gravely, Samuel L., 64
Graves, Earl G., 149–52
  salesmanship of, 197–98
  wealth and, 259
Gray, Albert E. N., 333
Great Depression, 64, 337–38
Green Bay Packers, 293
Green Power: The Success Ways of Arthur G. Gaston (Gaston), 44
Gregory, Dick, 331
Guinness Book of World Records, 330
Gumbel, Bryant, 10
Gunn, Harry E., 108

Hale, Clara "Mother," 95–97
Hale House, 95
Haley, Alex, 117–20
Hall, Arsenio, 299–301
"Hallelujah, I Lover Her So," 74
Halsey, George, 88
Handicapped Olympics, 122, 123
Hannibal, 10
Harlem, N.Y., Dunham's McDonald's franchise in, 275–76
Harlem Nights, 299
HARPO Productions, 267
Harvard University, 27, 35, 62, 248
  Fitzhugh's graduation from, 91
  St. John's graduation from, 123
  Woodson's graduation from, 246

Hayes, Bob, 126
Hazlitt, William, 325
Hebrews, 117
Height, Dorothy, 14
Heisman Trophy, 146
Henley, William Ernest, 138
Henson, Matthew, 240
Herndon, Alonzo F., 59–63
    background of, 60–62
    barbershop of, 60–61
    on creative thinking, 59, 62–
        63
    Hill and, 305
    mission of, 61
    persistence of, 156
    real estate investments of, 61
Herndon, Norris, 306
Hill, Jesse, 304–7
Hill, Napoleon, 6–9, 84, 340
on aim of common man, 12–13
Carnegie interviewed by, 6–7,
        194
    on creative thinking, 63–64
    on enthusiasm, 236
    on failure, 166
    on faith, 119
    on goals, 108
    on imagination, 52
    on infinite intelligence, 57
    on mind, 33, 266, 318
    on persistence, 148–49, 168
    on reading, 339–40
    on right mental attitude, 291,
        298
    on self-discipline, 324–25
    on success consciousness, 44
    writings aimed at Black
        America by, 7–8, 12–13
Holiday, Billie, 185
Holiday Inn, 274
Holmes, Oliver Wendell, 51,
        288
Homer, 341
Howard University, 89, 91, 312
Hubbard, Elbert, 173, 346
Hudson, Walter, 329–32

Hughes, Langston, 145, 321–22,
        340
Hunter-Gault, Charlayne, 153–
        54
Hurston, Zora Neale, 340
Huxley, Thomas, 4–5

IBM, 157, 228
"If" (Kipling), 136–37
Ignatius, Saint, 190
"I Got a Woman," 73
imagination, 51–79
    avoiding limitations on, 67–70
    and characteristics of infinite
        intelligence, 58–59
    dreams and, 51–53, 56–57,
        64–65
    Hill on, 52
    as idea centered, 77–79
    learning to mix efforts with,
        62
    and moving from slavery to
        wealth, 59–63
    and origin of ideas, 57–58
    power of, 53–56
    self-discipline and, 326
    and substance of things hoped
        for, 74–75
    success and, 77–78
    and unlocking inborn
        creativity, 66–67, 70–77
    visualization and, 71–74
Indiana University, 342
Inner City Broadcasting, 205
inner space:
    and changing your life by
        changing your thoughts,
        34–36
    and choosing your thoughts,
        45–47
    conquest of, 17–50
    handicaps and, 36–39
    mental laws and, 26–27
    mental world of, 24–26
    and power of choice, 47–49
    and prosperity as privilege, 43

quality of visualizations in, 75
and reasons for failure, 49–50
and thinking your way to
    success, 43–45
and wealth as thought, 39–42
International Black Writers
    Awards, 297
"In the Spirit" (Taylor), 65
"Invictus" (Henley), 138
Iowa State College, 111

Jackson, Jesse:
    imagination of, 55
    on right mental attitude, 296
    on self-image, 172
Jackson, Maynard H., 327
Jackson, Vincent "Bo", 146
Jackson Five, The, 247
James, Daniel "Chappie":
    background of, 220–21
    pleasing personality of, 221,
        223–24,229
James, William, 27, 29, 35, 332
    on enthusiasm, 248
    on imagination, 78
Jemison, Mae C., 67–70
Jesus Christ, 120, 130–31, 185
Jewel Foods, 143
Johns Hopkins University, 160,
    162
Johnson, Beverly, 154
Johnson, George E., 347–49
Johnson, James Weldon, 340
    desire of, 89
    enthusiasm of, 247
Johnson, John H., 97–98
    on punctuality, 231–32
    salesmanship of, 200–201
    self-reliance of, 187
    wealth and, 259, 260
Johnson, Lyndon B., 90
Johnson Products, 347
Johnson Publications, 97, 187,
    231, 259
Joint Center of Political Studies,
    10

Joint Chiefs of Staff, 310
Jokl, Ernst, 127
Joyner, Florence Griffith, 90–91
Julliard School of Music, 217
Justice Department, U.S., 198

Kansas City Royals, 146
Karbo, Joseph, 280
Kassorla, Irene, 158
Keats, John, 158, 287
Kennedy, John F., 206
Kennedy, Robert, 198
Kent State University, 258, 299
Kentucky Fried Chicken, 274
Kimball, Florence Page, 217
King, Don, 249–52, 259, 260
King, Martin Luther, Jr., 51–
    52, 236
Kipling, Rudyard, 136–37
Knight-Ridder Newspapers, 306
Kraft Foods, 143

Lady Sings the Blues, 247
Laws of Success (Hill), 7, 13
Lazy Man's Way to Riches, The
    (Karbo), 280
Lee, Spike, 154–55
Leflore, Ron, 45–47, 156
Lever Brothers, 83
Life, 200
"Lift Ev'ry Voice and Sing,"
    247
Lincoln, Abraham, 145, 190
Lincoln Center, 216
Lincoln University, 89, 305
Livingstone College, 146
Lombardi, Vince, 293–94
Los Angeles Raiders, 146
Lowell, James, 38–39
Luper, Clara, 255

McDonald's, 205, 274–78
McNair, Ronald, 136
MacNeil/Lehrer News Hour, 153
Magic of Thinking Big, The
    (Schwartz), 158–59

Maltz, Maxwell, 177
Man's Search for Himself
    (May), 104
Marcus Aurelius, Emperor of
    Rome, 34
Marden, Orison Swett, 164, 236
Marshall, Thurgood, 89–90
Marshall Fields, 201
Marsten, William, 4
Martin, Billy, 46
Martin Luther King, Jr., Center
    for Nonviolent Social
    Change, 306
Maslow, Abraham, 334
Mattel, 295
Matthews, James Brander, 3
May, Rollo, 104
Maynard , Robert, 310–11
Mays, Benjamin E., 105, 153,
    170
Merrick, John, 22
Methodist movement, 340
Metropolitan Life, 83
Metropolitan Opera, 88
MGM Studios, 295
Michelangelo, 236
Michigan, University of, 305
Michigan State University, 226
Middlebury College, 206
Military Academy at West
    Point, U.S., 21
Milton, John, 145, 340
Miss America contest, 131
Miss Black America contest,
    269
Miss Black Nashville contest, 269
Mr. T. (Lawrence Tureaud),
    164
Mohammed, 32
Moody Bible Institute, 37
Moore, Aaron McDuffie, 22
Morehouse College, 22, 105
Morgan State University, 197
Morrison, Toni, 340
Moses, Edwin, 136
Motown Productions, 246

Motown Records, 247
Motown Returns to the Apollo,
    247
Murphy, Eddie, 299

Napoleon I, Emperor of France,
    81
National Achievement
    Scholarships, 68
National Aeronautics and Space
    Administration (NASA),
    17, 69
National Association for the
    Advancement of Colored
    People (NAACP):
  Hill's position with, 305
  Johnson's role in
    establishment of, 247
  Marshall's work for, 89
National Association of Life
    Underwriters, 333
National Commission for
    Excellence in Education,
    11
National Council of Negro
    Women, 14
National Educational
    Association, 92
National Football League
    (NFL), 136–37
National Handicapped Sports and
    Recreation Association,
    315
National League, 92
Navy, U.S., 64, 311
Negro Digest, 200
Newton, Isaac, 26
Nightingale, Earl, 57
  on leadership, 335–38
  success defined by, 102
  top five percent theory of,
    103–5
  on wealth, 103, 264
Nobel Prize, 28, 135
North Carolina Mutual
    Insurance Company, 22

Northwestern University, 8–9, 113, 297
Novak, Michael, 255

Oakland Raiders, 136–37
Oakland Tribune, 310
Ohio State Penitentiary, 250
Ohio State University, 199
Olympics:
  Joyner's participation in, 90–91
  Moses's participation in, 136
  Thomas's participation in, 327
Oprah Winfrey Show, 267
outer space, 318–51
  dreaming and, 344–46
  job hunting and, 335–38
  leadership and, 335–43
  learning and, 341–43
  and person you are meant to be, 323–24
  self-discipline and, 326–38
  and standing up and stepping out, 322–23
  success and, 346
  ultimate resource and, 320–22
  wealth and, 324–26, 347–49
Oxford University, 123

Pabst Brewing Company, 199
Pacific Telephone, 228
Paige, Alicia, 259
Paracelsus, 18
Paradise Lost (Milton), 145
Paramount Pictures, 299–301
Parks, Henry, 198–200
Parks Sausage Company, 198–200
Patton, George, 289
Paul, Saint, 312
Payton, Walter, 75
Peace Corps, 69
Peary, Robert E., 240
Peete, Calvin, 127–28
Pericles, 341
persistence, 145–69
  and adversity and achievement, 164–65
  and blessings of failure, 159–60
  and conquering or being conquered, 165–68
  dreams and, 344–46
  as form of faith, 152
  and hitting the mark by failing, 163–64
  and lessons of failure, 158–59
  and making the grade, 168–69
  measurement of, 155–56
  power of, 147–51
  right mental attitude and, 301–3
  self-discipline and, 327–28
  selling and, 197–98
  and true nature of failure, 157–58
  and understanding failure, 156
personality:
  definition of, 213–14
  enthusiasm and, 237
  program of improvement through, 229–33
Pitman, Wylie, 72
pleasing personality, 211–34
  and appropriateness of attire, 230–31
  by avoiding criticism, condemnation, and complaining, 229
  effective speech and, 232
  first impressions and, 225–29
  flexibility and, 230
  formula for, 221–23
  Golden Rule and, 214–18
  integrity and, 230
  and likes attracting likes, 215
  punctuality and, 231–32
  secret of, 218–20
  self-discipline and, 327–28
  sense of humor for, 231
  and showing appreciation and giving praise, 218–25
  and showing interest in others, 229–30

tactfulness and, 230
traits of, 233–34
what it can do, 220–21
Powell, Colin L., 10, 310
Presbyterian Board of Missions, 37
Presidential Medal of Freedom, 88
Price, Leontyne, 88–89, 156, 215–17
Pro Bowls, 136
Procter & Gamble, 142, 205
Proctor, Barbara Gardner, 140–44, 260
Proctor & Gardner Advertising, 143
Pro Football Hall of Fame, 136–37
Prophet, The (Gibran), 345
Provident Hospital, 246
Psychocybernetics (Maltz), 177
Pulitzer Prize, 89, 119, 206, 340
PUSH, Operation, 172
Pygmalion (Shaw), 177

Rand, A. Barry, 282–83
Rand, Ayn, 35
Ray Charles Group, 73
Reader's Digest, 200
Reagan, Ronald, 96
Revlon, 200
Rhodes Scholarships, 123
Richie, Lionel, 247
right mental attitude, 40, 133–34, 287–317
changing your life with, 313–16
goals and, 292, 296–303, 307–9, 313
as habit, 307–9
meaning of, 301–3
mind conditioners for, 316–17
possessors of, 310–13
and pursuit of excellence, 304–7

real you and, 292
self-discipline and, 326
stage for occurrences in life set by, 289–90
toward yourself, 290–92, 309–10, 316
Riis, Jacob, 168–69
Robeson, Paul, 240
Robinson, Eddie, 163–64, 311
Robinson, Jackie, 92
Rockefeller, John D., Sr., 7, 186, 266
Romans, 312
Roosevelt, Eleanor, 170
Roosevelt, Franklin D., 6, 146
Roosevelt, Theodore, 321
Roosevelt, University, 296
Roots (Haley), 119
Roots (television series), 119
Ross, Diana, 247
Rowan, Carl, 206

Saint Augustine School for Deaf and Blind Children, 72
St. John, Bonnie, 121–23
St. John, Ruby, 121
St. Louis Cardinals, 92
Schlitz Brewing Company, 294
Schomburg, Arthur A., 239–40
Schwartz, David, 158–59, 160
Scotia Seminary, 37
Sears, Roebuck and Company, 143, 205
Secret of the Ages (Collier), 84, 93
self-image, 170–84
and being somebody, 172–75
and being worthy of success, 179–80
evaluation of, 171–72
guidelines for rebuilding or strengthening of, 183–84
love and, 179
and overcoming mental slavery, 180–81
and protecting your mind, 175–77, 181–84

right mental attitude and,
   295–96, 316, 317
scientists on, 171
and seeing yourself as you will
   one day become, 177–79
self-reliance, 185–210
   and being president of your
      own company, 187–89,
      192–94
   change and, 191–95
   faith and, 133
   and forward movement of life,
      189–90
   as personal responsibility,
      207–10
   and selecting area of interest,
      190–91
   self-help and, 203–4
   and selling yourself, 195–202
   and waiting for opportunities,
      204–7
Senate, U.S., Brooke's election
   to, 87–88
Shakespeare, William, 35, 236,
   319, 321, 340
Shanahan, Mike, 137
Shaw, George Bernard, 35–36,
   177, 323
   self-reliance and, 203
   on wealth, 255
Shell, Art, 136–37
Simon and Garfunkel, 201
Sivart Mortgage Corporation,
   297
Small Business Administration,
   143
Smiles, Samuel, 185
Smith, George, 64
Smith, Willi, 231
Smith Pipe & Supply, 64
Socrates, 63
Southern Michigan State Prison,
   45–46
Spaulding, Charles Clinton, 21–
   22, 156
Spelman College, 10

Stagg, Amos Alonzo, 163
Stalin, Joseph, 113
Stanford University, 20, 68
Steinbeck, John, 340
Stevenson, Robert Louis, 223
Stone, W. Clement, 24, 340
Street in Bronzeville, A
   (Brooks), 89
Stringley, Darryl, 207–8
Super Bowls, 75
Supreme Court, U.S., 90
Supremes, 201
Sutton, Percy, 205

Talladega College, 141
Taylor, Susan L., 64–65, 170
Teachers Insurance Annuity
   Association/College
   Retirement Equities Fund,
   226
Temple University, 1
Temptations, 201
Tennessee State University, 269
Think and Grow Rich (Hill), 7,
   12, 33, 84
Thirteenth Amendment, 111
Thomas, Debi, 327–28
Thoreau, Henry David, 12, 77–
   78, 107, 340
Thorpe, Jim, 146
Tonight, 299–301
Travis, Dempsey, 296–98
Travis Realty Company, 297
True, Herb, 158
Tubman, William, 134
Tucker, Sophie, 255
Turner, Debbye, 131–33
Tuskegee Institute, 62, 111
Tutu, Desmond, 134–35
Tyson, Mike, 249

Udall, Morris, 198
Ueberroth, Peter, 92
United Peanut Association of
   America, 112
Upshaw, Gene, 136

Veterans Administration, U.S. 314

Waldorf-Astoria, 273
Walker, Alice, 205–6, 340
Walker C. J., 53–55, 63, 156
Walt Disney Productions, 228
Walter Reed Army Hospital, 314
Wanamaker, John, 7
Warner, Glen "Pop," 163
Washington, Booker T., 48–49, 111, 121
Watson, Thomas, 157
wealth, 255–86
  attitudes toward, 284–86
  of Black Americans, 262–63, 347–50
  definition of, 261–62
  desire for, 82–85, 87–88, 113
  government in creation of, 260–61
  and how much money you want, 280–86
  master key to, 324–26
  from parents to children, 265–66
  peace of mind as, 266–67
  philanthropy and, 272
  relationship between creativity and, 62–63
  and service to others, 263–66, 273–80
  from slavery to, 59–63
  in Third World nations, 258–60
  as thought, 39–42
  top five percent theory of, 103–5
  your right to, 257–58
Wesley, Charles, 172
Wesley, John, 340
Westside Preparatory School, 92
Wharton, Clifton R., Jr., 10, 226–27, 229
Wheeler, Elmer, 241–42
White, Bill, 91–92
Whiting, Percy, 196
Wilder, L. Douglas, 187, 340
William Morris Agency, 87, 201
Williams, Daniel Hale, 246
Willie Davis Distributing, 294
Wilson, Woodrow, 6
Wimbledon Trophy, 23
Winfrey, Oprah, 10, 138, 267–72
Winfrey, Vernon, 269
WLS-TV, 270
Woodson, Carter G., 182–83, 245–46, 340
Woolworth, F. W., 7
Wright brothers, 133

Xerox, 282–83

Yale University, 160, 161

About the Author

Dennis Kimbro, Ph.D., lectures across the country for the Napoleon Hill Foundation and consults with a small business. He has written for *Success* and many other magazines. He lives in Georgia with his wife and three daughters.